Exposés and Excess

Exposés and Excess

Muckraking in America, 1900 / 2000

CECELIA TICHI

PENN

University of Pennsylvania Press

Philadelphia

10   9   8   7   6   5   4   3   2   1

Published by
University of Pennsylvania Press
Philadelphia, Pennsylvania 19104-4011

Library of Congress Cataloging-in-Publication Data
Tichi, Cecelia, 1942–
   Exposés and excess : muckraking in America, 1900 / 2000 / Cecelia Tichi.
     p. cm. — (Personal takes)
   Includes bibliographical references and index.
   ISBN 0-8122-3763-3 (alk. paper)
   1. Journalism—Social aspects—United States.   2. Social problems—Press coverage—United States.   3. United States—Social conditions—20th century.   I. Title.   II. Series.

PN4888.S6T53 2004
302.23'0973—dc21

                                          2003056363

We are now in a second Gilded Age. Instead of taking steps that would strengthen our democracy, we're heading backward to the wealth inequalities of a century ago.

—*Bill Gates Sr. and Chuck Collins,* The Nation, *January 27, 2003*

We have not grown too hubristic as producers and consumers; we have grown too timid as citizens, acquiescing to deregulation and privitization and a growing tyranny of money over politics. . . . But consumers are not citizens, and markets cannot exercise democratic sovereignty. The ascendant market ideology claims to free us, but it actually robs us of the civic freedom by which we control the social consequences of our private choices.

—*Benjamin Barber,* New York Times, *July 29, 2002*

What empires lavish abroad, they cannot spend on good republican government at home: on hospitals or roads or schools. A distended military budget only aggravates America's continuing failure to keep its egalitarian promise to itself.

—*Michael Ignatieff,* New York Times Magazine, *January 5, 2003*

The phrase, "narrative as rhetoric," means . . . that narrative is not just story but also action, the telling of a story by someone to someone on some occasion for some purpose.
—*James Phelan,* Narrative as Rhetoric, *1996*

Contents

Chapter 1

From *The Jungle* to *Fast Food Nation*
American Déjà Vu

In 2001, forty-five Vanderbilt University students, doubtless hoping for a film-and-literature course, enrolled in my "Twentieth-Century American Blockbusters."

These blockbusters were books, not movies, I explained that hot, late August day. The titles, I emphasized, deserved the name "blockbuster" according to the dictionary definition of experience so overwhelmingly forceful that it radically changes people's minds. The books appearing on the reading list, I pointed out, had changed public opinion on a range of issues. They included Rachel Carson's *Silent Spring* and Betty Friedan's *The Feminine Mystique*, both engines of the nascent environmental and feminist movements in the later twentieth century. Our semester together would let us investigate why certain books, both fiction and nonfiction narratives, have proved pivotal to social change. In a multimedia era, I wanted students to examine these narratives and their historical eras to discover how and why the book can be a social power tool.

We began with Upton Sinclair's 1906 best-seller *The Jungle*. The students were horrified by the disgusting Chicago packinghouse conditions represented in the novel. Like Sinclair's contemporary readers, the students of 2001 overlooked the heinous workplace conditions in favor of a self-interested focus on meat contamination, verifying Sinclair's wry remark that he had aimed for the public's heart and hit the stomach instead. Yet to a point all were sympathetic with the Lithuanian immigrant family struggling against impossible odds to earn their living as packinghouse workers in a socially corrupt and toxic environment. I informed them that President Theodore Roosevelt had read *The Jungle* and dispatched two agents to Chicago to verify Sinclair's claims, whereupon they reported "meat shovelled from filthy wooden floors . . . in all of which practices it was in the way of gathering dirt, splinters, floor filth, and the expectoration of tuberculosis and other diseased workers" (qtd. in Tindell and Shi 951).

Predictably, the class grimaced. In modern America where food sanitation is taken for granted, students shuddered complacently at the carnal medievalism of the early twentieth century. They seemed pleased to hear that *The Jungle* expedited passage of two important laws, the 1906 Meat Inspection Act, requiring federal inspection and sanitary handling of meat intended for interstate commerce, and also the Pure Food and Drug Act of 1906, which prohibited the manufacture, sale, or transportation of adulterated, misbranded, or harmful foods, drugs, or liquors.

The classroom feel-good moment was to prove, however, dangerously naive in its basic assumptions. As we discussed *The Jungle*, a writer named Eric Schlosser was shattering our beliefs about contemporary food safety in the United States in a book as dense with facts as it is stylistically elegant and narratively cunning. In 2001, Schlosser, a former student of the acclaimed nonfiction writer John McPhee, chronicled the extent to which meat processing conditions in 2000 matched those described in *The Jungle*. As the "Blockbuster" course went on, *Fast Food Nation: The Dark Side of the All-American Meal* was climbing the best-seller lists, informing readers of dire threats to health by a meat industry which, at the turn of the twenty-first century, was once again virtually unregulated, its working conditions as wretched as those described by Sinclair. *Fast Food Nation*, in short, proved that we'd gone forward into the past.

New Muckrakers, c. 2000

To be honest, the "Blockbuster" course, like my interest in Schlosser's book, was not happenstance but a deliberate foray into socially activist narrative. A kind of Rip Van Winkle feeling had been settling in mind since the late 1970s, a sense of seismic changes occurring in this country in waves of layoffs, healthcare woes, reported failings of public education, and widening income gaps—all reported as I went about my work in the classroom and library stacks, dimly sensing a grinding of sociocultural and economic techtonic plates but insulated from it as a tenured professor. Social change was in motion, however, and much of it negative. Writers must be at work recording the fuller contemporary story, writers of exposé and disclosure—new muckrakers.

Say the word "muckraker" in the opening years of the twenty-first century, however, and the listener's mind shuts as fast as it opens, for muckraking suffers both from too much and too little familiarity. The term floats freely in popular culture, but the texts themselves lack literary prestige, no matter how skilled their practitioners or schooled their readers over decades of varying regimens of taste. Students of

American history know that Jacob Riis's *How the Other Half Lives* of 1890 is considered the precursor of the muckraking movement, which arose in full in the first Gilded Age, specifically the opening years of the twentieth century, with essays appearing in such magazines as *Collier's*, *Cosmopolitan*, *Everybody's*, and *Ladie's Home Journal*.

Muckraking, however, was chiefly identified with Samuel S. Mc-Clure's *McClure's Magazine*, which featured not only Upton Sinclair but such names as Ray Stannard Baker (*Following the Color Line*, 1908), Lincoln Steffens (*The Shame of the Cities*, 1904), and Ida M. Tarbell (*The History of the Standard Oil Company*, 1902-4). These writers' own rubric for their common enterprise was exposé and disclosure. Both terms referred to a reportorial literature, produced in the public interest, in factual revelation of malfeasance and criminal behavior in politics and business.

As identifiers, however, neither "exposure" nor "disclosure" endured. Instead, *muckraker* proved to be the term with traction, assigned in a 1906 coinage by President Theodore Roosevelt. In a speech that year, Roosevelt modified an image from John Bunyan's *Pilgrim's Progress* to acknowledge the prevalent "filth" of corruption in business and public life in the United States and to assert the need to remove it with a Bunyanesque "muck-rake."

Immediately, however, Roosevelt warned listeners that those writers who relentlessly ply that rake threaten the social order and are agents of "evil" (reprinted in Weinberg 58–65). Roosevelt arguably hobbled the cohort of literary social critics even as he named them. The baleful presidential baptism didn't doom the movement, but its own decadence weakened it in the mid-1910s and 1920s. Such writers as David Graham Phillips relied increasingly on emotional appeal at the expense of factual accuracy and routinely invoked familiar spectres like "the trusts" or "the syndicates" as the public wearied of the formulaic repetition and lost interest. Exposé now bore the earmarks of stereotype.

By 1930, the influential Fred Lewis Pattee's *The New American Literature, 1890–1930* declared the movement to be "the last spasm of the Puritan conscience," initially honest but in its late phase "debauched" into a jeering cynicism (146). Extinction, it seemed, was virtually complete, and even today no muckraker questions appear on the literature sections of the SAT or GRE exams, those measures of cultural capital. No muckraker unit appears in the anthologies of American literature. Muckrakers, in short, are the "disappeareds" of American literature, the label lingering both as accolade and albatross, oscillating always between honor and opprobrium.

Without fanfare, however, the movement is enjoying a renaissance in this, the second Gilded Age. A c.2000 generation of muckrakers has taken center stage on best-seller lists. The publishers are mainstream houses such as Houghton Mifflin and Random House.* The new muckrakers' books have been reviewed in equally mainstream publications, notably the Sunday *New York Times*. Schlosser's *Fast Food Nation* is one, reviewed on January 21, 2001 as "a fine piece of muckraking, alarming without being alarmist" and stocked nationwide at Barnes & Noble and Border's Books. *Fast-Food Nation*, true to its subtitle, *The Dark Side of the All-American Meal*, shows in understated tones the "dark side" of modern American meat packinghouses, diabolical workplaces with soaring injury rates and abysmal hourly pay.

Fast Food Nation admittedly touched me in an autobiographic way. In college years, hadn't I myself earned good money working in the meat department of an A&P supermarket, wrapping chickens and beef cuts at a good hourly wage negotiated by the company's management and the Amalgamated Meat Cutters of America? Suppose as a young person today, I were to seek work in a packing plant. Would I have the union safeguards, literally speaking, the guardianship of my safety? No, according to *Fast Food Nation*, I'd be at mortal risk, most probably injured or disabled, certainly wretchedly paid. And despite those reassuring purple USDA Inspected stamps, I'd be one cog in a machine—call it Charlie Chaplin's *Modern Times* meets Hieronymus Bosch—producing meat often contaminated with fecal matter (*E. coli* 0157: H7), endangering the health, the very life, of consumers who fail to detoxify it by cooking it to a high temperature.

From Schlosser, I moved to Naomi Klein's *No Logo: Taking Aim at the Brand Bullies* (1999), also brought to my attention by a *New York Times* review (April 2000) and awaiting attention on my shelf. *No Logo*, a best-seller in Canada and Europe, is an account of transnational corporations' business practices which are hostile to the public interest. From Pepsi to Nike to Levi Strauss and others, Klein argues, these companies' marketing strategies operate to colonize the United States and other parts of the world by turning citizens solely into consumers, with life's choices accordingly narrowed to mere brand selection. With its case studies based in U.S. school districts, in Philippine free-trade zone factories, and in New York City's Times Square, *No Logo* exposes

---

* Some titles have proved overtly polemical, such as Gail Eisnitz's mid-1990s *Slaughterhouse*, an animal-rights activist's indictment of the meat industry, and Michael Moore's *Downsize This!* a caustic, jocular critique of corporate and political corruption culminating in an invitation to join "Mike's Militia," itself a call for citizen activism couched as a spoof of paramilitary groups. Other exposés had appeared from book publishers known for political stances, such as Regnery, the conservative-right publisher of Bernard Goldberg's best-selling *Bias*, as indictment of the news media's alleged liberalism. Or the leftist Verso (its motto: Books with an Edge), the publisher of Kim Moody's *Workers in a Lean World: Unions in the International Economy* (1997).

the dark side of corporate branding in an era in which corporations have jettisoned the factories producing products that bear their brands. Klein offers a first-hand account of the offshore manufacturing sites where upscale products are made under subcontract in sweatshop conditions by workers paid pennies and fired for union organizing and/or (if female) for pregnancy.

Like *Fast Food Nation*, *No Logo* tapped another autobiographic memory. As a summer worker in an Owens-Illinois glass bottle plant in West Virginia in 1960, I had packed glassware bound for Coca-Cola, Pepsi, Clorox, and a host of other companies. The union to which I paid hefty membership dues, the Glass Bottle Blowers Association, negotiated the hourly wage that allowed my fellow plant workers to own homes and drive late-model Chevies and Fords. It let me save for college.

That plant is long closed, a part of the 1970s huge wave of deindustrialization that left the former factories Rust Belt relics as it ushered in the service economy and ended material prosperity for vast numbers of blue-collar American workers. The factory work that supported a huge segment of our people no longer exists in the United States, and *No Logo* maps its newer far-flung remote locations, its worker degradation, and the relentless corporate branding that has superceded it.

"Why are you reading all those ain't-it-awful books?" I was asked in 2001, half in jest, by Dr. Hugh Tilson, former State Health Director, North Carolina Division of Public Health. Dr. Tilson and I were attending a music festival, and I'd just finished reading Laurie Garrett's *Betrayal of Trust: The Collapse of Global Public Health* (2000), a book Tilson knew and praised for its breadth and accuracy. Neither he nor I could have known that Garrett's book was the textbook prediction of the 2001 failure of the U.S. public-health system to deal with the anthrax bioterror scare episode in the fall, following the attack on the World Trade Center, when five people died from anthrax amid widespread confusion about safety procedures, treatment protocols, and the source(s) of infection.

So why, this physician asked on a warm April day in the North Carolina mountains, was an English teacher interested in reading about the collapse of public health? Why not stick to poetry and novels? Replying that a cultural-studies approach to literature requires a certain societal vigilance, I did not admit to the tremors registering on a kind of personal Richter Scale, one epicenter being the reality of contemporary minimum-wage work, revealed in another new muckraker narrative, *Nickel and Dimed: On (Not) Getting By in America*. Barbara Ehrenreich's first-hand authorial report from the field of low-pay, no-benefit jobs was staged by middle-class espionage via serial role-play as a waitress, house cleaner, and Wal-Mart clerk in Florida, Maine, and finally Minneapolis. Ehrenreich reports back to tell us of the "involuntary philanthropy" provided by low-wage workers ill-housed, ill-fed, and socially invisible too. Ehrenreich portrays these working millions as on-the-job "invisibles" in the richest country in the world.

Perhaps no single group has disappeared more completely from the American middle-class consciousness—my own included—than prison inmates. Yet in Nashville, where I live, the entrance to a residential development leads past an ice-blue glass high-rise, the headquarters of Corrections Corporation of America (CCA). To my mind, prisoners-for-profit seems decadent even in a marketplace culture, the incongruity more appropriate as material for standup *schtick*, perfect for a dark Lennie Bruce routine, the early *Saturday Night Live*, or Jon Stewart's *The Daily Show*.

But open the pages of Joseph T. Hallinan's *Going Up the River: Travels in a Prison Nation* (2001) to see the post–Cold War result of simultaneous public support of the prison-industrial complex and the abdication of citizens' responsibility for the American criminal-justice system, in which two million persons are incarcerated, the highest rate in the world, 700 per 100,000 citizens (while the Canadian and European countries' rates are 80 to 121 per 100,000). Prisons, as Hallinan notes, have spread over America like Wal-Marts, replacing shuttered manufacturing plants and military bases as vital centers of local economies.

In Nashville, the home of country music, the legends Merle Haggard and Johnny Cash recorded soulful songs of death row and hard time, but CCA conducts business on behalf of shareholders from the suburban office park, its NYSE stock quotations reported daily in the business pages of newspapers nationwide.

Exposing horrific prison conditions, *Going Up the River* provides a lesson in American literary history. Eldridge Cleaver's *Soul on Ice*, a prison memoir that a class of mine had read and debated in a recent course on literature of the 1960s, was produced, Hallinan reveals, at a point when prison reading and writing programs were advocated as rehabilitative. *Going Up the River*, however, chronicles the abandonment of all such programs and implies that a budding Eldridge Cleaver in today's punishing prisons would more likely become psychotic.

What lies inside the new muckrakers' pages? The due diligence narratives of grave problems now deeply embedded in U.S. culture and extending abroad. In toto, they address food contamination and monopolistic corporate takeovers of citizen space, including schools. They chronicle the collapse of the public health system in the United States and worldwide, the marketplace commodification of prisoners for profit, and a U.S. labor minimum-wage peonage that has become standard practice throughout the country. These books address crises in what some fear is a U.S. socioeconomic "race to the bottom."

Admittedly, the identification of this particular cohort of neo-muckrakers is my own. No reviewer of the various books named above has noticed the titles' topical kinship, except insofar as reviews praise all their writing as "gifted," "graceful," "lyrical," "valuable and illumi-nating," "eloquent," "vivid," and "good reading."

The writers named above did not set out to be a literary nonfiction group or movement. No impresario of an editor approached them at the verge of the twenty-first century to sign this group to publishing contracts and thus identify them as a "school." Among the five, Bar-bara Ehrenreich and Naomi Klein have a slight acquaintance, and Klein once shook hands with Eric Schlosser at a public reading. Otherwise, these writers share no regional base nor biographical con-nections nor professional affiliations except insofar as they earn their living as freelance and staff writers for newspapers and magazines as they write their books. Naomi Klein is a columnist for the Toronto *Globe and Mail* and *The Nation*, Joseph Hallinan a reporter for the *Wall Street Journal*, Laurie Garrett a reporter for *Newsday*, Barbara Ehren-reich a contributor to *The Nation*, and Eric Schlosser a staff writer for *The Atlantic* and contributor to *Rolling Stone*.

Each of these writers, nonetheless, has entered into an unintended collaboration, a fellowship defined by Edward Said as "independent intellectuals who actually form an incipient community." Based vari-ously in Washington, D.C., Toronto, Key West, and the New York area, each of these new muckraker writers thus worked by herself or him-self for years, researching and writing, helped by librarians and assis-tants but unaware that his or her individual project was one puzzle piece of a much larger movement diagnosing America's major mod-ern malfunctions.

Canon Fodder

Immersed in these new muckraker books of c. 2000, I became in-trigued by their century-old "parents." Amid revivals of everything from Broadway musicals to corsets, why no backward glance at the first-generation muckrakers? Were their Gilded Age books and maga-zine pieces as rabidly polemical as I'd been led to believe? Was Roo-sevelt right? Did they deserve their decades of all-around neglect? Ida

Tarbell, for instance, appears on a 2002 first-class U.S. postage stamp, honored as a woman journalist mainly for her *History of the Standard Oil Company* (1902–4). Why haven't feminist readers renewed an interest in Tarbell, whose own words in a letter of 1901 surely beckon students of American writing to take a closer look. "The work we have in mind is a narrative history of the Standard Oil Company," Tarbell wrote, "a straightforward narrative, as picturesque and dramatic as I can make it" (qtd. in Brady 125).

Drama, the pictorial, the linear—and "narrative" too. Such writerly key words cry out for notice in a contemporary moment when a melange of texts are scrutinized by English teachers, from political campaign speeches to real-estate classified ads. (And since when have literary critics allowed Teddy Roosevelt the final word on literary achievement and morality?)

So why, one asks, has critical attention bypassed the muckrakers all this time?

A response to *The Jungle* in my "Blockbuster" course of 2001 gave me the clue. From their classroom seats, the students in "Twentieth-Century American Blockbusters" objected to specific shortcomings in *The Jungle*. Its "two-dimensional" characters frustrated them, likewise its "excessive" language. Above all, its "melodrama."

To tell them that melodrama was now important in film studies required a too-quick reflex in my déjà-vu moment. My thoughts, instead, flashed on a turbulent recent history of "culture wars" and canon reform, of arguments pushing (and resisting) a major realignment of American literature's table of contents. To a seasoned college instructor in American literature, the students' critique was all too familiar as a rerun of the very terms used for decades to dismiss both whole genres and single authors, for instance, Theodore Dreiser. Until critics of the 1980s mounted a case for the rich complexity of Dreiser's novels, readers routinely ridiculed the onetime journalist for sentimentality and melodrama.

Students' objections to stylistic "excess" in *The Jungle* also recalled a decades-long minimal interest in an entire narrative genre, the sentimental novel. Its exponent, Harriet Beecher Stowe, was long ostracized for her allegedly bathetic *Uncle Tom's Cabin*. The august post–World War II *Literary History of the United States* (1946, 1953) proclaimed that when Ralph Waldo Emerson visited England, he "took wisdom to wisdom." On her trip, Mrs. Stowe was said to stir a voguish hysteria. Emerson appropriately moved Europe's "mind" while the lesser "Mrs. Stowe" had moved the lower-order faculty, the European "heart" (383, 583).

American literary studies from the 1980s onward, however, situate Harriet Beecher Stowe prominently with the higher canonical figures. Why? Because, as we know, Stowe and her sentimentalist cohorts enjoyed a vigorous and ongoing revival after critics showed that such authority as the *Literary History* was a political formation serving professorial caste interests. At the same time, sentiment itself was found to be a mentality crucial to the ethos of nineteenth-century thought in the United States, not a marginal but core value.

My 2001 students' complaints about *The Jungle* meant that some terms of denigration had not disappeared, but receded into latency. If "excess" was no longer viable for derision of the sentimental novel, it could still readily be deployed for muckraker texts. So this was critique-as-déjà vu! The object of derision, however, was not the female cohort of popular writers denounced by Nathaniel Hawthorne as a "d——d mob of scribbling women." Nor was it a male journalist-turned-novelist allegedly so unsophisticated that he dubbed his title character in *Sister Carrie* "our Little Knight." The butt of criticism was, instead, the writer identified as a muckraker. By extension, this time around, the literary scapegoat was not a Dreiser nor a Stowe. It was a group of writers producing a literature of social critique, branching from Sinclair's *The Jungle* to such texts as Jack London's *The Iron Heel* or Frank Norris's *The Octopus* and also to numerous nonfiction texts as well.

On Native (Burial) Grounds

Changes in reading tastes have a political side, which I learned first-hand when searching the case histories of commentary on the 1900s Gilded Age muckrakers. Their graves, I found, were dug by specific critics. Roosevelt lifted the first shovelful, but other pallbearers took their turn. This is to say that damning statements in landmark books dating from the mid-twentieth century made their mark and went unchallenged. A prime example is Van Wyck Brooks's *The Confident Years: 1885–1915* (1952), the fifth and final volume of Brooks's influential literary history of the United States. Its publication just at the beginning of the Cold War accounts for Brooks's anti-communist scorn for the muckrakers as followers of Russian immigrant anarchists still fighting the tyranny of Czarist Russia in Manhattan's Lower East Side.

Brooks's chapter, "The Muckrakers," characterized the movement in Cold War terms of alien invasion and infection festering in the body politic (see ch. 21). The "so-called" muckraking movement, Brooks wrote, was not engendered by art, but instead hatched in a 1900s socialistic and communistic world and "invade[d] all corners of the mind and spirit." Muckraking brought all discontents to a head, Brooks added, his phrasing compounding the alien attack with hints of infection. Their project, he wrote, was lamentably far afield of art. Brooks damned muckraking, in short, as politically dangerous (albeit ephemeral), anachronistic, and subliterary.*

A second major critical project, one even more influential, was Alfred Kazin's *On Native Grounds: An Interpretation of Modern American Prose Literature* (1942). Kazin judged the movement in terms reminiscent of natural disaster: "suddenly released in a flood," muckraking became a "long-awaited reckoning with the realities of the new industrial and scientific epoch," a "welled up . . . last tumultuous fling" of post-frontier energies (see ch. 4). Kazin saw muckrakers as opponents of monopoly capitalism, which he called an American behemoth overlaying the landscape, "absorbing everything for itself, brazen in its greed, oblivious to the human society on which it fed." The monopolistic trusts, Kazin wrote, were "those dragon's teeth, sowed in American individualism," now come to "haunt the national imagination and provoke a national effort toward reform."

Yet Kazin's rhetoric undercut this political analysis. The "spirit of active critical realism," Kazin wrote, "now swept through politics and journalism," and the American "native grounds" were thus inundated when a collective mental dam broke. The muckraking movement, for Kazin, was one raging intellectual and emotional tumult.[†] *On Native Grounds* interpreted the muckrakers as anti-imperialists who were nonetheless fascinated with imperialism, as writers more interested in colorful proletarian material than in workers' rights, as nostalgics avid to rewind American history to its preindustrial era of small farms and Main Street shops.[‡]

---

* Muckraking, to Brooks, enlisted "reformers and social workers" and "vague progressivism" which "generally led toward socialism—and communism later." Brooks acknowledged that the movement destroyed America's "fatalistic optimism" from the national past and was "historically vital." But yet he implied that muckrakers' retrograde, foreign, and crude politics were commensurate with their literary "superficial[ity]" which expressed only a passing, if historically recurring, national "mood."

† Kazin wrote that the flood waters roiled with inchoate intellectual flotsam and jetsam as the new "spirit of insurgence" flowed with "borrowed and conflicting European ideas," with "amorphous tendencies toward political reform," with "hopes for a different social order," with nostalgia, aspiration, impatience, all of which were "dammed up so long at the back of the American mind."

‡ Kazin thought of the muckrakers as rife with self-contradiction, as indicated by his chapter title, "Progressivism: The Superman and the Muckrake." The first term referred to Theodore Roosevelt's Nietzschean superhuman "gusto," the second to the reformers who, Kazin felt, borrowed that very life-force for their reformist fling. Kazin rehearsed a debate among historians of the United States about the political efficacy of the muckrakers' nonfiction narratives, but he scanted that literature in favor of

The 1940s–50s political climate in the U.S. doubtless also kept the muckrakers in eclipse because it fostered the New Criticism, which favored literary forms hostile to the muckrakers' own. Their literature of exposure positioned readily accessible meanings along narrative surfaces. In this sense Brooks's barb about muckrakers' "superficialities" rang true, even if he turned their salient and carefully honed feature—accessibility—against them. Muckrakers, in addition, directly addressed societal relations and problems, while New Criticism rejected such relations as unliterary and thus unworthy of literary critical talent.

Indeed, literature was instead seen by New Criticism as a form of knowledge accessible mainly through the interpretation of distinct linguistic features, principally metaphor and symbol, which were the nemesis of muckrakers who strove for discursive transparency. New Critical poetics sought structural tensions and their internal resolutions within the poem or novel, often with resort to epistemologies of irony. The best critical intellects were considered those adept in discerning depths of indirection, instanced in William Empson's 1966 *Seven Types of Ambiguity*. Reading taste changed accordingly, as the allusive *The Waste Land* of T. S. Eliot displaced the accessible *Evangeline* of Henry Wadsworth Longfellow.

This climate stifled potential interest in the once-admired muckrakers, who strove to produce meaning directly, explicitly, and without the need for critical mediation or intervention of any kind. Ray Stannard Baker had encapsulated its ethos in his preface to a coal-strike report: "It seems profoundly important that the public should know exactly—." Baker's word choice expresses the muckraker's goal, public information rendered with exactitude (qtd. in Weinberg 40).

In the interdisciplinary field of American Studies, meanwhile, the muckrakers fared no better because New Criticism made itself felt in the myth-and-symbol school, which argued that societal conflict could be codified in cultural symbols. Machines, gardens, and public figures such as Lindbergh or Andrew Jackson were now susceptible to literary critical deep penetration. No muckraker was offered as a cultural symbol, just as no muckraking text was plumbed for its divers types of

---

extended treatment of the muckrakers' novels. He wrote, "At *McClure's Magazine*, where the first muckrakers were provided with shovels, Frank Norris worked along with Ida Tarbell, Lincoln Steffens, and Ray Stannard Baker."

But all muckrakers, according to Kazin, failed to "transcend the normal boundaries of journalism in their day or in our own." *On Native Grounds* did not suggest what form that transcendence might take, or what its criteria might include. Instead, Kazin focussed his critique on the muckrakers' fiction, proving that the *Prose Literature* of his subtitle was really weighted toward the novel, that he had no fresh insights into nonfiction prose.

ambiguity. None could be, since the point of a literature of exposé was razor-sharp incision through veils of ambiguity and obscurity.

The Brooks–Kazin–New Critical critique has stood for more than a half century as American literary critical projects either ignored the muckrakers entirely or mentioned them only in passing, with Sinclair typically representative, a "master of exposure" and "propagandist" (Blair et al. 183, Hubbell 144).*

Literature versus Journalism: The Maginot Line

One study deserves notice for its particular term of attack: journalism. Jay Martin's influential *Harvests of Change: American Literature 1865–1914* (1967) reinforced the Brooks-Kazin pejoratives but also used a revealing term to attack these qualities: "journalism" (246).

Journalism. Echoing the Brooks-Kazin and New Critical critique, the term is a major epithet of derision to which the muckrakers have been subjected by self-identified literary critics. Consider Morris Dickstein's *Double Agent*, a 1992 study of the critic and society, to see how fraught the term is. "Even to link the words 'journalism' and 'criticism,' " Dickstein cautioned, "goes against the grain" of serious literary criticism (see ch. 4). *Double Agent* reinforces the distinction. While critics make carefully considered judgments involving root meanings, Dickstein argued, the journalist traffics in ephemera: "the word journalism suggests a day-to-day thing, as ephemeral as the paper it's printed on." Dickstein elaborated: "Though journalists themselves often lead feverishly active, even adventurous lives, in their work they're expected to be passive conductors of the world's ongoing business." Caught up in ephemera, the journalist acts in febrile haste in a mental stance of social passivity.

Dickstein spoke specifically of newspaper book reviewers working under tight deadlines and commercial pressures. But his terms reprise the censure of investigative writers whose work has appeared in mass-market magazines. From the longstanding literary studies standpoint, these writers are *merely* journalists. The literary critic, both in and out of the academy, has the higher calling, in the true meaning of vocation (from the Latin *vocare*). The journalist, on the other hand, is merely a voc-ed worker. (Programs in journalism and in English typically exist in separate academic departments, schools, or university colleges, an arrangement normalized over decades, with writers designated as "creative" separated from those in journalistic "training."

---

* One effort to reconsider the muckrakers' social role positions them as an "orientation device about America"—this in the 1988 *Columbia Literary History of the United States*, 578.

Self-styled "creative" writers reinforce the hierarchy, for instance, when the narrator of Gore Vidal's novel *1876* (1976), says, "The conversation of any journalist is always more interesting than anything that he writes" (165). Norman Mailer, as novelist and New Journalist, has taken a similar stance, arguing that "the best investigative journalism tends to rest on too narrow an ideological base—the rational, ironic, fact-oriented world of the media liberal." The superior genre, Mailer's own favorite, is realist fiction, which he calls "the most concentrated form of fantasy" (81). Those muckrakers whose fiction can be categorized by critics—not journalists, but critics—as part of the literary realist or naturalist school, such as Frank Norris or Jack London, can be critically redeemed. Otherwise, the literature of exposure is not bona fide literature.*

Despite this severe academic hierarchy, muckraker fiction has flourished through the twentieth century, notably John Steinbeck's *The Grapes of Wrath* (1939), but including such popular titles as John D. McDonald's *Condominium* (1977), a condemnation of criminally deadly shortcuts in the construction industry. In some areas of academic literary study, in addition, nonfiction narratives of disclosure have commanded attention in recent years. *Silent Spring*, one of my "blockbusters," has been studied as ecological literature and as feminist literature of domesticity. In addition, gay and lesbian studies has included Randy Shilts's *And the Band Played On* (1985), an account of U.S. government failure to recognize and assess the growing AIDS epidemic and formulate appropriate treatment policies.

This niche status, however, is the exception proving the rule. Critical interest in muckraker texts within literary studies has been desultory.†

Teachers of literature have thus been averse to inclusion of muckraker narratives, for instance, bypassing Ralph Nader's 1965 *Unsafe at Any Speed*, an indictment of fatal engineering flaws of General Motors' Chevrolet Corvair, the car in which a friend of mine found herself and her infant son suddenly flipped upside down in a roadside ditch in the early 1960s, both miraculously unhurt. Nader's book led to a new U.S. law, the National Traffic and Motor Vehicle Safety Act, and to the

---

* One study, dismissive of the "mere muckraker," tries to "rescue" literary journalism from muckraking with this status claim based on boundaries: "Narrative literary journalism can bear a resemblance to muckraking, and muckraking can clearly bear a resemblance to literary journalism. . . . As a consequence, if narrative literary journalism is not to be mistaken for sensational or muckraking journalism there is a need to understand what makes it distinctive among these journalistic discourses [and] equally important is a need to understand the overlapping and mutual concerns of these discourses." See Hartsock, *A History of American Literary Journalism*, 135, 134.

† Notable studies include Harold S. Wilson's *McClure's Magazine and the Muckrakers* (1970), Justin Kaplan's 1974 biography of Lincoln Steffens, and Christopher Wilson's *The Labor of Words: Literary Professionalism on the Progressive Era* (1985).

movement for seat belts, air bags, and crashworthy vehicles. Yet I my-self did not consider *Unsafe at Any Speed* for the "Blockbuster" course. Somehow it did not seem, well, literary. In choice of course books, the boundary articulated by Dickstein on behalf of all literary critics had held as a Maginot Line.

My students' complaints about *The Jungle*, however, cracked open new possibilities. Suppose such texts as *Unsafe at Any Speed* were to be subjected to different criteria. Suppose the firewall between journalism and literature were razed so that an assortment of texts could be examined from a different angle. Why not take advantage of narrative studies, an area of lively debate within what is loosely termed literary theory, with abundant work published by Hayden White, Peter Brooks, James Phelan, and others? Suppose narrative theory were to reopen the kind of "radical writing" that, according to theorist of narrative Christopher Nash "claims to strike at the root (social, for example) of things 'outside' the text"—which is to say, narrative able to intercede directly in the sociopolitical realm (199–218).

Suppose, moreover, that my own bent toward American and cultural studies were to prompt an examination of two generations of muckraker texts within the sociocultural contexts of each era—the turn-of-the-century moment of Sinclair, Tarbell, Baker, Steffens and others like them now positioned in relation to American muckraker texts of c. 2000, Schlosser and Ehrenreich, Klein, Garrett, and Hallinan.

Muckrakers c. 1900, c. 2000

Parallels between the two generations of muckrakers—of the 1900s and 2000s—must be acknowledged and explored in this project. Those of the Gilded Age of the early 1900s exposed and censured corporate trusts for their illegal business practices (for example, kickbacks and industrial espionage) and their virtual monopoly on commodities and services—steel, oil, rail transit. They did so in order to make clear the need for organized response to abuses of the democratic system.

The neo-muckraker texts of the c. 2000 Gilded Age similarly critique contemporary socioeconomic conditions in which marketplace capitalism (dubbed "extreme capitalism" by the cultural critic Thomas Frank) is shown to be hostile to democratic society. They expose the legislative and corporate contributive role in social crises which demand major public-sector campaigns for remediation. Their work has been prompted evidently by the demonstrable public-sector retrenchment from the civic commonweal in a late twentieth-century era of deregulation and privatization abetted by special-interest funding of legislative and executive election campaigns.

Differences between two generations of muckraker narratives must also be examined. The new group bears the stamp of their 1900s antecedents, but turn the pages, for instance, of Schlosser's narrative, and significant variation between the two generations is immediately apparent. In *The Jungle*, for instance, the main characters are all downtrodden workers whose bosses are purebred villains. *Fast Food Nation*, on the other hand, widens the spectrum of its dramatis personae by featuring several compelling biographies of self-made American entrepreneurs, such as John Richard Simplot, a one-time Idaho potato farmer who became one of America's richest men through a potato empire supplying the military and McDonald's. (Simplot's is the name responsible for the crispy golden-arch fries.)

Other differences are equally evident. In *The Jungle*, Sinclair made the cri de coeur of the Lithuanian-immigrant Chicago packinghouse worker the metaphoric "hog squeal of the universe." Sinclair's metaphor exploits his audience's assenting familiarity with the sensational tradition of nineteenth-century sentimental and melodramatic narrative. Its decibel level is high, its appeal to emotion direct and intense.

In 2000, in contrast, *Fast Food Nation* deploys an aesthetic image of slaughterhouse "Whizzards peeling meat off decapitated heads [of cattle], picking them almost as clean as the white skulls painted by Georgia O'Keeffe" (171). Schlosser, like Sinclair, presents a slaughterhouse which is alien, repellent, at best pruriently interesting to their bourgeois readers. Schlosser's art image, however, avoids such techniques of nineteenth-century sensationalism. His antiphony of narrative and metaphor works within an interpretive framework of emotional containment. It operates in accord with an understated narrative style typified by his former teacher John McPhee. It stabilizes the horrific for a reading community whose class identity is affirmed by reference to exhibition spectatorship of art. The reference to O'Keeffe signals a narrator who construes his readers as late twentieth-century art devotees aware of metropolitan museum showings, such as the Georgia O'Keeffe multi-city exhibit of the late 1980s (with ancillary gift-shop reproductions, coffee table books, and documentary TV footage). Each narrative, Sinclair's and Schlosser's, rhetorically shapes, and is shaped by, the reading community it serves.

Both groups, however, claim literary allegiance to their projects. The picturesque and the dramatic, Ida Tarbell knew, were prime components of her exposé of Standard Oil, not flourishes but integers. In

2001, Schlosser engaged fast food "both as a commodity and as a metaphor," the literary term given equal weight with its counterpart in commerce (3). Both generations of muckrakers have understood that a deep impression on the reading public is only possible if their stories are told well, faithful to facts but peopled with sharply drawn characters and compellingly paced.

Exposés and Excess investigates two generations of muckrakers for their narrative designs and the sociopolitical conditions that fostered their efforts, and just at a time of possible renewed interest in them. An edition of the 1961 anthology *The Muckrakers*, edited by Arthur and Lila Weinberg, is now reprinted, and the University of Illinois Press is soon to publish a new edition of Ida M. Tarbell's autobiography *All in the Day's Work*. In addition, Judith and William Serrin have compiled *Muckraking! An Anthology of Journalism That Changed America* (2002), with selections from the Stamp Act to the early 1990s, the project being the editors' tribute to "a journalistic tradition marked by depth of vision, passion for change, and bravery . . . journalism that has made America a better country."

To which *Gilded Ages, Civic Passions* adds: provided a richer literary record. It is precisely to present the neo-muckrakers as writers that this project includes original interviews with them.

Recording the writers' thoughts on writing is especially important in the age of composition on computers and email. Had Ida Tarbell lived in the electronic age, it's doubtful we would have her revealing statement on the plan to write a picturesque, dramatic narrative of Standard Oil, which was written in a letter to a young editor, John Siddall, now archived and available to researchers in the Petroleum and Research Center at the University of Wyoming at Laramie.

The electronic era of the throwaway—and recycle—society has largely eliminated such paper trails. The "delete" and "typeover" functions of a word processor instantly erase the editorial process, just as email has replaced the handwritten letters that formerly provided keen insights into the writing processes. To pursue investigative writing as creative and created, *Exposés and Excess* provides an opportunity to hear its writers-on-writing, a sort of *Paris Review* Writers-at-Work format for nonfiction narrativists.

This book opens, however, with a personal account of this observer's growing uneasiness that it might not be, as President Reagan once assured us, "morning in America." So many layoffs, so many closings in such big numbers in an era celebrated for free-market supremacy. And why does everything touched in the household, from a coffee mug to an American flag, say "Made in China"? Or Bangladesh or Pakistan or the Philippines, anywhere but here? Could the prosperity cycles be more faux than fact? Could the experts—the economists, the officials, the media—describe a virtual America, an America .com, disconnected from the one which most people actually inhabit? *Exposés and Excess* opens with a personal survey of the creeping quiet crisis and one citizen's overdue vigilance.

Chapter 2
Bulked Up and Hollowed Out
Looking Backward, Looking Forward

A special time in history: affluent and aggressive, prosperous and peaceful, wired and wild, and, ultimately, finite . . . The New Gilded Age: The New Yorker Looks at the Culture of Affluence, *edited by David Remnick, 2002*

—New Yorker *advertisement, 2002*

Indices of economic gloom gather like ghosts at a funeral. Portents are everywhere that America's latest Gilded Age may be coming to an end.

—*Steve Fraser,* Los Angeles Times Book Review, April 1, 2001

Middle class America . . . is best thought of not as the normal state of our society, but as an interregnum between Gilded Ages.

—*Paul Krugman,* New York Times Magazine, October 20, 2002

The Census Bureau said that the number of poor Americans rose last year to 32.9 million, an increase of 1.3 million, while the proportion living in poverty rose to 11.7 percent, from 11.3 percent in 2000.

—*Robert Pear,* New York Times, September 25, 2002

In the early 1980s, I agreed to edit a paperback reprint of Edward Bellamy's time-travel romance *Looking Backward—2000–1883* (1887), published in the era known as America's Gilded Age. A blockbuster novel of its own day, based on a love story and studded with technological wonders, *Looking Backward* called attention to U.S. sociopolitical problems crying for correction. It summoned help from organized citizen groups, business leaders, and public officials. Wildly popular among middle-class American readers in the late nineteenth century, *Looking Backward* is credited with contributing to the political activism of the muckraking movement of the early twentieth century. For me, this utopian novel turned out to be an important gauge measuring

America's social malfunctions of the 1880s–1890s. Surprisingly, it also became a guide to conditions giving rise a century later to equally urgent social problems and a new surge of investigative writing: muckraking.

Among the contemporary investigative writers considered here, only Barbara Ehrenreich was in print in the early 1980s when I began my introduction to Bellamy's novel, though her *Nickel and Dimed* was undreamed of. Joseph Hallinan was an undergraduate studying journalism and writing for the student newspaper at Boston University (where I was then teaching, though our paths never crossed). Eric Schlosser, a recent Princeton graduate, was writing fiction but planning a career as a playwright. Laurie Garrett had left doctoral studies in immunology at the University of California, Berkeley, to move into health and science broadcasting, first at San Francisco's KPFA, then to National Public Radio. Naomi Klein, a child of ten, was beginning a rebellion against her "granola family" by wearing satin pants, listening to Blondie records, and making crank calls to hairdressers.

I, of course, was reading Bellamy nearly two decades before the September 11, 2001, attack on the World Trade Center and Pentagon, although the America of *Looking Backward* was hardly innocent. The novel critiqued the America of of the 1880s as a social Darwinist society in which vast, unprecedented wealth concentrated among the Olympian few was poised against the catastrophic deprivation afflicting the general population. Bellamy represented 1880s American society as a metaphoric huge coach drawn by harnessed, toiling, dusty "masses of humanity" over a hilly, sandy road at a tortuously slow pace. "The driver was hunger, and permitted no lagging." Atop the coach, enjoying the cool breeze, sat those of privilege whose comfortable seats were "in great demand." Won through keen competition, these seats could be given as gifts or willed to heirs.

Yet Bellamy emphasized the instability of this sociopolitical arrangement for those elites enjoying the ride. He cautioned that "the seats were very insecure," since at any moment accidents or jolts, meaning economic panics and depressions, might tumble these passengers to the ground, whereupon they would be obliged to join the masses in dragging the coach. "It was naturally regarded as a terrible misfortune to lose one's seat, and the apprehension that this might happen to them or their friends was a constant cloud upon the happiness of those who rode" (38–41).

The tremendous appeal of *Looking Backward* was in part its assurance to readers that this socioeconomic precariousness was only temporary, as was the horrific toil of the vast numbers in harness for their daily bread. The coach journey, Bellamy explained, was but a primitive phase of an industrial and social evolutionary process certain to culminate by the year 2000 in a utopian, rationalized industrial nation of interest-group cooperation, stable employment, high productivity, and an equitable distribution of goods and services for the entire citizenry.

Much of the futuristic technology in *Looking Backward* (for example, radio and central heat) was in everyday use by the mid-twentieth century, though politically Bellamy's millennial America seemed fantastically idealistic and also highly regimented, as societies in utopian narratives usually are. (Bellamy, a newspaper journalist, had yearned to attend West Point, and his youthful dream of a military career lived on in the citizens' National Army envisioned in *Looking Backward*.) The dire socioeconomic miseries of the novel's 1880s, however, had been safely consigned to a benighted American past. Bellamy's grim opening pages portray a late nineteenth century U.S. convulsed by violent strikes, class discord, economic depressions, joblessness, hunger, ruinous greed, extremes of wealth and of poverty, social instability—all of this presumed to be banished from modern America. It had been rumored that desperate immigrant families in Bellamy's hometown of Chicopee Falls, Massachusetts, had lived in caves dug into riverbanks, but a century later, nobody was let to starve, homeless in America.

Or were they?

The early 1980s, in fact, were bringing disconcerting news of a new wave of homelessness in the United States even as I began my introduction to *Looking Backward*. It would take another twenty years for the 2000 Urban Institute report "Millions Still Face Homelessness in a Booming Economy" to state that 2.3 million adults and children face "a spell of homelessness at least once during a year."* By then, the homeless would be a naturalized feature of the social landscape, but in the early 1980s, the sight of homeless persons on U.S. city sidewalks was shockingly new. A Third World norm was suddenly visible in every city in this richest nation in the world. During a 1984 visit to San Francisco, the streets around the hotels near Union Square were suddenly lined with beggers—many of them not dark-faced but white, new modern-day Okies. A West Coast architect stirred controversy for a portable shelter he designed for homeless persons living on the street.

Hunger in the U.S. was also becoming a media topic in the early 1980s as I wrote my introduction to *Looking Backward*. The antipoverty Great Society programs of President Lyndon B. Johnson had

* In December 2002, the U.S. Conference of Mayors would underscore the food-and-shelter crisis of the opening years of the twenty-first century, reporting a 19% increase in demand for food aid over the previous year for working families and stating that "the lack of food and adequate shelter for the working poor is becoming an endemic problem" (*New York Times*, December 18, 2002: A18).

been reported to feed hungry Americans nationwide, but TV and newspapers of the early 1980s featured suburban parents and children loading their station wagons with bologna-and-cheese sandwiches, which they drove into such cities as Boston and Philadelphia and charitably distributed to the new class of hungry street people. On corners by city stoplights, one began to see the "will-work-for-food" hand-lettered signs held by day-laborer hopefuls (among them some drug addicts).

As the street-corner men became fixtures through the 1990s and beyond, hard evidence of hunger was developed by U.S. government and not-for-profit agencies. Their messages were nearly identical. The U.S. Department of Agriculture would find that from 1996 to 1998, ten million U.S. households lacked access to sufficient food to meet their basic needs. Second Harvest, a U.S. not-for-profit hunger relief agency, would report that 23.3 million people sought emergency food assistance in 2001. This agency stated that because wages had not risen enough in recent years to cover the increased cost of living, "food has become an unaffordable luxury." Although welfare reform of the 1996 Personal Responsibility and Work Opportunity Reconciliation Act had pushed seven million people into jobs, nearly half of those people, according to the Joyce Foundation (2002), were unable to meet bills, pay rent, and buy food since starting their jobs.*

Back in the early 1980s, seeing these first signs of a new, high level of societal distress, I thought about my birthplace, Pittsburgh, whose identity as Iron City and Steel City endured only in a brand of beer and a football team after the city's steel plants closed in the 1970s. Public officials had then promoted job retraining as the alchemy to turn former industrial workers into high-tech computer programmers in these years of the newly fashionable deindustrialization. Their actual new jobs, however, trended downward, as many ex-steel workers—the fortunate ones—took semi- or unskilled postindustrial jobs such as school bus driver or janitor, or fast-food restaurant worker, earning a small fraction of their former wages at the abandoned, rusting plants along the Monongahela and Allegheny Rivers.

My Boston University students of those years, most from upper-middle-class families far removed from such blue-collar woes, nonetheless also sensed something amiss in the U.S., though the symptom of their anxiety was a perplexing hostility to literature's hapless souls. In

* On *60 Minutes II* on January 8, 2003, viewers saw typical American food lines of hundreds of people awaiting food at two donation centers in Ohio—working people who were identified as a nurse, an Air Force career retiree, a home-improvement store clerk unable to feed his family on his minimum-wage job(s). One man recalled standing in such lines as a boy during the Great Depression.

a large lecture hall at Boston University, where I was then teaching, students showed marked antipathy toward fictional characters whose moral actions jeopardized their socioeconomic status. Silas Lapham, the anguished paint manufacturer in William Dean Howells's novel *The Rise of Silas Lapham*, drew their scorn as a business failure too weak to take all necessary measures—specifically, commit fraud and theft to prevent the collapse of his business empire. Edith Wharton's Lily Bart, the protagonist of *The House of Mirth*, was despised as too squeamish to commit the blackmail necessary for her economic survival, too spineless for a social Darwinist world indifferent to her peril. Business cunning would have saved the paint mogul, the students suggested, and Lily ought to have toughened up and played hardball.

The students, in short, rewrote the stories to upgrade the protagonists' survival skills. And my exasperation with this pattern of misreading grew steadily—up to the epiphany at the classroom lectern when I cried out, "I get it, you're scared, aren't you? Scared of the future . . . you're worried about your futures." Whereupon nearly two hundred heads nodded, the faces relieved and grateful to bare their secret and acknowledge in common the fears which each had harbored alone. For the most part affluent whites, these students feared the contagion of failure in an America whose social contract, they somehow sensed, was expiring. In their American lives, there was to be no Catcher in the Rye.

Additional sources of my students' fears weren't difficult to find. The late 1970s were notable for what the political historian Haynes Johnson calls "a deep sense of frustration, compounded by a series of political, economic, and military failures at home and abroad." In *Sleepwalking Through History: America in the Reagan Years* (1991), Johnson catalogues the events fostering the national "pervasive sense of pessimism" which gripped my students: the debacle of the Vietnam war, ending with the televised fall of Saigon, the Watergate scandal which drove Richard Nixon from the White House, the murders of Martin Luther King Jr., Malcolm X, and Robert Kennedy.

Against this background, moreover, the presidency of Jimmy Carter was marked by the capture of the fifty-two American hostages in Tehran on November 4, 1979, with televised crowds of Iranians in the weeks and months ahead routinely chorusing, "Death to America!" in front of the seized U.S. Embassy. (Soon the Reagan administration contended with its own scandal, as the media and congressional hearings revealed the Iran-Contra scheme in which weapons were to be exchanged for the hostages.) When the Iranian Revolution cut off oil supplies, gasoline shortages and high prices seemed to expose a new American vulnerability, and in addition, recession loomed while inflation raged, with interest rates climbing toward twenty-one percent, a rate not seen since the Civil War. "For perhaps the first time," says Johnson, "many Americans wondered if the United States had passed its peak" (see chs. 1 and 2).

Other worries would beset my students in the years to come. In the recession of the late 1980s and early 1990s, young Americans were advised that they might become the first generation to fail to surpass their parents in earned income and material standard of living. Some of my students' fathers were laid off, especially as banks consolidated and corporations merged. The Gulf War brought women students to the shocked realization that in the event of a national military draft, they would probably not be exempted. In those years, students nationwide graduated without job offers, competing instead for the unpaid internships which might, they hoped, be the wedge to career opportunities.

Later on, in the superheated economy of the late 1990s, some undergraduates in my office admitted to feeling pulled between service work (teaching, the ministry) and family expectations of financial success. One young man, attracted to social work, held a *Wall Street Journal* on his lap and wistfully conceded he was headed for investment banking. The economic rollercoaster nonetheless brought the early 2000s return of the recessionary cycle of the B.S./B.A. unpaid internships. In a spring 2002 presentation to the faculty, the director of Vanderbilt's Career Center startled us with an onscreen name of the corporation which in recent years had been a major employer of Vanderbilt graduates: Enron.

This is to say that those of us instructors who are years in the classroom enjoy repeated opportunities to appreciate students as barometers of sociocultural change. My first benchmark barometric reading, however, took place in that Boston University lecture hall at a moment which was powerfully coincident with the *Looking Backward* project. That classroom moment and Bellamy's novel thereafter moved me to look beyond rosy projections of politicians and economists on the new U.S. high-tech service economy. Popular culture provided useful, yet discouraging, terms. Suppose the Paul Simon song lyric about things "slip-slidin' away" applied to social trends well underway and relentlessly in motion by the early 1980s. Suppose the discord in the opening passages of *Looking Backward* were to point, to borrow a movie title, "back to the future." Suppose, to recycle Walt Kelly's *Pogo* comic strip mantra yet one more time, "We have met the enemy, and he is us."

Suppose, in fact, that a full century following the publication of Bellamy's *Looking Backward*, conditions were once again to become dreadfully ripe for the emergence of a muckraker movement in American literature. True, oil and steel monopolies were no longer lightning-rod issues as they had been in the late nineteenth century. But the corporate domination of large sectors of life in the United States and offshore was giving rise to public concern about a de facto colonization of private and public space and about brutal dictates of workplace conditions. The globalization movement of what Thomas Frank calls *One Market Under God* (2000) was an accomplished fact, seemingly blessed in a *New York Times* editorial of 2001 which elided capitalism and democracy in its advocacy of "marketplace democracy." Some argued, however, as Frank does, that collapsing those two terms is a dangerous move with potentially dire consequences for the public.

As for politics, no writer in the later twentieth century bannered "The Treason of the Senate," as had David Graham Phillips in his 1906 muckraking magazine article in *Cosmopolitan*, an "arraignment" of senators who "betrayed the public to that cruel and vicious Spirit of Mammon" (reprinted in Weinberg 71–83). Yet later twentieth-century critiques castigated special-interest lobbying and the funding of election campaigns with the goal of controlling elected officials at the highest levels of government. In 2002, Enron, a major corporate contributor to legislators and to presidential campaigns, was found to have manipulated electricity shortages and prices in California and reaped billions of dollars from that state's citizens. The names and faces differed, but muckraking literature was arguably cyclical, and its moment once again propitious.

But what about audience receptivity? Samuel S. McClure had been surprised when subscriptions to his new *McClure's Magazine* surged in response to investigative essays by Ray Stannard Baker, Lincoln Steffans, Ida M. Tarbell, and others. McClure and the *McClure's* writers stumbled into their mission: to tap strong pent-up public feelings about political and business-related wrongdoing and thereby focus attention on the need for civic and legislative corrective action.

By the 1990s, of course, TV news had trumped newsprint, including newsmagazines, and the downward slide of television news into entertainment—or infotainment—was scrutinized and deplored by journalists and scholars. David Halberstam's panoramic *The Powers That Be* (1979) had shown how print journalism relinquished its authority to television in the 1960s, the years when the premier news network CBS nevertheless produced muckraking documentaries such as *Hunger in America*, the 1967 report on malnutrition and hunger among low-income groups in the United States Such reports aired in prime time into the early 1970s, alerting millions of Americans to national crises, including environmental damage.

Halberstam, however, also revealed the economic and political pressures under which newspaper reporters and editors were working, especially during the Nixon-era Watergate scandals. Those pressures intensified through the 1980s and 1990s until the news media all but abandoned its basic public-service mission, which was defined by Leonard Downie, Jr., and Robert G. Kaiser in *The News About the News* (2002): "Good Journalism . . . enriches Americans by giving them both useful information for their daily lives and a sense of participation in the wider world" and "makes possible the cooperation among citizens that is critical to a civilized society." They add, "Journalists have a special role in preserving one of America's greatest assets, our culture of accountability" (see ch. 1). But Downie and Kaiser subtitle their book *American Journalism in Peril*, indicting local reporting as lazy and superficial, national reporting as prone to triviality and the "soft" side of the news.

Other faultlines in the news media have been mapped by James Fallows, the Washington editor of *The Atlantic Monthly*. In *Breaking the News: How the Media Undermine American Democracy* (1996), Fallows shows the extent to which in recent years journalism had become "star-oriented." Its leading figures now forfeited investigative and reportorial work for "power, riches and prestige" in a profit-driven industry in which prominent journalists align themselves with the interests of society's elites. Instead of muckraking, Fallows shows, journalists jokingly refer to their "buckraking" in lucrative appearances on the corporate lecture circuit. Their glibness now passes for intelligence and knowledge, and new ideas are hyped, then quickly discarded, especially by the weekly newsmagazines. TV news, he writes, is but a scandal machine with reporters in actors' roles, and the political talk programs more squabbles than debates (see chs. 1–4 and 6).

Important issues, Fallows goes on to argue, have become mere props for journalists' own political gamesmanship, a point corroborated in Joan Didion's *Political Fictions* (2001), which says that by the late 1980s, "the political process had already become perilously remote from the electorate it was meant to represent" and that "those inside the process had congealed into a permanent political class [whose] defining characteristic was its readiness to abandon those not inside the process," that is, the public (see chs. 1 and 6).

Other critics weigh in with similar concerns. Downie and Kaiser point to a conundrum: journalists' skills have never been higher, their technological tools never more sophisticated, and yet the commitment to exploit these for serious-issue purposes has never been lower. When the coauthors interviewed Dan Rather and asked, Who at CBS has the "ultimate power to make the important decisions," the veteran anchor replied, "They're all on the corporate side" (see chs. 1 and 5).*

The corporate-izing of news is apparent not only on TV but in newspapers, which are increasingly part of national chains, notably the Gannett Company, publishers of *USA Today*. Says Fallows, chain ownership "brings a counting-house mentality determined to 'downsize' newsrooms and cut expenses to satisfy quarterly earnings demands." Those living in cities whose local newspaper has been downsized knows this firsthand. Friends in Louisville, Kentucky, regret the decline of their *Courier-Journal*, now a Gannett paper. Following decades of the distinguished editorial leadership of John Seiganthaler, Nashville's *Tennessean*, also taken over by Gannett, has become a shell of its former self. (It was the *New York Times*, not the *Tennessean*, which in the 1990s investigated the financial corruption of Nashville-based Columbia/HCA, the Hospital Corporation of America.)†

Given all this, it is hardly surprising that in the late twentieth century, Americans showed little interest in the kinds of issues central to muckraking literature. Experts cited the ever-declining voter turnout on election day as proof that the U.S. public was sunk in a swale of apathy, which Robert D. Putnam's widely cited *Bowling Alone* (2000) seemed to corroborate in its analysis of U.S. patterns of disconnectedness of individuals from one another and their communities nationwide.

I, however, continued to take my cue from the Boston University students who confessed their sense of insecurity and societal jeopardy when sympathetically prodded. Against the grain, I decided to search for signs of social angst and concern despite widespread presumptions of public apathy, obsessive consumerism, and a craving for nonstop entertainment. Not surprisingly, I found signs that large segments of the U.S. public were indeed attuned to and worried about larger negative trends, just like my early 1980s students. Back in the 1910s, the poet Ezra Pound insisted on the idea of a "radiant gist," by which he meant the telling detail as portal to creative, key insight. What fol-

---

* The corporate-izing of sources of public information and its consequences is a major focus of Robert W. McChesney's *Rich Media, Poor Democracy* (1999), which maps the merging and vertical integration of a "holy trinity of the global media system," including AOL-TimeWarner, Disney, and Rupert Murdoch's News Corporation. McChesney shows how all of these invoke public choice of information as a public relations smokescreen, even as "corporate growth, oligopolistic markets, and conglomerates barely reveal the extent to which the global media system is fundamentally noncompetitive in any meaningful economic sense of the term" (see ch. 2).

† The media critics single out four newspapers that have withstood news dilution: *New York Times*, *Washington Post*, *Los Angeles Times*, and *Wall Street Journal*—the first three because of private stock ownership of their companies and the last because of financial-industry pressures.

lows is my reading of just such "gist" on the upramp to the twenty-first century.

Bulking Up

First ground-level sign of the times for me: baby carriages. The sidewalks and mall concourses of the 1970s had sported new lightweight, versatile umbrella-style baby strollers ideal for newborns to tots to three-year-olds. The popular, ubiquitous, cleverly engineered strollers folded tight and narrow, took up little space, cost little, were arguably democratic in the way in which John Kouwenhoven, years ago, identified democracy at work in material culture. (Kouwenhoven had contrasted the open-air English locomotive cabs exposing rail workers to foul weather against those of American design which sheltered them, and he ascribed the difference in design to an English class-bound society versus an American democratic one.)

The new lightweight American baby strollers surely were here to stay by popular demand, so I thought, clocking high mileage on three or four umbrollers, each pushed to the point of metal fatigue by the weight of two baby daughters on the sidewalks of Brookline, Massachusetts. Surely the umbrollers surpassed—and buried for all time—the preceding era of *Queen Mary* baby buggies, just as the Ford Model T had replaced the Stanley Steamer.

Wrong. Then came the 1980s, and new parents rejected umbrollers in favor of heavily padded Italian imported models—bulky, heavy, awkward to pilot, impossible to maneuver on stairs. These Euro imports were big, boxy, aggressive in their claims to space and cost ten times more than the umbroller. Two of these wide-load babies couldn't pass side by side on a walkway. Infant transport now marked the new era of the Yuppie, the acronym for the young, urban professionals who selected luxury limousines for their newborns.

These baby limos were my first "radiant gist," a later twentieth-century sign of America bulking up for fortification. The ultra-padded babies in their Euro deluxe carriages were not simply indulged by doting parents. Ideological passions were at work. Personal space, in fact, was set to enlarge explosively in marked and numerous ways, all of them rooted, I soon sensed, in anxiety-driven quests for fortifying security and safety in an era of deepseated though unacknowledged sociocultural fears. Ironically, this bulk-up happened as the electronic revolution increasingly made "micro" a byword, as silicon chips stored ever more prodigious banks of data and desktop and laptop personal computers packed multi-gigabytes of power and palm-size messaging devices were mainstreamed.

Even as the "e-"revolution surged, however, a counter movement evinced itself in a bulked-up America. By the turn of the twenty-first century, this bulking would extend from the baby carriages to other areas of life—automotive transport, housing, men's and women's bodies, even money itself. By the later 1990s, the students who admitted deep visceral anxieties in the Boston University lecture hall confessional moment were on the far side of their thirties. Their generation was by then a part of the movement to fortify by bulking up, a movement that would present itself in terms of recreation, practicality, health, fashion, and America's most sacrosanct values, individualism and freedom. Its impetus, however, would prove to be anxiety, uncertainty, fear that something basic in America was unraveling or eroding, leaving each of us to fend for ourselves against long and longer odds.

The Euro baby limos, of course, presaged the adult transport debuting in the mid-1980s, the sport utility vehicles or SUVs, many of their model names inviting owner-identification with rugged Western terrain and its native peoples. Magazine and TV ads appealed in terms of individualism and the pleasure of off-road ventures. SUVs photographed atop Western buttes or fording forest streams spoke the same message: no mere lack of pavement need stand between you and your life journey. No mere conventional road, moreover, will stop you from individualistic self-realization. In an SUV, yours is the road not taken.

Thus the names: Bronco, Grand Cherokee, Durango, Dakota, Tahoe, Santa Fe, Blazer, Range Rover, X-terra, Pathfinder, Escalade, Sequoia, Tracker, Liberty Sport, Highlander, Expedition, Navigator, Explorer, Mountaineer.* With most models built on truck frames, the SUVs share features of similar styling, including high-off-the-ground bodies with steroidal fenders, oversize tires, and often dark-tinted windows. Dwarfing and nearly outnumbering automobiles by the turn of the twenty-first century, SUVs burgeoned in shopping-mall lots, at movie multiplexes, at restaurant valet parking stands—which is to say drivers operate them primarily on interstate and suburban asphalt and concrete, not over off-road ruts and rocks and stream beds, thus proving that the most accurately named model is indeed the Chevrolet Suburban.

Environmentally conscious SUV owners have a schizoid relation to these vehicles, for their emissions level is high and gas mileage (averaging 13 m.p.g.) so poor that activists sometimes slap their bumpers

---

* The minivan, on the contrary, has been marketed as a practical family vehicle, the diminutive "mini" itself antithetical to the SUV.

with stickers that read: "I'm Changing the Climate. Ask Me How." In 2002, the Sierra Club pointed out that a changeover from the average new car to an SUV means extra energy output equivalent to a refrigerator door left open for six years, a bathroom light burning for thirty years or a color TV turned on for twenty-eight years. Christian groups in 2002–2003 protested that Jesus would not drive an SUV, and TV ads in early 2003 linked gas-guzzling SUVs to Middle Eastern terrorism.

Safety facts of the SUVs have proven sobering. Advertised for all-terrain driving, they are top-heavy with high centers of gravity and thus subject to deadly rollover in highway driving. (Twelve thousand persons were killed in SUV rollovers in the 1990s, making these the deadliest vehicles on the road.) The high, rigid SUV frames, in addition, make the vehicles lethal weapons in collision with cars whose hoods they override, putting automobile drivers at risk of decapitation and thus prompting some defensive purchases of SUVs on the grounds that one must join the SUV fleet to stay alive.*

The Ford Explorer became notorious in 2000–2001 for deadly roll-overs when its left rear tires (Bridgestone/Firestone brand) overheated and blew out at highway speeds. But the vehicle surely most indicative of the SUV craze and its values became the General Motors Hummer, introduced in 2000 and adapted from the Humvee, a military transport vehicle. The Hummer could climb a twenty-two-foot wall at a grade of sixty degrees or ford a stream to a depth of thirty inches. "Explorers have blazed trails, conquered wild environments," said one dealer's Web site in 2001, "Marco Polo, Magellan, Lewis and Clark. If they were alive today, they'd want a Hummer." Exploration and pioneering nostalgia, however, barely obscures the militarism fundamental to Hummer design. Despite an array of festive body colors from bright white to candy apple red, the Hummer (H1) is an infantry transport vehicle resembling a jeep crossed with a tank. Nearly seven-feet wide, it most pronouncedly identifies the SUV—all SUVs—as personal armored cars.

The basic SUV identity, the armored car, marks the era when all feel left to fend for themselves in America. The SUV ads promote independence and pleasure, but the buyers' motivation is—if my "radiant gist" reading were accurate—self-protection in an era of social uncertainties, in short, a vehicular response to fear. GM's ads for the Hummer,

* See Bradsher, *High and Mighty: SUVs—the World's Most Dangerous Vehicle and How They Got That Way*. In January 2003, Jeffrey W. Runge, administrator of the National Highway Traffic Safety Administration, warned about the SUV rollover problem in a speech in Dearborn, Michigan, at a point at which automakers had begun to shift manufacturing to crossover vehicles built on auto and minivan frames.

1. Hummer (H2), by General Motors, 2002.

said the *New York Times*, "suggest it as a fortress apart from the peopled world," and Hummer customers reportedly have boasted, "If someone bumps me, they're dead" (Nov. 3, 2002: B3). This and other SUVs were nothing short of automotive armor for perilous times, vehicular exoskeletons for personal protection when domestic news brought notice of homelessness, hunger and layoffs encroaching ever closer on the territory of the American middle and upper-middle class.

The same social angst expressed itself in the bulking and hardening of American bodies, both male and female. Bodybuilding in the United States had been identified in the 1940s and 1950s with Charles Atlas (b. Angelo Siciliano, 1892), who promoted his program for turning a "ninety-seven-pound weakling" scorned on bathing beaches by men and women alike into a sort of Mr. Universe, no longer puny and timid but a powerful, muscular male alluring to women and admired and respected (read, feared) by men.

From the 1980s, however, under the bywords of health and of the customized physique, the hardened and bulked human body gained in popularity and social status. Surgery, liposuction, peels, and botox would all be summoned to realize visions of ideal bodies, but one measure of social anxiety became the ideal of the invincible self whose physical boundaries are large and hardened, whose body expresses its power in enlarged musculature.

Two film stars, Jane Fonda and Arnold Schwarzenegger, became the exponents of this movement. Fonda identified herself in the 1980s as a health guru, establishing an exercise studio in Beverly Hills and producing *Jane Fonda: Total Body Sculpting* and other video programs to achieve the lean, hard, invulnerable body. Fonda's male counterpart, the Austrian-born bodybuilder Arnold Schwarzenegger, exhibited feats of astonishing muscularity in the action-thriller *Terminator* movies. Schwarzenegger and Fonda became the public faces of a fitness movement measured roughly in the proliferation of its niche magazines, including *Muscle & Fitness*, *Abdominals*, *FightSport*, *Muscular Development*, *Women's Physique World*, *Men's Workout*, *Natural Body Building*, and *IRON-MAN*, in addition to encyclopedic books such as *Bodybuilding 101: Everything You Need to Know to Get the Body You Want*.

From one such magazine photo to another, hardened bodies bulged with glistening fat-free muscle and veins coursing like rivulets over boulders. Some were bulked up with muscle-building supplements, the testosterone-related anabolic steroids which increase muscle mass. These controlled substances (anabolic from the Greek, "to build") are known to cause side effects such as liver disorders and a mood swing called " 'roid rage," but the injected or orally taken steroids are used by

2. Altoids advertisement, Callard and Bowser, 2002.

professional athletes to enhance sports performance and by white- and blue-collar workers, women, and adolescents, all seeking, according to a medically based ESPN report, increased muscularity.* The bulked-up body even became an ad image promoting breath mints.

Indications are that the bulked-up bodies, like the SUVs, are a response to a collective societal sense of personal vulnerability. Titles of some bodybuilding programs provide clues to larger societal meanings. Though some are humorous (for example, *Bottoms Up!*) and others straightforward (*Fat-Burning Workout*), several of the programs promote the idea of muscle converted into hardened nonhuman materials. Bone, evidently, is not nearly hard enough, for metal and rock are the featured bodily goals—thus *Abs of Steel, Buns of Steel, Legs of Steel, Crunch Killer Legs, Going Ballistic, Lethal Abs, Lethal Buns, Rock Hard Abs, Quick Toning Lower Body of Steel, Minutes to Granite Abs,* and even (in the e-device era) *Thumbs of Steel.* One program promises a body of titanium, likewise supporting the idea that human flesh can be transmuted into the hardest metal alloy or rock or carbon fiber ballistic material and thus become impregnable to damage or injury by attack.† Strength, health, and attractiveness are the stated goals, but autonomy and invincibility appear to be deeper motives, as if the body itself can become the carapace, the protective armor against any and all assaults, making the modern American everyperson an invulnerable superhero, not to save endangered others in the community but his or her own imperiled nearest-and-dearest and self.

The glistening abdominal as radiant gist points us to yet another site of the bulked-up, fortified American life of the 1980s–2000s: megahouses. The oversized houses known as McMansions or faux chateaux became the hallmark of U.S. residential realty beginning in the late 1980s in California and spreading nationwide in the 1990s from Westport, Connecticut, to Versailles, Kentucky, to Tampa, Florida, and Nashville. These are houses of 5,000 to 10,000 square feet, dwarfing neighboring homes of an average 2,200 square feet as they fill their lots to the lotline, as one Tampa resident says, with "wall-to-wall cement." Community tax bases, land use, zoning regulations, architectural aesthetics, and historic preservation of existing housing often razed to make way for the new construction—these are the explicitly stated issues in conflict over the outsized houses, addressed in such newspaper reports as a 2001 *New York Times* article by Lisa W. Foderaro:

* Comparison of G.I. Joe toy figures between 1982, 1992, and the mid-1990s shows increasing steroidal muscle bulk, itself a childhood model for the ideal male body (see *New York Times,* December 2, 2002: A1, A19).

† Strengthening credit-card plastic, Discover Bank in 2002 offered the trademarked Discover Titanium Card.

"Suburban communities are grappling with a new quandary as houses continue to mutate into ever-larger forms: how big is too big, and what can suburban communities do to try to rein in the monster house next door?" (March 19, 2001: A1).

One real-estate writer explains the successful formula for McMansions: symmetrical structures on clear-cut lots with Palladian windows centered over the main entry and brick or stone enhancing the driveway entrance, plus multiple chimneys, dormers, pilasters, and columns—and inside, the master suite with dressing rooms and bath-spa, great rooms, breakfast and dining rooms, showplace kitchen, and extra high and wide garages for multiple cars and SUVs. Though construction quality may be subpar and materials shoddy (from faux stucco to styrofoam crown molding and travertine compounded from epoxied marble dust), McMansion buyers are eager; the real-estate writer locates them in the generation of my angst-ridden Boston University students: "mostly young, mobile, career-oriented, high-salaried 30- and 40-something individuals" who are too time-squeezed to hire an architect but seek "a luxury home" that they might soon (and easily) sell whenever "it's time to move on."

Moving *on* in this realtor's parlance implies promotions, still higher incomes, and ever-larger future McMansions, thus suggesting the basis for yet another nickname for these (and even more luxurious) structures: trophy house. "Trophy" situates the owners as financially successful winners, among them doubtless some of my former students. Once terrified to empathize with the hapless characters in American novels, their generation has, in adult life, triumphed in the new economy. Theirs are the prizes.

Yet as Edward J. Blakely and Mary Gail Snyder note in their book *Fortress America* (1997), anxieties are at work in the era of SUVs, bodybuilding, and McMansion housing: "People are feeling insecure; they want their home to be a fortress" (18).

These authors, both specialists in urban and regional planning, map the burgeoning of gated communities throughout the United States, especially concentrated in the Sun Belt states of the Southeast and Southwest, but "found nearly everywhere" (rare only in such largely rural states as the Dakotas, Vermont, and West Virginia). The United States nationwide is, in their words, "forting up" in an era of "dramatic demographic, economic and social change" and "fear about the future of America." Blakely and Snyder continue, "Many feel vulnerable, unsure of their place and the stability of their neighborhoods in the face of rapid change." This recent phenomenon of "walled cities and gated communities," they find, "is a dramatic manifestation of a new fortress mentality growing in America." As of the late 1990s, middle-class

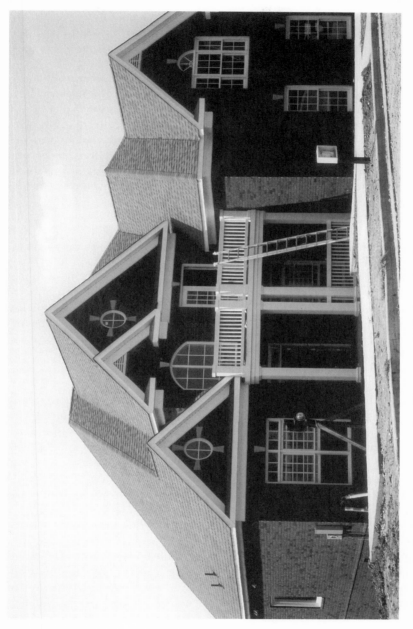

3. McMansion house under construction, Tennessee, 2002. C. Jamie Adams.

homeowners in "inner-ring suburbs and smaller cities were also turning to gates," and *Fortress America* estimated that more than three million American households had sought this new "refuge" (see ch.1:
1–14; chs. 4 and 6).

Fear of crime is cited by the numerous gated-community inter-
viewees in *Fortress America* as the single most important reason for forting up, though "realistically, crime is a far greater problem for
lower-income people than for the better off," according to 1989 data
from the National Crime Victimization Survey conducted by the Bureau of Justice Statistics. The survey showed city residents to be one
and one-half times more likely to be victimized by burglary or violent
crime than are suburbanites (see pp. 126–29). Whatever the actual
crime threat, say Blakely and Snyder, "Fear is real" and drives the
surge toward Fortress America.

Blakely and Snyder extend the findings of *noir* demographer and
cultural critic Mike Davis, whose *City of Quartz* (1990) many of us include in college courses in cultural or environmental studies. Davis
identified "Fortress L. A." as a harbinger of the nation's "massive privatization of public space" together with its "voracious consumption of
private security services . . . whether in the fortified mansion or the
suburban bunker" (see ch. 4). (Davis's militaristic terms point readers
also to the department store and boutique windows of the 1980s–
2000s, when military camouflage-pattern clothing, ammo belts, and
combat boots were fashion items for men and women, creating a limi-
nal mix of fashion and survivalism.)

Meanwhile, insecurities expressed in home fortification increasingly
include an inner fort from which the community is excluded: the
panic room. Within the McMansions, if not modest condos, the post–
Cold War version of the home bomb shelter has reemerged in the
guise of a safe room, an interior space to which occupants can retreat
from criminal trespassers behind multibolt steel doors, reinforced
concrete walls, and Kevlar insulation. This safe—or panic—room was
featured in the Jodie Foster film *Panic Room* (2002) in which audiences
identified with the woman whose home is under siege by criminals.
(For those of modest means, a 2002 *Home Decorators* mail-order cata-
log, which retails rugs, lamps, and end tables, also sold a "Simulated
Security Camera" for indoor or outdoor use, no wiring required.
"Comes with warning decal for door or window.") When one out of
every one hundred forty-five American citizens is imprisoned—totalling
nearly two million persons—*crime* is a mandate to fortify. The fear of
crime has created a boom in prison construction in the United States
in the later twentieth century, prompting Joseph Hallinan, one of the

new muckrakers considered here, to subtitle his book *Travels in a Prison Nation*.

Crime, then, is the explicit, stated fear, the demonic word all can utter freely without a nanosecond of hesitation or self-censure. As one *Fortress America* interviewee says, "Crime is an issue that unites everyone."

Suppose, however, that the dreaded epithet, crime, were to be considered a socially permissible word for something far more difficult to say, something taboo. Granted that crime is a real and deadly dangerous threat to inner-city neighborhoods, as Blakely and Snyder acknowledge. Suppose that for others, however, crime is a substitute for a whole lexicon of fears and anxieties that are much more difficult to articulate, either publicly or in the deepest recesses of the mind. Suppose, in sum, that crime is actually a diversionary term for a complex of cultural malfunctions that demand attention and redress, lest the United States become, as some economists predict, not a model for democracy but a Third-World country split between an elite minority and legions of the desperately poor.

MONEY

Suppose, now, that instead of "crime," a different but equally dreadful core vocabulary of fear is put in play. In *Fear of Falling: The Inner Life of the Middle Class* (1989), Barbara Ehrenreich explored a spate of fears metastasizing in the American middle class in the late twentieth century. Ehrenreich puts the case in terms of a stark Manichaean economic split, namely, an American class system indexed solely by money, by "who has it and who doesn't" (201).

Ehrenreich's American great divide of money's haves versus have-nots provides another radiant gist, this one glistening like sunlight on a gold coin's face but shadowed darkly on its backside. Have or have-not, the nexus is money. The social and individual litmus test is money. All roads lead to, or from, money. Though many of us who teach and write from faculty positions in colleges and universities have differentiated individuals and groups by race, ethnicity, and gender, Ehrenreich beckons us to a different, either/or heuristic. While intellectuals have warned for years against the oversimplifications of binary thinking, Ehrenreich summons us to utilize this binary for urgent knowledge and its ramifications. Humanists have pored over subtly nuanced differentiations of consumer goods, folkways, and speech patterns as indicators of class status, a critical practice exemplified in Paul Fussell's *Class: A Guide Through the American Status System* (1983). Ehrenreich, however, warns that these are largely diversions from the fundamental criterion of the contemporary class system: money. As of the late 1980s, she goes on, "those who 'had' had more than ever, and those who 'had not' were more numerous, and more undeniably miserable" (see chs. 5 and 6).

Ehrenreich's paradigm was elaborated in the mid-1990s by two academic economists in *The Winner-Take-All Society* (1995). Robert H. Frank and Philip J. Cook, of Cornell and Duke Universities, subtitled their book *Why the Few at the Top Get So Much More Than the Rest of Us*, an analysis of the new economic star system in every endeavor from business to thriller fiction to the sports and entertainment media and academic life itself. They warn that "winner-take-all markets attract too many contestants, result in inefficient patterns of consumption and investment, and often degrade our culture." If these costs are to be avoided, they advise, "firms and individuals must somehow be restrained from taking advantage of readily available profit opportunities" (see chs. 1, 2, and 6).

Restraint, however, seems nowhere in evidence, and the cleavage of monied haves from have-nots goes far to explain a phenomenon observable through the 1980s, 1990s, and beyond. Previously, the "M" word was considered conversationally crass, and its tchochkes (for example, bathroom tissue as a scroll of dollars) irredeemably vulgar. More recently, however, the SUVs, the "crunch killer legs," and the fortress houses in gated subdivisions signal a growing popular obsession with money, a kind of American climate in which all seasons became the season of money. As plastic credit cards increasingly replaced cash in transactions for goods and services, money became a kind of cultural fetish.

Signs of the explicit societal great divide, based solely on money, seemed everywhere in American popular culture as the new century drew closer. Money was not now like the Depression-era whimsical rain shower of "Pennies from Heaven" nor a melding of wealth into romance as in the moment in *The Great Gatsby* when Daisy Buchanon's voice is identified as the sound of money. Nor was it the wish-fantasy of the Parker Brothers' *Monopoly* with its miniature pastel cash, nor a reprise of Walt Disney's whiskered rich comic-book character Scrooge McDuck, who in 1950s comics dived into the deep end of his vat of coins for his daily swim. Nor was this new fixation on money a version of the postwar-era festival of the late 1940s *Howdy-Doody* TV show, in which live-audience kids in the Peanut Gallery were invited to plunge hands into penny bowls and candy bowls to retrieve fistfuls of bright copper as delightful as an equal fistful of chocolate M&Ms.

Money in the late twentieth and early years of the twenty-first century lost all such sense of whimsy or playfulness. It became, instead, a deadly earnest indicator of identity, personal legitimacy, and authenticity— above all, of desperately sought security.

"Greed . . . is good. Greed is right. Greed works." Thus the signature line in Oliver Stone's *Wall Street*, the 1987 Hollywood film in which Michael Douglas played Gordon Gecko, the junk-bond king, based on the career of the actual junk-bond sovereign (and convicted felon) Michael Milkin. Said Al ("Chainsaw") Dunlap, the ex-CEO of the Sunbeam Corporation, "The Best Bargain Is an Expensive CEO." In the late 1980s and 90s, commercial airplane aisles were gauntlets of business-class male passengers with cuff links and suspenders patterned with dollar signs. Newsstands sprouted new money magazines (*Money*, *SmartMoney*), while money programs on radio and TV burgeoned (*Moneyline*, *Your Money*), as the financial-advice columnist Jane Bryant Quinn appeared in *Newsweek* magazine and author-advisor Suze Orman became a TV personality with the best-sellers *The 9 Steps to Financial Freedom*, *The Courage to Be Rich*, and *The Road to Wealth*. By the new century, *The New Yorker* magazine was publishing a special "Money" issue, while the *Washington Post* investigative reporter who had launched his career on the Watergate scandal, Bob Woodward, wrote a paean to Alan Greenspan, chairman of the Federal Reserve Bank. He titled it *Maestro*.

Greenspan seemed the *genius loci* of the stock market bubble of the 1990s, which has been dubbed a "collective insanity" by the finance writer John Cassidy. His 2002 book *dot.con* (as in Herman Melville's title *The Confidence-Man*) is subtitled *The Greatest Story Ever Sold*. It recounts the propagandizing of a "New Economy" by Wall Street analysts who propounded "an economic vision favorable to Internet companies." Millions of Americans, Cassidy shows, were egged on by the stock analysts and the media, especially the bull-market's cheerleader CNBC, and by the Clinton administration's promotion of the new Web- and Internet-based capitalism for the new century. These naive investors dreamed orgasmic "web dreams" of stock-market riches reaped from investment in publicly traded Internet start-up businesses. These ranged from the online grocers Webvan and Peapod.com to the pet-supplies retailer Pets.com.

The new Internet companies did not appeal to investors on the basis of company assets (few had any) nor of revenues, which paled in contrast to expenses. Instead, they boasted that their very lack of assets made them desirably frictionless. They promoted the promise not of imminent profits but of growth sustained by infusions of venture capital and of shares bought and sold on the NASDAQ. The exponential rise in Internet firms' stock prices lured unprecedented numbers of Americans to the market, and by the late 1990s, as consumer credit-card debt grew (reaching $2.7 billion by 2001), the discount broker Charles Schwab had six million customers and was enrolling another 100,000 monthly. The dot-com "Euphoria" ran its course only when the Federal Reserve raised interest rates in March 2000, after which the bubble burst into what Cassidy, echoing 1929, calls a "crash." This was a " 'winner-takes-all' model," writes Cassidy, in which "the Internet economy would end up looking more like a television quiz show in which the victorious contestant takes home all the prizes" (see chs. 9, 12, 17, and 20).*

TV and movies exploited precisely this winner-take-all money mentality. Peekaboo versions of the monied life in *Life Styles of the Rich and Famous* won high ratings, while a Darwinian quest for high-stakes cash was broadcast in the so-called "reality" TV's *Survivor*, in which a million-dollar prize was awarded to each of the single surviving contestants not ostracized by group members living for weeks in harsh conditions in remote places. The quiz show *Who Wants to Be a Millionaire* also won highest ratings in 2000–2001, as did the short-lived *Who Wants to Marry a Millionaire* (canceled when it was found that a judge's restraining order had been served on the millionaire bachelor in an abuse case). Its 2002 TV sequel, of sorts, *The Bachelor*, featured a Harvard- and Stanford-educated management consultant, the scion of a CEO, who ultimately chose the winner—publicized as his potential bride—from a competing pool of twenty-five women sent to Malibu to vie for his favor, most of them from such working-class work worlds as bartender, dancer for the Miami Heat, power-tools sales clerk. One writer called this the man-catching superfecta.

For millions in the United States, one American dream machine of affluence became legalized gambling as the basic costs of food, shelter, and clothing far outstripped the minimum wage and pushed huge numbers into the bottom of what demographers saw as an hour-glass-shaped U.S. society, both top- and bottom-heavy with a pinch-waist middle. Gambling venues ranged from tribal reservation casinos such as the Connecticut Pequots' Foxwoods resort (boasting 300,000 square feet of games from roulette to bingo) to riverboat casinos as in Tunica,

* Though the Internet bubble got major media attention, the telecommunications financial scandals had greater adverse impact. According to a *Wall Street Journal* assessment, "Hundreds of telecom executives . . . sold at least some portion of their stock and made hundreds of millions, while many investors took huge, unprecedented losses. It dwarfs the much more highly publicized Internet boom and bust. And the economic and personal damage in jobs lost and bankruptcies is far worse" (*Wall Street Journal*, August 12, 2002: A7).

Mississippi, to state lottery scratch cards and multistate Big Game super lotteries whose sales from 1996 to 2002 reached $3.7 billion, each ticket fanning visions of celebrity-grade wealth at an odds of 76 million to one. David Baldacci's best-selling 1997 thriller *The Winner* exploited this fantasy of lottery winnings as the "beautiful, dirt-poor" protagonist wins a $100 million jackpot in a scheme embroiling her in deadly danger, testing her mettle, and persuading readers at last that the plucky heroine has earned the fortune.

Inevitably, in "One Market Under God," to borrow Frank's title once again, divinity was summoned to inspire the American broke and the poor with confidence in the imminence of God's material bounty in their lives. The deity simultaneously assured the prosperous of the rectitude of their good fortune in *The Prayer of Jabez* (2000). This self-help inspirational best-seller is based on a short, obscure Old Testament prayer (1 Chronicles 4: 10) in which Jabez implores the God of Israel for blessings, safeguards from evil, guidance, and—this the crux—to "enlarge my territory." The *Prayer*, says author Bruce Wilkinson, "will show you how to break through to abundance." Rev. Wilkinson asserts that had Jabez worked on Wall Street, he might have prayed, "Lord, increase the value of my investment portfolios." When Christian corporate presidents ask Wilkinson, "Is it right for me to ask God for more business," the minister answers, "Absolutely!" explaining that God awaits that very question, which brings Him "delight" (see ch. 3). (Management books of the 1990s also included this title: *Jesus CEO*.)

Had the delighted Lord God of the *Prayer of Jabez* arisen from Catholicism with its doctrine of transubstantiation of bread to body of Christ, a certain New York City dining experience of 2002 would perhaps have been thought divinely blessed. Gold and banknotes were literally consumed at New York's World Economic Forum (known as Davos for its decades-long site in the Swiss alpine ski resort). This annual gathering of global business and political titans and their think-tank and entertainment-industry entourages became Davos-in-New-York 2002. Among the invitation-only parties, a select group were literally offered a taste of money, described by the caterers as an art installation consisting of a silver tureen of clear broth into which was dropped little gold-leaf-flecked meatballs and pasta sheets with a U.S. $100 bill printed on each. "We offered people a taste of money" which "was quite consumed," explained the caterer, whose partner explained, "The guests licked their plates."

Other artists challenged this normalization of a hyper-money environment, Barbara Kruger with block capital letters spelling "MONEY" on t-shirts and "Money to Burn" against a cigarette background, while

J. S. Boggs created hand-drawn, precisely-produced renditions of bills. Their *trompe-l'oeil* effect is recognized only when a viewer—often a retail clerk or cashier—is requested by Boggs to treat the art text as authentic cash. The transaction is foiled at the sight of the blank backside of the paper "bill" or else a closer look at the motto, which isn't "In God We Trust" but "Red Gold We Trust." Critiquing a money-obsessed culture, Boggs, Kruger, and other artists both reinforce and index it.

Scholarship, too, showed certain influence of the new money era. The English historian Jason Goodwin published *Greenback: The Almighty Dollar and the Invention of America* (2002). H. W. Brands, a historian known for his book on the citizenly forefather Benjamin Franklin now wrote on the history of the California gold rush of 1848. *The Age of Gold: The California Gold Rush and the New American Dream* (2002) argues that as of the 'Forty Niner moment, "a new American dream began to take shape," one "of instant wealth" (442). This new "age of gold," writes Brands, "was also the age of speculation, corruption, and consolidation" whose "sordid" side was offset by its "enormously creative force" (443). It seemed inevitable that the late twentieth century would give rise to a new biography of John D. Rockefeller, replacing the "robber baron" identity with the frankly admiring *Titan* (1998).

One figure in the late twentieth century and the opening years of the 2000s seemed particularly synonymous with money: the corporation chief executive officer or CEO, typically from realms of media, venture capital, telecommunications, or corporate reengineering. Whether his or her company prospered or lost value or even sank into bankruptcy, whether its stock spiked or collapsed à la what *Fortune* magazine called "The Enron Disaster," the CEO of 2000s was increasingly represented in the media for "scoring big paydays," as the *Wall Street Journal* put it in 2002.* The *Journal* reported the CEOs' "bounteous bonanza," or "Who Made the Biggest Bucks," ranging over seven CEO pay packages in 2001, from the $706.1 million of Lawrence J. Ellison at Oracle Corporation to the $49.4 million of Jeffrey C. Bible at the Philip Morris Companies, to a grand total of nearly $1.9 billion (April 4, 2001: B7).† Lush retirement deals sustained the imperial

---

* These included CEOs of failed businesses such as WorldCom and Kmart, whose multimillion-dollar company "loans" were "forgiven," as was the $19-million loan of Salomon Smith Barney's fabled telecommunications analyst, Jack Grubman, named in a *New York Times* editorial of August 2002 as "the maitre d' to the late 90's telecom party" (August 10, 2002: A10).

† In 2002, the ratio of the average company employee's compensation to that of the CEO approached 1:500 (a ratio that in 1985 was 1:70. In contrast, Japanese executives' earnings ratio was 1:12, with average annual salaries $300,000 to $500,000, figures in line with European chief-executive pay, according to East West Consulting, an executive search firm based in Tokyo.

CEO lifestyles. The *New York Times* reported extraordinary perks of the self-styled "fat-cat" John F. ("Jack") Welch of General Electric, who in retirement was to receive a lifelong use of business jets and a fully staffed "palatial" GE-owned New York apartment supplied with food, wine, and flowers, plus V.I.P. boxes for baseball, opera, and tennis at Wimbledon. "Because of his relationship with G.E., he and his wife also got discounts on diamonds and jewelry settings" (September 6 2002: C2). WorldCom's CEO Bernard Ebbers, who was shown to have built his business empire on "a mountain of debt" from huge loans from major banks, bought himself a 132-foot yacht, the *Aquasition*, with a remote control helm set in an on-deck hot tub (*Wall Street Journal*, December 31, 2002: A1, A6).

CEOs of U.S.-identified corporations, notably Welch and Louis Gerstner of IBM, became celebrities with multimillion-dollar book advances and were profiled under such reverential, Mount Rushmorean titles as *The Mind of the C.E.O.* In June 2002, the *New York Times* reported that even felony convictions would not necessarily dislodge such CEOs, since contract protections limit the kinds of felonies for which top executives can be dismissed: "The contracts have made the executives nearly immune from dismissal, ensuring them that they will receive millions of dollars when they leave their posts, under almost any circumstances" (June 9, 2002: section 3: 1). In this era of "imperial capitalism," wrote the business professor Rakesh Khurana in *Searching for a Corporate Savior* (2002), corporate boards of directors helped to create a "distinctly American cult of the C.E.O." whose ascendence bears similarity to the self-coronation of Napoleon (qtd. in *New York Times*, September 22, 2002: section 3: 6).

To some extent, canonical American literature of the later twentieth century has acknowledged and critiqued this fixation on money. Toni Morrison, for example, issued a prophetic caveat in her mid-1970s enduring *Song of Solomon*, which features Milkman, a young man who is driven by his father's message that money provides life's only freedom. Milkman risks his life in a failed multistate quest to find a buried trove of gold nuggets, only to realize that the journey itself is the experiential rite of passage, that personal freedom is unrelated to the gold.

A complementary message appeared in Tom Wolfe's *The Bonfire of the Vanities* (1987), featuring a "Master of the Universe," a Wall Street top bond salesman named Sherman McKoy who revels in a luxurious life of everything-money-can-buy, until tripped up and finally ruined in the domino-effect aftermath of a skirmish with young black men in the Bronx 'hood. Wolfe continued to explore the rich man's fall in *A Man in Full* (1998), in which Charlie Croker, a rags-to-riches Atlanta construction magnate, loses his fortune—his mansion, hunting lodge, stud farm, art collection, executive jet—yet finds solace and personal renewal in classical stoicism of Zeno. (Ever the ironist, Wolfe has the neo-Stoic Charlie become a motivational speaker under contract to the Fox Network as the novel concludes).

The critique of money's corruption on a grand scale made its appearance in other later twentieth-century fiction, some of which historicized the topic in order to school readers in antecedent eras of greed and graft. Gore Vidal reprised the Gilded Age of the Tweed Ring and of the Grant and McKinley Administration political-financial scandals in his novels *1876* (1976) and *Empire* (1987), the third and fourth of Vidal's six-volume American chronicle spanning U.S. history from the Revolution to the era of Hollywood and media conglomerates. In *A Conspiracy of Paper* (2000), the debut novelist and literary scholar David Liss displaced the 1990s stock-market bubble from Wall Street to eighteenth-century London in a mystery plotted on a financial boom in a much-heralded new economy.

Despite this belletristic interest in money, however, prominent novelists for the most part have engaged different concerns in the years of America's intensifying popular focus on money. Following *Song of Solomon*, Morrison went on to exploit racial hauntings in *Beloved*, passion and spirituality in *Jazz*, and intergenerational conflict in *Paradise*. Jane Smiley similarly directed attention elsewhere following the publication of *Moo* (1995), her satirical sendup of a Midwestern flagship state university, Moo U., which is enmeshed in a corrupt, environmentally catastrophic gold-mining scheme. The gold mine, however, figures only in a subplot, and post-bovine *Moo*, Smiley turned her novelistic skills to the equine world of *Horse Heaven*.

Other prominent U.S. writers in belletristic traditions have similarly veered away from money as a cultural core issue. Thomas Pynchon and Don DeLillo, for instance, have been repeatedly drawn to sociopolitical codes and conspiracies; Ann Beattie and Ann Tyler to problematic personal relationships; David Foster Wallace to consumerist and other addictions, and to narrative deconstruction; Barbara Kingsolver to bio-environmentalism; Russell Banks and Richard Russo to working-class life, to its dynamics per se and to elegiac treatment of its passing in a bygone America. Ethnically identified writers such as Sandra Cisneros or Oscar Hijuelos or Sherman Alexie have focused on the representation of ethnicities and Native American cultural complexities. Certain younger writers have addressed the pathologic effects of affluence. The school of Jay McInerney and Bret Easton Ellis stratify characters via brand names and fashion details. On the whole, however, the literary establishment has not as yet turned attention to the hows and whys of money increasingly becoming an idée fixe in American popular culture from the late twentieth century onward.

A major point has been thus largely missed so far by novelists who are surrounded by this dizzying obsession with money up and down class strata and across ethnicities and gender and region in the United States It is that money—whether in hand or only dreamed of—had now become one means of forting up in fearsome times. In the new environment of money, societal purchase solely meant purchasing power. Money was now a rarer and rarifying passport to the good life, a talisman and redoubt for fortress America—and for those without it, a wish-fantasy and shimmering mirage in a time of parching, life-threatening drought in a minimum-wage world, which Ehrenreich chronicles first-hand in *Nickel and Dimed: On (Not) Getting By in America*, and which Naomi Klein and Eric Schlosser engage in *No Logo* and in *Fast Food Nation*.

I thought long and hard to recall when in the course of American literary history money had been so important, so urgent as a measure of winner-take-all power and do-or-die survival. Was it in the letters of the chronically cash-strapped Thomas Jefferson? Or the mid-nineteenth-century poems of Walt Whitman and Emily Dickinson? Critics have written fully of the Transcendentalists' deep ambivalence toward (and complicity with) the capitalist marketplace, and Ralph Waldo Emerson, for instance, penned such aphorisms as "Always pay; for, first or last, you must pay your entire debt." His cohort Henry David Thoreau, who failed despite his best efforts to succeed in commercial publishing, created in the naturalist's *Walden* the exemplary good life launched on a bare-bones cabin construction budget. Harriet Beecher Stowe and her sister Catherine Beecher wrote *An American Woman's Home*, a best-selling housekeeping manual on living well on minimal cash.

Texts in which money is a forefront, critical issue, however, show up on American literature's historical table of contents under the "naturalism" school of the late nineteenth and early twentieth centuries—the very years that gave rise to the muckraker literature. In *The Souls of Black Folks* (1903), W. E. B. Du Bois writes, "To be a poor man is hard, but to be a poor race in a land of dollars is the very bottom of hardship." In the era of robber barons and monopoly trusts, the *McClure's* muckraking writer and novelist Frank Norris presented a psychopathological case study of a nation afflicted jointly with gold fever and societal instability. In *McTeague* (1899), Norris's character Trina, a petite and charming dentist's wife, transits from thrift to miserliness as her marriage disintegrates when her husband, a self-taught dentist, is effectively laid off, barred from practice in a new age of medical licensure. Trina's household scrimping and her lottery winnings prompt chilling, erotic avarice as she secretly buries her face in the heap of gold coins that she polishes and gathers lovingly toward her, her cheeks cooled by the metal even as she jingles small coins in her mouth, sucking and stacking her playthings by the hour. "Ah, the dear money, the dear money," she whispers. "I love you so! All mine, every penny . . . . and I'm going to get more, more, more" (238).

In a late nineteenth-century America of extremes of wealth and poverty, Norris's confrere, the journalist-turned-novelist Theodore Dreiser, also scrutinized "the true meaning of money" which, said Dreiser in *Sister Carrie* (1900), "yet remains to be popularly explained and comprehended" (see chapters 1–8). The novelist theorized that money ought to a form of stored energy, then turned from physics to sociology to say it functions as "a usurped privilege" and thus as a causal factor in social, religious, and political "troubles," an oblique reference to labor strikes, sectarian church battles, and stark class divisions.

Sister Carrie enacts the division that Ehrenreich would articulate nearly a century later. The title character Carrie is economically launched with money early on when she is ferried over the squalor of factory-toil wage slavery by the "soft and noiseless" greenbacks seductively proferred by a salesman-dandy as a "loan." Thereafter as a kept woman and later as a successful stage actress, Carrie lives in comfort and material luxury.

But the novel's more arresting character, the character who earned Dreiser praise as the first American novelist to represent the actual experience instead of the spectacle of poverty, is George Hurstwood. An upper-middle-class manager in mid-life, a family man and homeowner—in sum, a paragon of Victorian respectability and prosperity—Hurstwood becomes besotted with the charming Carrie, then impulsively steals ten thousand dollars from his Chicago employer and flees with her to New York City. Readers then enter into his steady, relentless slide into mental depression and poverty as he depletes the stolen cash and struggles through a series of failed businesses and short-term jobs, the last as janitor's helper in a hotel basement and as "scab" streetcar motorman during a transit strike. Finally destitute, he lives day-to-day, begging on the streets, pitiful and sick and ragged as he queues up for one night's bed in a shelter for men. The Hurstwood whom readers first meet as an upper-middle-class man of business with custom-tailored suits and softly lustrous calfskin shoes finally succumbs on a city sidewalk in a freezing winter night, his last utterance, "What's the use?"

Hurstwood not only anticipates Ehrenreich's binary split but exemplifies precisely the "terrible misfortune" mapped in Bellamy's *Looking Backward*. The former manager loses his seat of coach-top class privilege and plunges into the dust with the "masses." True, readers might prefer to ponder Hurstwood's moral weakness, his criminal theft, the role of desire and sexuality in the novel, representations of the urban scene, and so on. Readers can also explore Carrie's performativity, her stage success based on the objectification of popular longing, her lack of inner resources, etcetera.

In terms of money, however, Carrie is freed of the sweatshop ergonomic Hades and cosseted by cash throughout. Hurstwood, on the contrary, represents the problematics of money enmeshed with class status in America. His downward slide demonstrates the precariousness of class position and economic viability in this nation. Severed from genealogy, class status depends on a monetary scaffold that is subject to collapse in economic recessions, depressions, under- and unemployment. These threaten the Hurstwoods of 2000s as they did those of late 1800s and early 1900s. Dreiser arguably tapped readers' suppressed anxieties on this point. His plotline depends for its impact upon reaching readers' underside of angst fed by actual marketplace conditions, the very conditions that engender the pathological obsession in Norris's Trina. Dreiser's statement is clear: the "fear of falling" is legitimate and justified. It can happen. Destitution lurks.

Contemporary U.S. versions of Hurstwood's fall are of course quite different in important ways. Passion for a new life with Carrie is the manager's impetus, and theft its trigger, and thus Hurstwood does not necessarily typify whole populations. Dreiser makes Hurstwood a psychological case study but leaves unsettled the extent to which he is a sociological type.

Hurstwood's downward trajectory and disintegration, however, was neither singular for his time nor unrelated to vulnerabilities caused by the structural changes occurring on a vast scale in the United States in the late twentieth and early twenty-first centuries. Kevin Philips, in *Wealth and Democracy* (2002) calls this the "financialization" of America. For middle- and increasingly for upper-middle-income U.S. citizens, there have been disturbing, unbidden changes over which citizens feel they have little or no control, as newspapers (for example, of 2001) run such feature articles as "Grounded By an Income Gap: Inequality Just Keeps Growing in the U.S." Amid the collapse of the telecommunications industry the *Wall Street Journal* reported in August 2002 that a homeless shelter in a north Dallas suburb now saw "the shell-shocked faces of telecom workers who have lost their homes." One woman, an engineer, likened the job-loss situation to "the black plague," explaining, "it goes from the edges in—closer and closer—and finally gets here" (August 19, 2002: A8). Symptomatic, palliative efforts at self-protection during an era of socioeconomic shift is evident in the widespread fetishizing of money and the personal bulking up. This bulking, this upsizing, appears to be a push precisely against the movement to which it is collectively, euphemistically, and diametrically opposed—namely, downsizing.

TOWER OF GLASS

Suppose Bellamy's coach were deployed yet again to pose a sort of contemporary test. If the author of *Looking Backward* were to return in 2000, his metaphor would surely need updating for the later twentieth- and early twenty-first-century years. What new figure would he choose?

His best bet, for me, a glass high-rise corporate office tower. Installed in its top-floor suites, readers would find executives identified as world-class figures (as New York's real-estate magnate Donald Trump proclaims his Trump Tower to be "world class"). The glass tower, however, would be rife with the very same anxiety attributed to those sitting atop the coach in the primitive, draconian days more than a century ago. The CEO and topmost managers have assuredly secured their own personal fortunes (though perhaps through dealings later to subject them to prosecution by the Justice Department or shareholder suits pursued by top litigators). A new Bellamy scenario, however, would show those workers in offices and cubicles on the tower's other floors listening intently for the swing of the ax, audible in headquarters' announcements of "mergers" or "new cost-cutting efficiencies" or the euphemistic "rightsizing."

Each announcement would send multitudes of tiny managerial figures in business suits tumbling from the tower windows in a free-fall toward the ground in a "race to the bottom" where they would mingle with the four million blue-collar workers who have lost U.S. manufacturing jobs since 1979, some of them in inner cities that, according to sociologist William Julius Wilson's *When Work Disappears*, now suffer "devastating rates of joblessness."

The metaphoric tower, like the coach, is validated by social conditions of its contemporary moment, in this instance, the fall of tens of millions into joblessness. An in-depth *New York Times* report of 1996 cited "the most acute job insecurity since the Depression . . . an unrelenting angst that is shattering people's notions of work and self and the very promise of tomorrow"—this from *The Downsizing of America*

(1996), adapted from a *Times* series on job loss in the United States.*
In 2001, the *Wall Street Journal* assessed the "forever altered" lives of the
middle- and upper-middle-class unemployed, who sound like victims
of a tsunami: "People have been forced to move. Friends and relatives
are separated. Living conditions have deteriorated. And relationships
have frayed—particularly in households where layoffs have hit more
than one person." In spring 2002, the *Journal* began a series on the
etiquette of layoffs, "How to Tell People You've Been Laid Off (And
How to Cope with Their Sympathy)" (May 2, 2002: D1). One jobless
reader wrote to describe his neighbors' support, which reminded him
of "stories his grandfather told of people pulling together during the
Depression" (May 9, 2002: D2). Another *Journal* piece was headlined:
"Office Vultures Circle Still-Warm Desks Left Empty by Layoffs" (August 14, 2002: B1).

To explore the 2000s version of Bellamy's metaphor just a little further, gaze from the glass office tower suite or from the rooftop helipads
that airlift CEOs to and from their world-class corporate jets. From on
high, those workers in straits at ground level represent an unfortunate
side effect of necessary business efficiencies, a kind of collateral damage, regrettable but inevitable. Take the "down" elevator and step into
the shadow of the glass office tower, however, and glimpse those same
workers up close via published newspaper vignettes of 2001–2002—
for example, the *New York Times*' Joe McCaughey, 44, a Minneapolis
construction worker earning $7 per hour in 2002 and living mostly in
a battered station wagon with a propane heater and mounds of blankets in a city in which the average monthly income of homeless adults
is $622, while the average rent for a one-bedroom apartment is $664
(January 5, 2002).

* On the U.S. mainland, between 1979 and 1996 U.S. Department of Labor statistics
show that "more than 43 million jobs have been erased in the United States," with victims of layoffs outnumbering victims of violent crime by fifty percent (this according to
New York Times analysts). In the opening years of the new century, the layoffs continued
in relentless, numbing numbers, with the *Times* reporting on December 30, 2001, that
"corporate America announced roughly a million layoffs in 2001," an unprecedented
scale of downsizing. At "Motorola, 40,000 jobs, at Boeing, 30,000, at American and
United Airlines, 20,000 each." Wall Street jettisoned 43,000 jobs in the financial industry, and Dell Computer had its first-ever layoffs, 5,400. From October 2000 to 2002, the
number of Americans left newly jobless reached 2.3 million. By August 2002, one million additional workers had lost jobs, and the *Wall Street Journal* reported that the U.S.
Bureau of Labor Statistics disclosed in August 2002 that 8 million applicants were competing for 3.5 million available jobs: "This time the data suggest that millions couldn't get
a job even if they moved, upgraded their skills or took a job they once thought beneath
them." Hurstwood's fall is thus the spectre which haunts the American middle class and
validates its "fear of falling" in a modern deregulated economy as in the unregulated
one of the first generation of muckraker literature.

Or catch a sidewalk glance at Deborah A. Williams, a laid-off sock-factory worker in Georgia. "Lacking health insurance," says the newspaper, "she is postponing surgery to remove a stomach tumor." Williams is one of 41.2 million Americans without health insurance, together with another twenty million who are underinsured. These figures prompt Dr. Richard Roberts, chair of the American Academy of Family Physicians, to ask rhetorically, "What's wrong with this picture?"* In a time when the very term healthcare has become a prefix to "industry," Ms. Williams, 43, says, "All I can do is hope and pray that something comes along real soon." The "something" so urgently needed for Ms. Williams and for everyone else is graphed in Rudolph Mueller's *As Sick as It Gets: The Shocking Reality of America's Health Care* (2001) and by Laurie Garrett on a global scale in her muckraking *Betrayal of Trust: The Collapse of Global Public Health.*

As for work, Deborah Williams is reported to have spent $22K of her $34K (401K) retirement fund to meet expenses while taking a "basic hospitality course" at a hotel that she hopes will hire her (January 16, 2002). She and Joe McCaughey could easily play a cameo role in *Sister Carrie*, in which Dreiser had theorized that industrial-era management operated under one idea: "the idea being that something was gained by giving them as little and making the work as hard and unremunerative as possible."

Against hard times and a societal cold shoulder, recall Sister Carrie insulated by the "soft" greenback comfort. That same yearning for softness was measured by late twentieth-century "soft" TV network news and by the media and business press's soft euphemisms on "career misfortune," an "unkind" economy, and "uncertainty ahead." Softness, moreover, was central to the most popular and commercially successful artist in the nation in the closing years of the twentieth century and and beyond: Thomas Kinkade, the Christian "Painter of Light."

* Perhaps the former Surgeon General Dr. David Satcher intends to find out and speak out, for on January 15, 2002, he accepted an appointment to Morehouse College to head a center on public access to healthcare. On the day of the Satcher announcement, however, the *New York Times* published an article on the newest trend in health care, the "boutique" or "concierge" private medical practices serving the upper-middle class: "Doctors' New Practices Offer Deluxe Service for Deluxe Fee." For an annual fee of four thousand dollars, patients will get round-the-clock cell-phone access to doctors, same-day appointments, nutrition and exercise physiology examinations at patients' homes or at health clubs, and doctors to accompany them to specialists. Similar boutique practices are opening in Arizona and Florida and are expected to appear throughout the nation. Asked about this new type of personalized medical care during a presentation at Vanderbilt University in January 2003, Dr. Satcher replied that he had no objection to "boutique" physician services, providing that the U.S. citizenry at large were afforded high quality preventive medicine and medical care across lines of race, ethnicity, gender, and income disparity.

Not one single image of a corporate glass high-rise tower finds its way onto a Kinkade canvas. On the contrary, his nationwide franchised galleries now sold reproduced, museum-frame images of Cotswold-style cottages, gabled Victorians, and rockbound lighthouses. All glow with the beckoning warmth of sheltering home. Each image idealizes American family and community life transcendent of economic vicissitudes. Kinkade became an upmarket version of the popular Currier & Ives lithographs, also from a Protestant Christian tradition. In Bellamy's and Dreiser's day, Currier & Ives images hung on parlor walls of middle-class Americans under such titles as *A Home in the Country*, *A Home on the Mississippi*, and *The Western Farmer's Home*. One difference has emerged across the centuries: a 2001–2002 gated subdivision rising north of San Francisco, its developers constructing a Thomas Kinkade Community whose houses are copied from the paintings and whose furnishings and artwork are all licensed by Kinkade. Thus in Vallejo, California, does McMansion forting up go soft and fuzzy.

The credit-card industry, in 2002, likewise recognized strategic advantages in its own Kinkade-like initiative for debt collection from certain delinquent cardholders (whose debts are unsecured). Steady customers now downsized and struggling to make ends meet received their regular credit-card bills as usual. But in addition, they got specially commissioned Hallmark cards encouraging those who experienced "life's unexpected detours" to rearrange their payment schedules. As personal bankruptcy filings rose to a record 1.5 million persons in 2001–2002, Discover Financial Services, a division of Morgan Stanley & Co., became the first credit-card company not to threaten but to woo customers who were suddenly stressed financially. The Hallmark cards conveyed messages of sympathy and inspiration, one showing a gushing mountain stream in a forest, another a sunrise in the mountains. "THE NEW DAY is another beginning," says the latter's text, "a chance for starting over . . . a time of hope and promises."

Let us revisit the McMansion real-estate writer's smooth phrasing on "a luxury home" easily sold whenever "it's time to move on." For these honeyed words presuppose owners' upward trajectories and their increasing success. The layoff numbers and such titles as *The Downsizing of America*, *Fortress America*, and *White-Collar Sweatshop*, however, make us read the realtor's words in reverse. Walter Mosely frames our rereading from an African-American historical viewpoint when he observes in *Workin' on the Chain Gang* (2000) that American middle-class whites are now subject to the sudden job ruptures that have beset blacks and other minorities for centuries in the United States. Mosely offers the survival strategy passed along for generations from black father to black son, the very same words which at once repeat and repudiate the realtor's own: *"you got to be ready to move on, son"* (43). Ready to move on, no matter how good the current job presently, how rosy the outlook or seemingly benign the employer. Brace yourself for involuntary transience and its hiatus.*

Davos Man

Brace yourself, in short, for instability. The sociologist Richard Sennett calls the impact on workers in the era of the new capitalism the *Corrosion of Character*, the title of a study of *The Personal Consequences of Work in the New Capitalism* (1998). Sennett, in fact, finds that the new instability is not happenstance but the direct result of a particular mentality that is dictating the terms of the new economy and thus the lives of all within it. (Those who opt out are said to live "off the grid"). If Matthew Josephson's 1934 book title gave the late nineteenth cen-

---

* The Congressional Budget Office finds that in 2001, adjusted for inflation, the families in the middle of the U.S. income distribution rose from $41,400 in 1979 to $45,100, a 9% increase. Meanwhile the income of families in the top 1% rose from $420,200 to $1.016 million, an increase of 140%. In April 2002, two research groups, the Economic Policy Institute and the Center on Budget and Policy Priorities, examined household incomes at the peak of each of three income cycles—the late 1970s, late 1980s, and late 1990s—and found that in forty-four states, the gains in the top twenty percent of households outstripped that of the bottom twenty percent. In September 2002, the U.S. Census Bureau reported, according to the *New York Times*, that the "most affluent fifth of the population received half of all household income [in 2001], up from 45 percent in 1985," while "the poorest fifth received 3.5 percent of total household income, down from 4 percent in 1985." The "increases in poverty [in 2001] were concentrated in the suburbs, in the South, and among non-Hispanic whites" (September 25, 2002: A1, A19).

In February 2002, the *New York Times* reported unprecedented requests by "hard-pressed" middle- and upper-middle-income parents for tuition refinancing for their children's college educations. The article quotes a representative of a company that assists colleges and universities with billing: "People are saying that they're being laid off, their stocks are down, and they're looking for ways to pay the bill" (February 3, 2002). A study commissioned by the National Center for Higher Education, supported by the Ford Foundation and the Pew Charitable Trusts, also reported in 2002 that "state spending on higher education and financial aid lagged behind steep rises in tuition," that poor families were spending 25% of their annual income for their children to attend four-year public colleges in 2000, compared with 13% in 1980. Middle-class families' tuitions costs had nearly doubled from 1980, from 4% to about 7%. "For the wealthiest families, there was no increase from the 2% spent in 1980." In January 2003, the *Wall Street Journal* reported that "families in record numbers—having maxed out on federal student loans—are turning to private lenders such as Citibank and Sallie Mae to cover tuition payments." Private borrowing, the *Journal* reported, "jumped to about $5 billion in the 2001-02 school year, a 39% increase from the year earlier and up from $1 in 1995-96" (January 8, 2003: D1, D3). The *New York Times* reported in the same month that "student borrowers now amass an average of $27,600 in educational debt, more than three and a half times what they compiled a decade ago in unadjusted dollars." The *Times* reported that the percentage of graduating seniors who had taken out education loans had jumped from 46 to 70% in a decade and that "the growing debt has begun to encroach on other major purchases like homes" (January 28, 2003: 1A).

tury its name as the era of the Robber Barons, Sennett may provide the rubric for the new era, for he proclaims this the moment of Davos Man (yes, named for the business titans at the Swiss alpine village World Economic Forum).

Davos Man, epitomized in Microsoft's Bill Gates, has specific character traits, according to Sennett. These include a "ruthless" competitive spirit and a lack of attachment to long-term or permanent structures, coupled with a willingness to destroy what he has made as he ventures restlessly into new things. He has also a "tolerance for fragmentation," and the "confidence to dwell in disorder," to "flourish in the midst of dislocation." Davos Man thrives, in short, on instability of his own causation. Indeed, he is its prime agent. Instability is Davos Man's métier and elixir of life.

The sociologist finds, however, that fragmentation, disorder, dislocation—in short, instability—is terribly "self-destructive" to those "ordinary employees" who are working "lower down" in a world of Davos Man's creation. For everyone except Davos Man and his minions, Sennett finds, this is not an era of societal efficiency nor of the "dynamic change" as celebrated by the Yale School of Management dean—but one of corrosive instability (see ch. 3).

For a student of American literature, this is indeed a moment of reprise, for "instability" casts itself both backward and forward. *Looking Backward* declared 1880s America to be "an age of instability," and the term proliferated in U.S. fiction in the 1900s and 1910s. "Instability" then meant not only the mysterious atmospherics which produced unpredictable killer storms but also the socioeconomic jeopardy of a cutthroat competitive business climate, which subjected individuals, families, and communities to dislocations all were powerless to resist. Instability became a hallmark of naturalist fiction, from Dreiser and Norris to Hamlin Garland, Robert Herrick, and Stephen Crane, whose stories and characters enact this social and individual precariousness and dislocation. *Looking Backward*, however, was one of the first popular texts to declare the United States to be captive to a "barbaric industrial and social system," which was as "unstable" as a drifting iceberg.

Plus ça change? Let us put an individual face on Davos Man, who appeared in a *New York Times* business-section profile of March 27, 2002. He is a former New York Citigroup businessman who is now "thinking big" as the new chief of a formerly profitable but heretofore "somewhat sleepy" insurance company in St. Paul, Minnesota. Part of this new CEO's plan to raise the stock-market value of the company includes eliminating eleven percent of the company's jobs and "axing an array of clubby perquisites" which previously made the company a "pleasant" place to work.

Pleasant no more. Though the new CEO is described as affable and down to earth, a man who "fetches his own coffee," he is also a "demon boss," commended by one Citicorp analyst for his "cold," objective scrutiny. Having left his wife and children back in New Jersey, he is "free" to "round up handfuls of employees frequently for impromptu dinners" where plans are made for a "lean, hard-charging financial conglomerate," starting with the ouster of employees from "plush" office buildings, the termination of an art rental program at headquarters, and cutbacks in lush atrium and office foliage. (Apparently this CEO has yet to implement one new cost-saving workplace design idea, six-by-six office cubicles reserved by barcoded employees in a time-share arrangement. This plan supposedly will save corporate real-estate costs in the next phase of corporate cubicle culture which has been satirized in Scott Adams's *Dilbert* cartoons and said by one 2002 business writer to be "sillier, stranger and scarier than anything we could make up.") For now, the Minneapolis CEO "inspires thriftiness" by occupying a "small," sixth-floor office (presumably sans green plants), having "abandoned the executive suite atop the 17-story headquarters."

But the new regimen of thrift evaporates at his compensation package, which includes $9.4 million in stock and cash plus 1.5 million in stock options valued at $29.8 million. His starting pay is $1 million per year with as much as $2 million in bonuses. Corporate austerity clearly stops here. The compensation package of the profiled CEO, in fact, exposes the modest office as a sort of Potemkin Village in reverse. The material culture of the business is stripped down by executive order. A skeletal work environment prevails for all, meaning those employees not laid off, at least not as yet. Hidden behind this ascetic front, however, is the CEO's fortune, secured from the moment of his appointment. His green may not be the ficus, but financially it's winner-take-all ultra lush.

Yet questions lurk between the lines of the flattering newspaper profile. What about the wife and children conveniently left back in New Jersey, doubtless in a trophy house—do they stoke the home fires while he campaigns at the front? Do they miss him? Or is he in absentia primarily the family pipeline to the material, high-status good life in a deal brokered with the New Jersey spouse, her agenda the lunching-shopping-salon/spa life so savagely satirized in the early 2000s best-selling narrative *The Nanny Diaries*?

As for those Minnesota "handfuls" of employees so readily rounded up for "impromptu" dinner with the boss—do some of them yearn instead to exit the long work day at dinnertime, to have their meal off the company clock? Are they, like the boss, "free" of family obligations? Or do they have partners to come home to? Or children to play with, bathe, help with homework and tuck in for the night before starting another lean-and-mean corporate day in the art-free environment stripped of the potted plants? The CEO is "an acknowledged insomniac," virtually boasting of sleep deprivation. But do the employees sign on for sleep disorders too? None were quoted in the profile, perhaps because the CEO is said to be a man who "bristles at criticism."

And what about those 11% of the insurance-company workers, some 1,150 scheduled to be laid off by the new CEO in the name of cost-cutting efficiency? In spring 2002, the *Wall Street Journal* featured a woman who could easily be one of the Minnesota employees about to be laid off by Davos Man and his vassals. Employed since her high-school graduation by AT&T, this divorced Chicago-area woman had "built a stable life" for herself and her daughter and purchased a "modest three-bedroom home." Laid off in 1994, she was forced to sell the home. Then in her forties, she was "devastated" (March 27, 2002: A1).

After a series of part-time, short-term jobs, however, she landed back at AT&T, this time at a $9.50-per-hour data-entry job on night shift, though she worked her way up once again, tripling her wages and even buying a condo. This woman typifies those workers who, plummeting from the glass tower, are caught in mid-air—rescued or reprieved by new employers, or, as in her case, by the same employer. Twenty-seven of the forty-three million who lost jobs between 1979 and 1996 were indeed rehired, according to *The Downsizing of America*, though with one major problem: over two-thirds earn substantially less than they did in former jobs and are often reemployed as contingent workers (freelancers, temporaries, or contract workers) without healthcare or other benefits.

Spokespersons for those at work include Barbara Garson, Jeremy Rifkin, and Jill Andresky Fraser, a finance writer and author of *White-Collar Sweatshop: The Deterioration of Work and Its Rewards in Corporate America* (2001). Fraser interviewed employees from entry-level through mid-upper management, from recent college graduates through Generation Xers and baby boomers. She sought to resolve a "nagging" contradiction: how to reconcile the "buoyant optimism" of the chief executives, the Davos Men whom she regularly interviewed as a finance writer, over and against the "bleak" workplace stories and remarks from sources outside the executive offices (see introduction and chs. 1, 3, and 4).

Fraser found that within a reportedly strong economy, employees experienced "ever-increasing workloads, time pressures, unrealistic

employer expectations, declining levels of career and financial security," in addition to "less emotional attachment to the workplace [and]
less time and energy for family." Yet computerized monitors kept
these employees under the constant surveillance. Lawrence Mitchell
in *Corporate Irresponsibility: America's Newest Export* (2001) calls this a
workplace "monitocracy" in which working people are treated "as little more than disposable chattel, destroying their economic futures
and personal satisfaction simply to increase stock price by a few
points" (see chs. 1 and 9). (Those few points are critical, however, to
CEOs who stand to gain or lose millions in this point spread because
their compensation plans are pegged to company stock prices.) *White-
Collar Sweatshop* ruefully concludes that "by the dawn of the 1990s, the
sweatshop corporation had become an integral part of the United
States business landscape."

Does the story of the rehired AT&T woman worker at least have a
"white-collar sweatshop" ending, meaning a steady income? No. Laid
off once again, this woman exposes the myth of upgraded skills as the
route to ongoing employment viability. She cites her record of continual
retraining as no defense against the sudden, second layoff—which struck
her at age fifty. Now she, too, sounds like a character ready for a Dreiser
novel, female kin to Hurstwood as she watches daytime TV and reads
popular romance novels and says, " 'To hell with it.' I'm burned out. . . .
It's too late for me." As of March 2002, mother and daughter (also laid
off repeatedly) entered a six-month financial countdown toward savings depletion, to be followed by the mother's retirement savings.
Both murmur vaguely about government aid as a last resort. (The
daughter reports overhearing commuter-train conversations about
impending layoffs at various companies and says the malls are packed
with people who ought to be at work. When not job-hunting, she cruises
the malls, charging clothing on her credit cards, then returning most
of her purchases, sobered by the double meaning of her sobriquet as
bag lady.)

Reconsider our Davos Man (b. 1953), who received his business degree from the University of Pennsylvania's Wharton School in 1974,
which puts his formative adult years in the 1970s, a period which
Bruce J. Schulman captures in *The Seventies: The Great Shift in American
Culture, Society, and Politics* (2001). This was a decade of a post-1960s
declining faith in government programs, a skepticism about a world
shaped by large-scale public projects, and a deep and thorough "suspicion of the instruments of public life" which gave rise, Schulman
shows, to a "new respect for capitalism" and "an unusual faith in the
market." He identifies a major sociocultural shift in the United States:

"Entrepreneurship replaced social and political activism as the source of dynamic cultural and political change in the United States. The political realm emptied out . . . [as] Americans relied less on the instruments of democratic governments, almost forgetting what it is that politics does, what only the public sphere can accomplish." Schulman continues, "This implosion of American public life and attempt to reconstruct the nation as a congeries of separate refuges revealed itself across the political spectrum and among all demographic groups." It energized "the political left as well as the right. It appeared in the suburbs and cities, in religion and secular life."

Beginning in earnest with the 1972 presidency of Richard M. Nixon and culminating in Ronald Reagan's presidency of 1980–88, says Schulman, "Politics aimed more and more to protect and nourish privatism." He continues, "All sorts of Americans, even those with dreams of radical reform, looked to the entrepreneur and the marketplace as the agent of national progress and dynamic social change." Schulman sums up, "A broad consensus had emerged: Americans affirmed the superiority of the private sphere to the public sector; entrepreneurship, not political activism, marked the path to personal liberation and social transformation." The 1970s shows how privatization indeed became "gospel" (see ch. 9).

The 1970s Davos Man's gospel is accordingly distilled into four "pillars of imperishable wisdom," which *Harper's* editor Lewis Lapham enumerated in dry irony in a post–September 11, 2001, essay: first, the doctrine that big government is "by definition wasteful and incompetent, a conspiracy of fools," bureaucratically cumbersome and inclined toward Marxism. Second, in the era of the free market, "global capitalism constitutes the eighth wonder of the world," sacred in its mysteries and omniscient in judgment. Third, politicians and statesmen are supernumeraries in a world properly guided by economists and policymakers from realms of finance. And fourth, history has reached its post-Soviet terminus at which any new political ideas are null and void in an unending, transcendent era of global markets (8–11).

Our 1970s Davos Man's credo is thus deregulation and privatization, which sanctifies "private," as the hallowed prefix to such terms as "beach," "practice," "school," and "sector." The polar antithesis "public" connotes scorn and derision, as in public school, which means dilapidated buildings and inferior education.

"Public" is thus the pejorative prefix to such terms as "transportation," "housing," "defender," even "service" (excepting IPO or initial public offering). As Naomi Klein argues in *No Logo*, however, public

spaces afford Davos Man prime colonizing opportunities for his corporate mission. Events or spaces previously set aside for public use are
now opportunities for privatization under the branding of a corporate
logo. Perhaps the insignia of the St. Paul insurance company that
Davos Man now heads will soon brand sporting events or an am-
phitheatre, just as Miami's Orange Bowl became the FedEx Orange
Bowl, a skating competition the State Farm Figure Skating Champi-
onship, a Houston golf tournament the Shell Houston Open, New
York's Jones Beach the Tommy Hilfiger Jones Beach, and so on. Perhaps the St. Paul CEO will follow the example of corporate branding
in high culture, in which the Philadelphia Orchestra has moved from
its former home, the Academy of Music, to its new space named for
the telecommunications sponsor: Verizon Hall.

Corporate heraldry often blazons in the name of charitable causes
as companies seek favorable public relations. Davos Man's new insecurity, however, is evidenced in the unprecedented security measures
taken for the Davos 2003 World Economic Forum, including a no-fly
zone and military orders to shoot down "unauthorized" aircraft.
Davos 2003 brought "the tightest security moves in Switzerland's history," including 2,000 Swiss soldiers, hundreds of police, military units
from Liechenstein, and German soldiers on "alert status." The entrance to the Davos Forum's Congress Center was "better protected
than most borders," and the personal bodyguards of Davos Man—or
Men—were granted "permission to use firearms" (*New York Times*,
January 16, 2003: A7).

In an era obsessed with security, Davos Man's angst could also now
be measured in a new forting up of corporate boardrooms—turning
them into panic rooms. "Bulletproofing boardrooms," according to
the *Wall Street Journal* in June 2002, has become a lucrative niche business in the opening years of the twenty-first century. Over a weekend,
construction workers line the boardroom floors, paneled walls, and
ceilings with armored steel and bullet-resistant fiberglass not only to
deter potential terrorists but also "angry shareholders or pink-slipped
employees" (May 23, 2002: B1). One more potential company expense for the St. Paul CEO to ponder: savings on the ficus, but extra
costs for the armored steel plate to ward off the nightmare of jobless
former employees on the attack.

By the Book

Is a post–Davos Man era possible? Can new social arrangements sup-
plant his? Can social change render his moment obsolete? The "new
day" promised in the Discover Company greeting cards, the "time of

hope and promises" and "chance for starting over"—is this "new day" possible in broader socioeconomic terms?*

More to the point here, can the new muckrakers provide a map to such a "new day"? Specific to this project, what role do the new muck-raking projects have in social diagnosis and civic activism? What part can they play in this era of TV and computer screens, when the tradi-tional book format, their format, is sometimes dismissed as marginal, even archaic—when books themselves are produced by the very cor-porate conglomerates that control broadcast news? What role might books on workplace conditions, prisons, public-health failings, corpo-rate takeovers of public spaces, or food production play as fulcrum in a socially pivotal moment?

Two events suggest an answer, the first a traditional book signing at Vanderbilt University's Freedom Forum First Amendment Center in 1999, when Tennessee's U.S. Senator Fred Thompson joined the for-mer *New Yorker* political writer Elizabeth Drew in a discussion of her new book, *The Corruption of American Politics* (1999). In the Q&A, Thompson observed that the percentages of citizens actively interested in public affairs issues were small, but their numbers actually quite large, in the millions. He talked, in short, of the multiplier effect, the leverage that minorities—of writers and readers—can exert on behalf of large num-bers of their fellow citizens.

Leveraged by books, certain popular groundswells for change have ample precedent in recent American history. Who knew that mid-twentieth-century American women would read Betty Friedan's *The Feminine Mystique* and be energized for gender-based social change? Who expected Rachel Carson's *Silent Spring* to initiate the environ-mental consciousness movement, which would hold firm as a national value into the twenty-first century? Who, for that matter, would have thought that a book titled *Unsafe at Any Speed* would initiate a national auto-safety movement still in progress in the era of air bags?

Bearing all this in mind, fast-forward to an evening lecture at Van-derbilt in spring 2001, when the featured speaker was Ralph Nader. Requiring my students to attend, I took a seat in one of the univer-sity's largest lecture halls, which was packed to capacity, standing-room only and many without tickets turned away. The attendance alone was stunning at this event on a campus known for political con-servatism. These students were far too young to know Nader's reputa-tion as a consumer advocate. A few might have worked for his Green

* In February 2003, a *New York Times* reporter filed a story from the World Economic Forum headlined, "Whatever Happened to Davos Man?" He described the gathering of "corporate chieftains . . . fearful of war and darkened by a global economy that has de-fied all attempts at revival" (February 2, 2003, section 4, p. 2).

Party presidential campaign of 2000, and some in the audience doubt-less had been assigned to hear the third-party candidate who was widely held responsible for splitting the Democratic party vote, which sent George W. Bush to the White House—in short, the spoiler.

But what drew this enormous crowd? And what kept them long be-yond the single courtesy hour that they commit to an "extra-credit" or mandatory course-related event? And why the hushed atmosphere? The Vanderbilt campus prizes courtesy, but these students were be-yond polite and respectful. They hung on every word as Nader graphed the difference between "growing up corporate" or "growing up civic." An hour passed, then two. Well into the third hour, hardly anyone had left. "Do not let the desire for material things trivialize your life," urged Nader to the seated students who really sat at his feet, allowing this man to be their guru, this muckraker of the 1960s who had burst on the scene with *Unsafe at Any Speed*.

A large part of Nader's impact was his timeliness at a moment of new cultural receptivity. Another was his skill in narration, the prime ingredient of muckraker literature. Nader told us fact-based, socially pointed stories with great skill. I remembered that similar narrative importance had been attached to a project with a focus similar to Nader's. This was a Fordham University study, its very title suitable for posters for Nader's talk: *The Social Health of the Nation* (1999). Wasn't this the focus of Nader's narration? Wasn't he crafting a story based, like that published study, on "leading indicators" of social health? Wasn't he addressing "bread-and-butter health and well-being issues that in-volve us every day."

Nader, the narrator, had overcome the problem that was pointed out by the authors of *The Social Health of the Nation*. They had worried that too often social data are released to the media and the public in "inaccessible" forms, in "raw data," "technical language," or "unre-lated pieces of information" (see introduction and chs. 1 and 2).

They insisted, instead, on the need for "narrated" information, the kind that Nader now offered his audience. In book form, such nar-rated information had been produced by a number of influential social critics, as the Fordham group knew. They named Michael Harrington's 1960s *The Other America* and John Steinbeck's 1930s *The Grapes of Wrath*. Then they named one founding text of the first generation of muck-rakers, Upton Sinclair's *The Jungle*.

Nader's lecture and my mental segue to *The Jungle* takes us back to the generation of the muckraker founders. "At the turn of the cen-tury," says *The Social Health of the Nation*, "America faced what might be considered the first of the nation's modern social crises. Problems of increasing crime, poverty, child labor, and the rapid spread of infectious diseases led many to believe that the nation needed to chart its social state."

Charting the social course was the mandate of the first muckrakers, not only Upton Sinclair but Bellamy, Dreiser, Tarbell, and others. Theirs was a tipping point leading to legislation of the Progressive era, the New Deal, and the Great Society programs of the Johnson administration. What lessons can be learned from these founders? How did they respond to their cultural moment? What liberties did they take as writers and critics? What constraints bound them? And what techniques of narrative writing did they establish and provide as a legacy to their successors of the late 1900s through the early 2000s? These were the clipboard questions to address by now "looking backward" to their era.

Chapter 3

Muckrakers c. 1900
Civic Passions, "Righteous Indignation"

> *The fundamental critical achievement of American Progressivism was the business of exposure, and journalism was the chief occupational source of its creative writers. . . . The muckraker was a central figure.*
>
> —*Richard Hofstadter,* The Age of Reform, *1955*

> *Roosevelt was quite wrong about this band of about two dozen or so writers who penned nearly 2,000 articles in soap opera-like serial installments that had the public gasping at their revelations. The muckrakers' gaze was neither up or down; it was squarely straightforward—at a reading public that was both enthralled and dispirited by their exposés.*
>
> —*Robert Miraldi, ed.,* The Muckrakers, *2000*

The muckrakers grew up in a world identified by two titles: *The Gilded Age* (1873) and *The Robber Barons* (1934).* One signifies a ruling aristocracy based on theft and plunder. The other profiles an entire era's cheap glossy reality—its gilding—which belied its obsession with gold and the desperation of those without it. The era's subheadings have become a standard textbook trio: urbanization, industrialization, and immigration—all vivified by a montage of images which appear routinely in high-school history texts, in the pages of gift-book editions, and on TV.

I can close my eyes and see them—the dark hulking steel mills of my native Pittsburgh, and the nose-to-nose steam locomotives mark-

---

* *The Gilded Age* was coauthored by Mark Twain and Charles Dudley Warner, a novelistic mix, as one critic put it, of Swift and Horatio Alger, Jr., meaning that its social satire of U.S. greed, hypocrisy, and political corruption was undercut by an advocacy of opportunism and also a genteel blunting of its satirical barbs. An exegesis of "gilded" is found in Louis J. Budd's introduction to the Penguin edition (2001). Matthew Josephson's *The Robber Barons* was titled from an 1880 pamphlet by "embattled farmers of Kansas who . . . applied the name of Robber Barons to the masters of the railroad systems" (rpt. 1962; ix).

ing the completion of the transcontinental railroad, with the ceremonial golden spike driven at Ogden, Utah, on May 10, 1869. I see also the cartoon caricatures of political bosses such as William Marcy ("Boss") Tweed and industrial kingpins Carnegie and Rockefeller, each as bloated as a Macy's Thanksgiving Day Parade balloon.

The mind's eye also brings up lithographs of warring strikers, which look like the Civil War battlefront woodcuts by Winslow Homer, even though they actually represent the 1892 Battle of Homestead, Pennsylvania, in which striking steel workers fought the company's hired Pinkertons on the shores of the Monongahela River. Add to these the Jacob Riis photographs of tubercular child workers in sweatshops and his street scenes of New York's Lower East Side. A contrasting image surges, of course—the formal dinners of the tuxedoed and bejeweled rich whites at sumptuous Fifth Avenue or Newport oceanfront mansions designed by McKim, Meade, and White or Richard Morris Hunt. Haven't I myself toured the gold-and-marble Newport "cottages" and heard the volunteer docents exclaim on the rivalrous Misses Astor and Vanderbilt, both staging duelling dinners with souvenir diamond table favors? Wasn't it the desperate thirst for fashion's novelty that prompted one Gilded Age all-male formal dinner on horseback, each gentleman served on a tray set above his saddle pommel, something like an infant's high chair?

Add, too, a mind's eye's magazine illustration of an African American lynched in the post-Reconstruction South as the mob parties on. For a soundtrack, play a recording of the lines from William Jennings Bryan's passionate defiance of the gold standard and its proponents at the Democratic party convention of 1896: *"You shall not press down upon the brow of labor this crown of thorns! You shall not crucify mankind upon a cross of gold!"* These Gilded Age images, in sum, capture extremes of wealth and power, energy and initiative, corruption, fatality, social upheaval, and misery of the era of the 1870s through the 1900s in the United States.

In sum, these images form the indelible imprint of the decades when Ida Minerva Tarbell (b. 1857), Lincoln Steffens (b. 1866), Ray Stannard Baker (b. 1870), Upton Sinclair (b. 1878), and their cohort came of age. In many ways, these are the images that the muckrakers engaged, illuminated, challenged, and finally deconstructed via narrative. Their projects addressed a literate middle class caught between rocks and hard places. On the one hand, this public feared yet envied the Croesus-rich robber barons with their business and banking pools, rings, and monopoly trusts, and they also disdained the politicians colluding in larcenous machine politics. Yet on the other hand, the same public feared and despised the disruptive and infectious immigrant hordes pouring inland from the coasts.

How did these muckrakers gain critical, analytical perspective on all this? How did they come to view their culture through a refractive lens? How did they define their collective mission as investigative, narrative writers able to captivate the reading public and activate its civic energies?

"I did not intend to be a muckraker," Lincoln Steffens was to say in his *Autobiography*. "I did not know that I was one till President Roosevelt picked the name out of Bunyan's *Pilgrim's Progress* and pinned it on us" (*Autobiography* 357). Steffens's remark was not entirely disingenuous. At the beginning of his career, he, like Sinclair, Baker, Tarbell, and others lacked contemporary investigative narrative skills and found no models available for emulation. In his autobiography *American Chronicle* (1945), Baker would speak retrospectively of "a new and powerful impulse in social criticism which Matthew Arnold called 'The New Journalism.'" But neither he nor the others initially saw a clear path toward their narratives of disclosure, even though they worked as professional writers, notably newspaper reporters (31).

Far from a "New Journalism," newspapering was stuck in a new moment of the 1890s industrial-era standardization, as Christopher Wilson explains in *The Labor of Words* (17–39). As a New York *Post* reporter, Steffens felt straitened among men who worked "like machines," all alike and "without style." He loved his assignments but felt "as a writer, permanently hurt by [his] years on the *Post*." (Steffens nonetheless resisted his mother-in-law's advice that if newspaper journalism failed him, there was always literature [*Autobiography* 179].) Baker, too, chafed at the newspaper format, in retrospect amazed at the disjunction between fact and feeling in his early work on labor strife in the 1890s. Had he managed to combine the two, he now saw, the combination "would have been literature," meaning encroachment on turf forbidden to a reporter (*American Chronicle* 40).*

Stymied by the journalism versus literature split, which had become naturalized and reinforced through the nineteenth century, these writers struggled early on between these two mutually exclusive realms even as pent-up public angst and anger grew over worsening economic and social conditions. Ida Tarbell was schooled in the sciences, got bored by her initial "timid . . . dashes into journalism" for the upstate New York *Chautauquan* magazine, and began writing a novel based on the turbulent history of the Pennsylvania oil regions where she grew up, only to abandon the novel in frustration and embark upon a project on the "science of society" (see Tarbell's *All in the Day's Work* [1939]: 76, 84, 203).

* Baker later wrote fiction under the pseudonym David Grayson.

Baker and Upton Sinclair, for their part, planned a leap from reporting into literature, as if to emigrate to another country. Disgusted with newspaper "hack-work," Sinclair fled to Canada to write his first "painfully crude performance," a self-published novel entitled *Springtime and Harvest* (1901), which yet expressed, he felt, "a new moral impulse" (Sinclair, *The Brass Check*, 18–19).

These writers recorded their frustrations as they sought to produce utilitarian, yet belletristic representations of complex social problems that at first, they knew, exceeded their grasp. Steffens acknowledged that the larger "picture" of high finance took shape intellectually only years after he'd left his Wall Street beat at the *Post*. Tarbell broke off her "science of society" opus after three chapters because she saw the need to know a lot more about history and social theory. Covering the violent Pullman Strike of 1894 for the *Record*, Baker set down the facts as he saw them, "but could not in the least degree make up [his] mind what ought to be done" (*American Chronicle* 38). Sinclair vaguely trusted that *Springtime and Harvest* would somehow, ineffably "convert the world to ways of love and justice" (*The Brass Check* 18).

"Magazining"

A propitious and momentous shift in magazine publication gave these writers a third way. A glance at the roiling state of late nineteenth-century magazine publishing shows the change from the genteel and conservative to the popular, mass-market " 'magazining' for the masses" (Regier 11). The muckrakers' moment was especially fortuitous because, in the 1890s, *McClure's* and rival Frank Munsey's *Munsey's*, together with several others, revolutionized American magazine publishing. They thrust cheap, mass-market magazines into circulation previously held by a conservative, literary foursome. *Atlantic, Scribner's, Century*, and *Harper's Monthly* were "four periodicals [which] were models of the sedate, exclusive, and not wholly indigenous culture of the latter part of the nineteenth century" (Wilson 40–62).

The muckrakers had been children of that older order. All through his "frontier" boyhood, Ray Stannard Baker read "with keen interest" the *Scribner's Monthly* and *Harper's Magazine* to which his father subscribed (*American Chronicle* 77). Ida Tarbell's father likewise subscribed to *Harper's Weekly* and *Harper's Monthly* while eking out his living as a river boatman, then as a builder of petroleum tanks and independent oilman in Rouseville, Pennsylvania, where he housed his family in a log cabin. On a hill over Oil Creek, young Ida lunched with *Harper's* on her lap, the upmarket *Monthly* introducing her to Thackeray, Dickens, and George Eliot, the popular *Weekly* acquainting her with Wilkie

Collins (while beyond the family ken, she read the "forbidden" *Police Gazette*) (*All in the Day's Work* 12–13).

Samuel S. McClure, however, spoke for a new generation of magazine editors and publishers. He denigrated the "literary" style and format of these older Eastern periodicals whose desk-bound editors traditionally awaited mailed submissions from which to pick and choose. Along with a new generation of business-minded, entrepreneurial editors whose own biographies were patterned by the Horatio Alger novels, McClure proceeded to reinvent the American magazine and redefine its editor-publisher.

He became a transatlantic talent scout and impresario, travelling constantly through Britain and Europe and the United States, signing talented writers and making deals, always on the prowl for fresh ideas and material in science, literature, and the arts. He was a "promotional spirit . . . creating a public need and then filling it with a designed product" (Wilson 50). McClure called this "magazinizing."*

Financed through advertising revenue, the magazine revolution measured its success in burgeoning subscriptions—and in the ambitious admiration of younger aspirant writers. As of 1893, William Allan White later recalled, new *McClure's* monthlies lay invitingly stacked on the counter in a bookstore where young noncomformists like himself gathered in Emporia, Kansas. *McClure's* was "something new and different," recalled Baker, a Chicago reporter who recognized the content as "fresh and strong and different." In 1897, when McClure invited him to come to New York to "plan out a series of articles," Baker exclaimed, "If a dream ever came true, this was it!" (*American Chronicle* 77–78, 79). The actual muckraking moment, however, was yet in the offing. The new, "different" magazines conveyed a sense of cultural in medias res immediacy—but had not yet become

---

* A detailed account of the magazine revolution is also to be found in Louis Filler, *The Muckrakers*, 1939 (rpt. 1978), chs. 2 and 3. Filler indicates that older magazines published some articles anticipatory of the muckraking era. See also Harold S. Wilson, *McClure's Magazine and the Muckrakers* (1970), which explains the financing and editorial politics of the magazine and profiles its pre-muckraking contents. One of Wilson's most engaging arguments is that in the 1890s, it was the socially conscious fiction in *McClure's* that augured its muckraking epoch (see pp. 123–27).

Frank Luther Mott's *A History of American Magazines* remains a mainstay of scholarship, vols. 3 (1865–85) and 4 (1885–1905) profiling those magazines that were predecessors to *McClure's* and *Munsey's*, such as the smaller-circulation *The Nation*, founded in 1865, *The Forum* (1886–1930), and the reformist *The Arena* (1889–1909). Mott's survey, in addition, indicates the extent to which other general-interest magazines such as *Collier's* (1888–1957) and John Brisben Walker's and thereafter William Randolph Hearst's *Cosmopolitan* (1889–1925) published muckraking articles, especially in response to proven public receptivity. Mott calls these the "brilliant group of ten-cent illustrated monthlies which made the latter nineties a distinctive period in American magazine journalism" (4: 485).

4. Samuel S. McClure, c.1906. Courtesy Brown Brothers.

venues for a literature of exposure. Their pivotal moment had not arrived.

The Making of Muckrakers

In the 1990s, the future muckrakers were nonetheless schooling themselves, somewhat unwittingly, for their moment of narrative innovation. Reporting for the Chicago *Record* on the march of Coxey's Army of unemployed men to Washington to appeal for federal aid in the depression year of 1894, Baker began to feel that the movement was "a manifestation of the prevailing unrest and dissatisfaction among the laboring classes" and surely a sign of disordered "national blood" (*American Chronicle* 19). In Chicago, he also learned that sensationalist demagoguery of religious leaders was at best ersatz social criticism.

His cohorts were also learning. An avowed socialist, Sinclair rejected the choplogic of the charge that a slaughterhouse was not an opera house—a critique implying, as he knew, an effete sensibility on his part and permission for Chicago's packers to continue to process meat under filthy conditions. Tarbell was jolted from the cozy *Chautauquan* culture by a minister who thundered, "You're dyin' of respectability." She determined to flee to Paris and earn her living by writing despite deepseated fears that she "had not the endowment nor the passion nor the ambition to be a writer" (*All in the Day's Work* 79, 87). Steffens was learning the practical problems of investigation: his interview subjects would divulge nothing important if allowed to speak without interruption.

Much of the literature of disclosure would depend heavily, nevertheless, upon personal speech from total strangers. Marching with Coxey's Army from Ohio, Baker made acquaintance with individual unemployed men and "soon had them talking" (18). Tarbell, persuaded by Samuel McClure to return from Paris and work full-time for his magazine, gained interview expertise when she agreed to write a biography of Lincoln based on personal reminiscences of the thirty-years'-dead president (one of her subjects: Lincoln's son, Robert). Steffens's numerous accounts of political bosses' and business chieftons' admissions of corruption—their "confessions and underworld gossip"—attest to his brilliant navigation of empathy and provocation (*Autobiography* 444–45).

Face-to-face interviews, one stock-in-trade of investigative narrative, did not, however, always yield useful material—and here my own interest came into play, since I planned to conduct interviews with writers of the c. 2000 investigative narratives, Ehrenreich, Garrett, Hallinan, Klein, Schlosser, none of them personal acquaintances. One journalist had told me of a frustrating experience interviewing one of these five, hinting about the person's hostility to women.

In a worst-case scenario, suppose I were to encounter the situation described by William Hard (*Collier's*, 1908), who reported meeting the gaze of Speaker of the House of Representatives Joseph G. ("Uncle Joe") Cannon of Illinois, finding a man who had "the most knowing eyes in any human head" but from whom "no reporter has ever got an even momentary flicker of self-revelation." Hard's frustration points to the seldom-acknowledged variable of a research project requiring resources beyond the library, the hall of records, and nowadays the Web. It also points to possible gaps and fissures beneath the muckrakers' narrative gloss.

Facts

Whichever muckraker one may choose to read, one salient criterion is palpable on the narrative surface: a commitment to verifiable fact. In 1892, Clarence Darrow declared a shift in public taste away from the romance of "fairies and angels" in favor of "flesh and blood." Said Darrow, "The world . . . to-day asks for facts." "Ugly facts," Baker called them, while Sinclair boasted that, whatever its literary status, *The Jungle* was "packed with facts" (qtd. in Davis 14).*

Fact was the muckrakers' antidote to rumor and to sensationalist yellow journalism. Baker recalled that through the later nineteenth century, the American public suspected or believed the truth of various "soap-box" orators' and politicians' campaign charges and countercharges of corruption and privilege. The charges, however, had remained "largely unsubstantiated" (*American Chronicle* 183). Committed to substantiation, the muckrakers were yet vulnerable to charges of amateurism. These writers were not expert in the subject areas of their work. Against opponents' charges of flawed data, exaggeration, and falsification, they armed themselves with factual claims. Our own late twentieth-century skepticism of facts as manipulable and "massage-able" by bevies of PR flacks and "spin doctors" had not yet entered public consciousness. Perhaps such skepticism ought not to prevail even now, according to Hayden White, the historian and theorist of narrative who insists that historical discourse must yield to assessment of its claims of truth value or else "lose all justification for its claim to represent and provide explanations of specifically real events" (45).

White refers to the muckrakers' obligation to verifiable factual accuracy, a prime part of the "contract" with readers. Mark Sullivan, a sometime *McClure's* muckraker, capsuled their fact-based method in *Our Times: America Finding Herself* (1927). He sounds like a professor of journalism. The muckrakers, says Sullivan, "spent months of investigation before printing a brief article of five or six thousand words. They investigated everything, confirmed everything. . . . [They] took

---

* See also *American Chronicle* 185; *Brass Check* 36.

their material from what they themselves saw, or from sworn testimony in lawsuits or legislative investigations. They made it a point to talk with everybody who had important, firsthand information. Almost always they discussed their material with the man accused, or the head of the corporation they were investigating."

The jeopardy of libel, Sullivan says, imposed its own rigor, for "manuscripts were almost always subjected to scrutiny by lawyers," since "most of the articles and books written by the Muckrakers would have been libellous if incorrect." But the public were the muckrakers' arbiters. Again, Sullivan: "they put out their product as *fact*, and asked the public to accept it and test it as such" (478–79). The result, according to Richard Hofstadter, was that "it now became possible for any literate citizen to know what barkeepers, district attorneys, ward heelers, prostitutes, police-court magistrates, reporters, and corporation lawyers had always come to know in the course of their business" (156).

To pinpoint the muckrakers' crucial kinds of facts, I've turned to categories proposed by James Phelan, who observes that the changeability of facts in certain texts does not prove that facts do not exist but that "there are multiple facts and multiple ways of construing facts" (17). Phelan locates in literary fiction areas in which "the line between fact and interpretation is extremely blurry" and also those in which facts "depend on the employment of interpretive faculties."

"Blurry" facts and relativistic interpretations were anathema to muckrakers committed to exactitude and directness. Their confidence in factual accuracy was in keeping with the new, late nineteenth-century era of professional statisticians, who claimed superior powers of precise social analysis.* The muckrakers rejected, or at least minimized, those "facts" fraught with ambiguity or those that would allow readers free rein for individual interpretation. Their investigative narratives sought consensus, even unanimity of response. In the muckrakers' domain, prized facts to be utilized were those "that will not be disputed" (see Phelan 16). In this, indisputable fact, the literature of exposure claims one crucial basis of its legitimacy.†

---

* A recent discussion of the problematic uses of statistics by Jacob Riis is Weinstein's "How Many Others Are There in the Other Half? Jacob Riis and the Tenement Population."

† Muckrakers defended their veracity, Sinclair saying he had been to Chicago "not as a blundering amateur as the packers charged," but as a researcher in "text-books on bacteriology" and assisted by a British investigator from the *Lancet*, this man "the world's greatest authority on packing-houses" (*The Brass Check* 33, 28). "I realized my witness had more feeling than facts," said Steffens of a banker who promised to disclose Wisconsin Governor Robert (Bob) LaFollette's dishonesty. The banker "blew up in a rage . . . but I could not write rage," wrote Steffens. "If he had facts, he could not

The public, however, did not receive these narratives like bolts from the blue. A patchwork of "primary schooling," so to speak, helped ready the public to accept the muckrakers' narratives.* Nearly twenty years before *The Jungle*, for instance, alerts were sounded on problems of food, beverage, and medicine contamination. Women's clubs and farmers in the late nineteenth century had lobbied for the creation of state agencies with oversight over food and dairy products in the new industrial era of factory-processed foods. Sullivan's *Our Times* chronicles the drumbeat of warnings in 1900s magazine articles, in speeches and writings of public-health officials from the 1880s, and even in a 1904 St. Louis World's Fair pure-food booth at which thousands of visitors saw fabrics dyed with chemical dyes extracted from brightly colored processed foods. Visual images played a part too, for instance, the 1905 *Collier's* drawing of a skull imprinted with these words: "The Patent Medicine Trust. Palatable Poison for the Poor." In the aggregate, these texts were opening acts for *The Jungle*, the audience thereby prepped for its message.†

The new magazines' serialization was also important to public education over time. As a newspaperman, Steffens had worried about stories "which ran so long . . . that the newspaper readers lost track of them." The new magazines and their openness to serial installments held the promise of the longer length needed for adequate treatment of complex subjects. The monthly, said Baker, "could take time" and "was not required to print 'spot news' " (*American Chronicle* 93). Said Steffens,

---

handle them" (*Autobiography* 454). Steffens's own facts were checked by a *McClure's* attorney, who "always said [his] evidence was not sufficient and that his articles should not be published" (405). Samuel McClure himself agonized obsessively about factual accuracy of the content of each issue of his magazine.

Steffens provides a gauge of the muckrakers' individual self-protection when he describes storage in "a safe place" of unpublished documents, "against the always possible libel suit that might be brought" (*Autobiography* 405). Steffens ingeniously (and strategically) also protected himself by gathering far more incriminating evidence of wrong-doing against political malfactors than he published, and letting them know it—thus gaining their gratitude for withholding at least some damaging information.

* Harold S. Wilson writes, for instance, "The country at large, the press in general, and the government were already [in 1903] preparing for battle with the two hundred odd trusts that had arison behind the Dingley Tariff of 1897" (129). These trusts included "tobacco, petroleum, sugar, linseed oil, iron and steel, copper, beef, starch, flour, candy, chewing gum, candles, ice, glucose, crackers, whiskey, anthrocite coal, fertilizers, tin cans, farming tools, locomotives, writing paper, school furniture, sewer pipe, glassware, rubber goods, buttons, leather, electrical supplies" (see Regier 4).

† Sinclair's perplexity at having hit the stomach instead of the heart of his audience may be attributable to reader reception already biased toward themes of food contamination. No parallel program of public education on issues of workplace conditions existed prior to publication of *The Jungle*. A full account of the influence of Sinclair and other muckrakers on federal pure food and drug legislation is found in Crunden, *Ministers of Reform: The Progressives' Achievement in American Civilization 1889–1920*, 163–99.

the magazine could "tell the whole, completed story all over again and bring out the meaning of it all with comment" (*Autobiography* 358).*

Steffens's phrase "all over again" points to a crucial element of audience impact. Contents of the daily newspaper could wash out of mind, but the monthly installment could set what psychologists call a reinforcement schedule. Serial publication kept a topic upfront for a monthly interlude long enough for readers to find time to read and absorb the import of the narrative. In addition, each installment opened with a refresher on the preceding months' material.

A repeatedly rewarding experience for readers, however, was key to successful reinforcement; repetition must be gratifying.† Dickens, George Eliot, Stowe, and others worked that vein with proven success. Nineteenth-century British nonfiction also had fared well in installments, including Carlyle's *Sartor Resartus*, Arnold's *Culture and Anarchy*, and much of Ruskin's major work. Could U.S. readers sustain interest in the history of the Standard Oil Company over eighteen months? Or stay engaged in exposés of municipal corruption in St. Louis, Minneapolis, Pittsburgh, Philadelphia, Chicago, New York, Cleveland, and Cincinnati, followed by whole states (Wisconsin, New Jersey)? The question was open and unanswerable at the beginning of the new century.

Successful serial publication, let me note, also brought readers (and writers) the synergy of a certain practice continuing in wide use today—book publication of magazine articles, the articles themselves a marketing and publicity campaign for the forthcoming book. When McClure, Phillips & Co. published Steffens's 1902–4 *McClure's* series on municipal corruption, titled as *The Shame of the Cities*, the project claimed domestic space on the home book shelf as well as the magazine rack, meaning expanded markets in both print formats. (Ehrenreich's *Nickel and Dimed* shows this legacy today, for it began as a *Harper's* magazine article to which readers' letters and emails became a kind of market test indicating whetted interest in an expanded version of the project. Eric Schlosser's *Fast Food Nation* was launched by a *Rolling Stone* piece, and his second book, *Reefer Madness*, on drugs and the U.S. legal system, began as a 1994 article in the *Atlantic*.)

---

* *McClure's* was especially generous in this regard, for Samuel McClure salaried his full-time writers, paid their expenses, and put no pressure on them to rush their projects—the equivalent today of generous multiyear foundation fellowships. Ida Tarbell, for example, traveled extensively and researched the Standard Oil Company for five years at a then-respectable salary of forty dollars weekly. It is estimated that each of her installments cost McClure two thousand dollars.

† Recently, studies of the serial format, notably Kenneth M. Price and Susan Belasco Smith's *Periodical Literature in Nineteenth-Century America* (1995), have argued its importance in the history of the book and examined such techniques as repetition of actions and scenes, techniques of visualization, and mnemonic devices to prompt recollection of characters, scenes, and plot.

Unguarded Gates versus The Shame of the Cities

The muckrakers exploded shibboleths advanced as truth in public discourse over decades in the nineteenth century. Personal interest has drawn me to one of these in particular: the truth claim that society's failings were caused by the barbarous, feckless lower classes, principally immigrants. Like millions of U.S. citizens, I am interested in my immigrant ancestors and how they have been represented. My German great-great grandparents settled in industrial Pittsburgh, so by definition they belonged to the "dangerous classes" savaged by the Reverend Charles Loring Brace in 1872, when Brace deplored mass urban populations as uneducated drunkards and brutes. Their female counterparts were the city "street girls" who became prostitutes "cursed" with venereal diseases.

My great-great grandfather Joseph Hepp worked in Pittsburgh's George Westinghouse plant manufacturing air-brakes for railroad trains. Would rage or despair have filled him at the statement of the social reformer Josiah Strong, who wrote in 1885 that "crooks" were imported on every immigrant vessel, that "immigration not only furnishes the greater portion of our criminals" but "seriously affect[s] the morals of the native population" (qtd. in Davis 228, 235, 247). Suppose "Papa" Hepp, as his daughters (my great-aunts) called him, had read this 1888 nativist polemic on the 1886 Chicago Haymarket riot:

Capitalists engaged in mammoth manufacturing enterprises like McCormick and others, in order to secure cheap labor to the exclusion of native skilled workmen, have imported to this country thousands of foreigners who, after gaining a foothold in the land, have turned upon their employers in organized bands with measures intended to be revolutionary.

The troublesome element consisted largely of the ignorant lower classes of Bavarians, Bohemians, Hungarians, Germans, Austrians, and others who held secret meetings in organized groups armed and equipped like the nihilists of Russia, and the communists of France. (McLean 12)

No family stories about strikes or anarchy have been passed down through generations of my relatives. But "foreigners" like Joseph Hepp, who was described to me as a gentle man devoted to opera and *Lieder* and the occasional evening in a *Bier Garten*, became visible to American-born middle classes mostly during labor strikes and riots, which were reported in nineteenth-century newspapers and such magazines as *Harper's Weekly*. These periodicals were dependent, then as now, on the support of advertisers and subscribers, their owners allied socially with peers in business and industry. Not surprisingly, most

representations of immigrant strikers who disrupted business as usual
were starkly negative.

Here, once again, was something tapping my own experience—this
of the late twentieth century. My two jobs as a member of different
AFL-CIO unions had passed uneventfully in the 1960s, but membership in the American Association of University Professors led to strike
action in 1979 at Boston University. No, we weren't "foreigners" (except insofar as the professorial stereotype leans more toward Einstein-
ish otherworldliness than to all-American McBurgers and football).
The issues that culminated in our strike were based on a need to secure worker rights and a faculty salary policy. (Some B.U. instructors'
salaries qualified them for food stamps.) As we faculty walked the
picket line day and night, the city's newspapers, however, virtually
printed the press releases issued by the university administration, por-
traying us, the striking faculty, as merely greedy and selfish. As for
strike violence, we had our whiff. I well recall the big dark sedan that
gunned its engine, aiming straight for our picket line like a charging
bull—the colleagues in its path springing back at the last split-second
while others pounded on the fenders in fury.

After that spring in 1979, it has been easier to imagine the distor-
tion of events and motives in portrayals of immigrant actions of the
previous century. It is not surprising to find that in 1886, *Harper's
Weekly* called the Pennsylvania coke workers "Hungarians" content to
live in "squalor" as they had in Hungary and "the most difficult class
of laborers . . . to pacify when they are enraged" (Gilje 124–25).*

Investigating corruption in American city government, Steffens
knew how deeply held and self-serving these status-quo beliefs. Middle-
class American readers of the Gilded Age had embraced the view expressed by Thomas Bailey Aldrich, editor of the *Atlantic Monthly* from
1880 to 1890, in his verse, "The Unguarded Gates," an anti-immigra-
tion "cry to keep out the alien sinister races." On his research travels,
Steffens repeatedly heard directly from the "educated citizens of
cities" that "foreign populations" or "ignorant foreign riff-raff" were
the source of municipal corruption.

In reality, he found, this was untrue. The foreign riff-raff had no
vote: "foreign population and labor, the irresponsible propertyless

---

* Paul Gilje's *Rioting in America* (1996) chronicles the widely reported explosive violence of the late nineteenth- and early twentieth-century strikes, notably the national
railroad strike of 1877, the Homestead strike of 1892, the Pullman (Illinois) strike of
1894, and Ludlow (Colorado) massacre of 1914. Many less publicized outbreaks also occurred, based on class conflict, abysmal working conditions, wage disputes, and the determination of owners-managers to maintain total control by enforcement of police,
military, and strikebreakers. Says Gilje, "The saga of these epochal struggles barely
scratches the surface of the violent strike activity" (117).

Rockwood

1440 Broadway, N.Y.(40th St.)
Holland Building

5. Lincoln Steffens, 1894. Courtesy of the Bancroft Library, University
of California, Berkeley.

voters were disenfranchised" (*Autobiography* 400, 467). Steffens offered proof that vice and graft of every sort was conducted by, also condoned from, the top of the social scale, perpetrated by the elites—the leaders in government, business, and industry—together with the "good old American stock" that had "sold out" (*Autobiography* 467). "The 'foreign element' excuse," Steffens wrote, "is one of the hypocritical lies that save us from the clear sight of ourselves" (*Shame of the Cities* 5).

How to overturn such stereotypes and enable self-reflection without infuriating the "good old American stock" or losing its attention? Steffens has left a desultory but useful textbook on the craft of narrative, and it speaks directly to the problem raised a century later, in 1999, in Fordham University's *The Social Health of the Nation*, which lamented that too often social data were released to the media and the public in "inaccessible" forms. In the 1900s, the muckrakers understood that narrative vitality depended on sparing readers what the Fordham project termed "raw data" or "technical language." Steffens, when researching corruption in Pittsburgh (entitled "Hell with the Lid Lifted"), was given a file of incriminating data, but "didn't print much of it" because "it was too detailed and dull." He added a telling point: "The public won't read figures" (*Autobiography* 405). "My task," he said, "was to select a few of the multitudinous facts to show the truth about—any State in the United States" (445). Steffens also gave Upton Sinclair advice on keeping readers' credibility: "I have a rule in my own work: I don't tell things that are unbelievable even when they are true" (qtd. in *The Brass Check* 32).

Civic Melodrama

Muckraker narratives were meant for civic incentive. They promoted civic activism. Within a Christian context, as one critic has written, "Progressive Era muckrakers practiced the literature of exposure because they hoped it would bring about the moral regeneration of a corrupt, overly materialistic American society" (Good 157). Steffens wrote that *The Shame of the Cities* was published and reprinted in book form "with a purpose . . . which was and is—to sound for the civic pride of an apparently shameless citizenship" (3). Other narratives might activate erotic desires or spiritual introspection, but those of the muckrakers were meant to stimulate recognition of citizenly identity and its obligations.

This activism can be regarded as civic melodrama, to use a word that I had spoken in student days in English classes, back when "melodrama" and "sentimental" both prompted a knee-jerk scorn that bonded teacher and student. In class back then, these two epithets got a student a warm, momentary upgrade from an instructor. You might never master the seven types of ambiguity in formalist study, but you got credit instantly for spotting the appalling sentimental and melodramatic on the literary radar.

Since that time, of course, the sentimental has been revalued, reclaimed, and canonized. And melodrama in recent years has also become a major critical term—a keyword—in film studies, especially in analysis of such films as Douglas Sirk's (for example, his *Magnificent Obsession*). Film scholars, in turn, credit Peter Brooks's 1976 *The Melodramatic Imagination* with rehabilitating the term and providing them crucial terms of argument.

Brooks, in fact, has defined the mentality of melodrama in terms vital to the muckraker narratives. In a historical moment when melodrama was still utterly pejorative, he undertook a literary-critical examination of narratives (and plays) of Balzac, Henry James, Dickens, and others. Brooks found in them a "moral manichaeism [as] the basis of a vision of the social world." That world is a "scene of dramatic choice charged with the conflict between light and darkness, salvation and damnation" (5). Melodrama's conflict, Brooks found, is spiritual and its mode is one of "high emotionalism and stark ethical conflict" (20, 12). The societal stakes of melodrama, according to Brooks, are socially urgent and critical: "to recognize and confront evil, to combat and expel it, to purge the social order" (13). The phrases virtually paraphrase the muckrakers' own statements of purpose, and thus *melodrama*—amended as "civic melodrama"—can serve as a kind of "radiant gist" by which the *McClure's*-era muckraker narratives can be best understood.

As in popular stage melodrama of the nineteenth and early twentieth centuries, the muckrakers portrayed a world of societal ideals that had been frighteningly threatened or assaulted. The social script, so to speak, called for the forces of civic virtue to combat the villainous assailants, to defeat them and restore the good order of an earlier era—or to project an ideal, yet attainable, society into the future, as Bellamy did in *Looking Backward*.

Considering the popularity of melodrama in nineteenth-century America, moreover, we expect to find its plotline and its traits in muckraking narratives. In *Melodrama and the Myth of America* (1993), Jeffrey D. Mason summarizes characteristics known to define the genre, including thrilling incidents, an uninhibited show of spectacle, an "open display of violence and catastrophe," and "exaggerated expression of emotion" (17). (If these sound archaic or dated, one might consider their applicability to the admired contemporary literature of magical realism.) Popular late nineteenth-century melodramas such as *The Dangers of the City*, *The Hidden Hand*, and *Through the Breakers* exhibited these qualities. Muckrakers who were appalled and angry at robber barons' and political machines' assaults on democracy would have found their thematic imperative in this line from Owen Davis's *The Silver King*: "Oh God! Put Back thy universe and give me yesterday!" (qtd. in Russel Nye, *The Unembarrassed Muse*, 158).

Muckraker prose style, not surprisingly, shows its debt to stage melodrama, whose development and pervasiveness from the Enlightenment through antebellum America has been chronicled in David Grimstead's *Melodrama Unveiled* (1968). Because Steffens's "typical American business man" has damaged democracy, he is thereby a villain to be exposed in fraught emotional terms. He is "a bad citizen . . . buying boodlers . . . defending grafters . . . originating corruption . . . a self-righteous fraud" (*Shame of the Cities* 5). The most melodramatic, however, of the muckraker texts is probably *The Jungle*, in which violence and catastrophe recur repeatedly in the industrial scenes of combative struggle between the honest, hardworking, familial immigrant Lithuanians pitted against the murderous capitalistic industrial system, which has corrupted popular democracy so pervasively that the only political solution for the future is socialism. Sinclair made it his narrative duty to supply the "metaphors of human destiny" on behalf of his nonpoetical characters (and also readers) (42). At the packinghouse, cattle are herded to the slaughter in a "river of death," while the hogs emit a "terrifying shriek":

It was all so very businesslike that one watched it fascinated. It was pork-making by machinery, pork-making by applied mathematics. And yet somehow the most matter-of-fact person could not help thinking of the hogs; they were so innocent, they came so very trustingly; and they were so very human in their protests—and so perfectly within their rights! They had done nothing to deserve it; and it was adding insult to injury . . . swinging them up in this cold-blooded, impersonal way, without a pretence at apology, without the homage of a tear. Now and then a visitor wept, to be sure; but this slaughtering-machine ran on, visitors or no visitors. It was like some horrible crime committed in a dungeon, all unseen and unheeded, buried out of sight and of memory. (44–45)

The bystanders, Sinclair insists, cannot long witness this scene without becoming philosophical and resorting to "symbols and similes." But it is Sinclair who supplies the emotionally wrought, universalizing, melodramatic metaphor for the voice of doomed victim-workers—the often-quoted "hog squeal of the universe" (45).

As a civic melodrama, *The Jungle* reflects reading tastes formed from

6. Upton Sinclair, c.1905. Courtesy Culver Pictures, New York.

popular entertainment over decades. To readers long habituated to the conventions of stage melodrama, Sinclair's narrative voice was unexceptional. It was his message on systematic production of food contaminated by every conceivable waste from rat droppings to rendered human flesh that gripped Sinclair's readers. The vehicle for that message is melodramatically emotional in accordance with the customs of the genre. Sinclair's novel might even be regarded in this context as the narrative culmination of a century of melodrama.

Ray Stannard Baker, however, comes close to offering a theory of narrative voice congenial to twentieth-century readers who were schooled in the sparer style that became Hemingway's hallmark—and that anticipates Eric Schlosser's narrative voice in *Fast Food Nation*. The relation between the text and its readers is dependent, Baker argued, on the author's dispassionate tone. (Schlosser would tell me something similar, that ranting is unnecessary when the facts speak for themselves.) The effectiveness of narratives of exposure, said Baker, depended precisely on a restrained account of a "complete picture, the truth, vividly and dispassionately set forth." Baker was responding to a reader's complaint about the absence of " 'red-hot invective' " in his indictments of "thieves and traitors who ought to be in jail."

But the narrative must not be a performance of rage, Baker wrote, lest it become solely a spectacle, with readers-audience passive onlookers or voyeurs (*American Chronicle* 185). (One factor in the decline in popular appeal of the literature of exposure in the late 1910s and 1920s might have been narrators' rhetorical emotionalism precisely at the point when that tone began to be thought histrionic.) The dispassionate presentation, on the contrary, opened space to stimulate readers' own emotional engagement and participation—that is, to enter the state that Ida Tarbell called the activist's "righteous indignation."

Baker's first conscious foray into dispassion was particularly precocious—and a window on the muckrakers' class-based code of values. "One day," Baker says, "I tried a new method altogether." This was in summer 1894, when the young reporter had been filing reports on court proceedings and events in Pullman, Illinois, stemming from the Pullman strike. Acquainted with the workmen's families from his many on-site visits, Baker ventured suddenly into the "new method." His innovation was to "tell their [that is, the workers'] stories, exactly as [he] heard them . . . hot out of life" (*American Chronicle* 41–42). He began:

The broad-shouldered Swede lives at 522 North Fulton Street. His name is Andrew F. Rall and he has not been in the country long enough to speak any English. He and his wife and five little white-headed children are crowded into two small rooms, for which he is charged ten dollars a month rent. He owes thirty-eight dollars to the Pullman company and the milkman has a bill of four dollars. . . . Yesterday morning he and his family sat down to the little oilcloth-covered table in his front room and ate a loaf of bread—the last in the house—and drank some water. Yesterday afternoon the children were whimpering for something to eat and the mother was urging them to be quiet until the father came home. She did not know that he would bring an empty basket. (*American Chronicle* 41–42)

7. Ray Stannard Baker, c.1905. Courtesy Culver Pictures, New York.

In response, readers deluged the newspaper with donation checks for families of striking workers, a prelude to the "astonishing" public response to the articles that Baker and his cohorts published in *McClure's*. "Partly by chance, partly by a new technique of reporting which demanded thoroughness of preparation and sincerity of purpose," said Baker, "we had put our fingers upon the sorest spots in American life (*American Chronicle* 169). Direct contact with society's "sorest spots" defined Baker's new role as muckraker.

The above vignette (for that matter, any muckraker narrative) does not, of course, represent a simple act of verisimilitude. The scene was carefully selected and shaped to appeal to middle-class readers who heretofore had agreed with the artist Frederic Remington that the Pullman strikers were a "malodorous crowd of foreign trash" (qtd. in Lichtenstein et al. 142).

Baker presents the striker's family at its dining table as a version of mealtime respectability in the homes of the Chicago *Record*'s readers. The worker's debt, we notice, is to the milkman, not the tavernkeeper. And the dollars owed to Pullman are doubtless family expenses. The children pitifully whimper but do not bawl, nor does the mother raise her voice, much less strike a child in frustration. Neither mother nor children venture out to steal food—which is to say that the plot of this short narrative serves strictures of middle-class conduct. The Chicago *Record* readers' outpouring of donations to what soon became the strikers' *Record* Relief Fund were tributes to—investments in—their own reflected values.

These were largely the muckrakers' own values transmitted continually in the texts. Norms of middle-class respectability are pronounced, for instance, in *The Jungle*, in which the Lithuanian immigrant family pool their resources to buy a Packingtown two-story house, pictured on a placard with porch, scrollwork trim, curtained windows, and familial image of "husband and wife in loving embrace" near their first-born's cradle. The assortment of home furnishings and housewares that they soon buy is strategically chosen by Sinclair, from beds to dishes and a scrub brush. This material vocabulary of family life communicates domestic respectability, combining comfort, propriety, manners, and sanitation.

The muckrakers' narratives are also filled with approving markers of middle-class status, such terms as "Americans of good stock and more than average culture," as McClure put it, or the "better element" found in C. P. Connolly's account of law and lawlessness in Montana (Weinberg, *The Muckrakers*, 4, 107). Or references to the "best" of whites and of negroes versus the "criminal class" of each race, as cited repeatedly in Baker's *Following the Color Line* (1908), a compilation of magazine essays on racialization and its precipitant crises in contemporary America (4, 14). Tarbell's *History of the Standard Oil Company* commends exemplary individuals, such as the president of the Petroleum Producers' Association, Captain William Hasson, whom she identifies as "independent in spirit, vigorous in speech, generous and just in character" (1: 111).

Narrative

The muckrakers explicitly identified their projects as narratives. "Swift-moving, hard-hitting narratives," Baker called his "exposure" texts (*American Chronicle* 183). Further West, C. P. (Christopher) Connolly identified "The Story of Montana" (*McClure's*, 1908) as a romantic narrative. He compared his project to *The Count of Monte Cristo*: "the story of the crimes and passions which seethed about [Butte hill] makes a narrative almost as romantic as the adventures of Edmond Dantes" (see Weinberg, *Muckrakers*, 105). Confronting the Standard Oil project, which she had earlier attempted as a novel, Tarbell subsequently asked this question: "Was it possible to treat the story historically, to make a documented narrative?" (*All in the Day's Work* 205).

Tarbell's question, posed in 1900, directed me to a consideration of narrative itself, which has been a topic of vigorous debate in literary studies from the mid-1980s. Among the many discussions of the complexities of how a story can be told, a few are especially useful in approaching the muckrakers. Hayden White's above-cited *The Content of the Form: Narrative Discourse and Historical Representation* (1987) helps because the muckrakers worked as contemporary historians who were self-conscious about their productions as narratives. The muckrakers' concerns about crucial elements of a story's pace, its pictorial composition, emotional stimulus, and documentation are well taken, White argues, because they are basic to any definition of narrative.

White explains why this is so. In the discourse of historians, he says, the facts (those truth-value elements) are displaced onto literary fictions' very "grounds" (47). These grounds are a kind of prose soil made up in part of the figures and tropes necessary to all narrative, including history, and therefore to be found in its production processes too. Says White, "A narrative account is always a figurative account, an allegory" (48).*

---

* White adds, "To leave this figurative element out of consideration in the analysis of a narrative is to miss not only its aspect as allegory but also the performance in language by which a chronicle is transformed into a narrative. . . . It is the success of narrative in revealing the meaning, coherence, or significance of events that attests to the legitimacy of its practice in historiography" (48, 54). In addition, White reminds us of

Reading White's and other scholars' anatomies of narrative once again brought back student my days, notably John Barth's fiction-writing class at Penn State. The narrative elements debated nowadays by scholars are, in fact, virtually the same ones that students of fiction-writing have always grappled with, even at the most elementary level. Under Barth's guidance, our first-year class—English 12—had dissected Joyce's *Dubliners* and Eudora Welty's "Why I Live at the P.O." in order to find clues for portrayal of actual places, character development, incitement of motion and conflict, and figurative language from a deliberately chosen point of view. We were also encouraged to work toward an elusive and mysterious but vital thing which baffled us when Barth named it: voice.

Memories of English 12 in Pennsylvania's Nittany Valley surfaced when I reread an essay by another former teacher, J. Hillis Miller. In his "Narrative," an essay in *Critical Terms for Literary Study* (1995), Miller cites "personification" as a key element of narrative—"whereby character is created out of signs" (75). Following my Barth-days memory and Miller's anatomy of narrative, it seemed now wise to seek in the muckraker texts the traits identified as the vital organs of narrative, starting with personification. Recall William Hard's secretive "Uncle" Joe Cannon, whom Hard proceeds to characterize through facial features, from the "short, stiff" beard that creates a look of combativeness and concealment, to a "long, cruel nose," "florid complexion," and eyes that "might as well have been forged at Pittsburgh out of real steel" (Weinberg, *Muckrakers*, 97).

Or see Steffens's more extensive characterization, in "The Shame of Minneapolis," of Albert Alonzo ("Doc") Ames, thrice mayor of the city, a "tall, straight and cheerful" surgeon who was a "genial, generous reprobate," and known to be "good to the poor" because he "gave not only his professional service, but sympathy and often charity." Steffens writes, "So there was a basis for his 'good fellowship.' There always is; these fellows are not frauds—not in the beginning."

Steffens then shows the "other side" of this "naturally vain" man who abetted corruption and whose "loose life" lost him the support of respectable "good" people so that he "came to enjoy best the society of the barroom and the streets." Ames first neglects, then abandons his

---

Paul Ricoeur's statement that a narrative is "a means of symbolizing events," that "one cannot represent the meaning of historical events without symbolizing them" (53). White's and Ricoeur's statements affirm the necessary inclusion of tropes and figures as building blocks of literary form, including historical narrative. Symbol-making, they agree, is inherent in the production of historical writing.

family, appearing uninvited at his wife's funeral "in a carriage on the street . . . with his feet up and a cigar in his mouth." His third term as mayor was "a career of corruption which for deliberateness, invention, and avarice has never been equaled" (*Shame of the Cities*, 1904, 65–69).

Figuration of language, another element named by Miller, is also present in the narratives of exposure, just as it is in novels, short stories, and other fictions (including the haltingly primitive fictions of my student days, when we struggled to elevate such objects as lightbulbs and oysters into metaphors and symbols). Of Montana's Anaconda copper mine, itself a figuration, Connelly says in *McClure's* (1906) that it was named by a former soldier who had read that General George McClellan "was enveloping Lee's army 'like a giant anaconda.' " When the veteran located his claim, "he gave it the name which had quickened his fancy as a soldier. It has since become a name to conjure with in the copper world" (Weinberg, *Muckrakers*, 108).

The scene or "initial situation" as Miller puts it, is also a crucial narrative element, providing a vivid sense of place and a forum for action (75). Consider this from Connolly, the Butte, Montana, prosecuting attorney who describes the area around the newly opened Anaconda mine:

Fortunes were made and spent in a day. An army of men descended into the mines daily to strip them of their treasure; huge forests were despoiled of their timber to stull [support] and shore up the excavations and protect the earth above—for these copper veins are often one hundred feet wide. Immense smokestacks began to vomit their clouds of smudge from scores of furnaces scattered over the hill; the moan and clank of huge pumps could be heard in the depths, forcing the water to the surface; the pound of hammers and the steady impact of drills sounded everywhere, while the earth trembled and bellowed with distant underground explosions. Great hollows, like cathedral naves, were scooped out, where the treasure had lain in the rock-ribbed earth. Horses and mules were blindfolded and lowered into the mines— where their hides, like the gray beards of the old miners, soon took on the greenish color of the copper which saturates everything below the surface. Their Butte hill soon became a veritable underground city. (Weinberg, *Muckrakers*, 110–11)

Setting the scene, Connelly also projects the plot: "The story of copper is largely woven around the passions, hatred and ambitions of two men who were by nature antagonists" (*The Muckrakers* 106).

Here I come to this matter of plot, the term that arises at the very word, narrative, even though college and university workshop programs in creative writing have all but abandoned it in recent years, evidently regarding plotting as a déclassé function best left to nonliterary commerical fiction, romance novels, mysteries, and the like.*

Scholars, however, feel differently. Plot interests them. Peter Brooks, once again, provides useful insights. His *Reading for the Plot* (1984) has called attention to narrative's recently undervalued infrastructure, the plot, that is, "what shapes a story and gives it a certain direction or intent of meaning" (xi). Brooks reminds us that our "common sense of plot . . . has been molded by the great nineteenth-century narrative tradition that, in history, philosophy, and a host of other fields as well as literature, conceived certain kinds of knowledge and truth to be inherently narrative" (xi). This he calls the "golden age of narrative," a period from the mid-eighteenth century through the mid-twentieth, when Western societies "felt an extraordinary desire for plots, whether in fiction, history, philosophy, or any of the social sciences" (xii, 5). That was the period, Brooks goes on to say, of plotting with a "good conscience," meaning the "confidence that the elaboration of plot corresponded to, and illuminated, human complexities" (see ch. 5: 115).

Brooks adds an observation relevant to the muckrakers, that the "pre-eminently nineteenth-century genre [is] the detective story." In classic detective fiction, it is essential that the "detective repeat, go over again, the ground that has been covered by his predecessor" (238, 24).

My ears perk up at this, my own bailiwick, detective fiction. Plot is its sine qua non, and, for many practitioners, myself included, a constant struggle whether one writes in the (tea)cozy tradition of Agatha Christie or à la the thrillers of Patricia Cornwell and Dennis Lehane. In all detective fiction, the mantra is *plot plot plot*, and guide books on fiction writing often devote two or more chapters to the subject. Says Donald Maass in his *Writing the Breakout Novel* (2001), "Plot is the organization of the story: its events and their sequence" (133).

Essentials of plot, Miller finds, include a minimal three "personages," the first two being a protagonist and an antagonist, the third "a witness" (75). What stirs the story?: "a change or reversal" of the initial situation (Miller 75). Something has gone awry; let the plot action begin. Closer to the muckrakers is another scholar's emphasis on the plot's moral core— a narrative "that moves from an unstable inaugural condition that *is* but *ought not*" (Harpham 403). Something has indeed gone awry, and the plot will show an effort to repair it, to bring about a state of things as they *ought* to be. A new stability is called for to instate or reinstate the appro-

---

* Recently, I was intrigued to hear Leah Stewart, a young novelist and Vanderbilt University colleague in creative writing, say that her M.F.A. writing program excluded all exercises in plotting, so that when drafting her first novel, she resorted to mystery fiction, especially Elizabeth George's novels, to learn plotting techniques for her *Body of a Girl*, which has been well received by literary critics.

priate order of things. For the muckrakers, the shameful cities will become efficiently well-administered municipalities, working conditions and food processing will become humane and hygienic, the monopoly trusts will break up to permit fair business competition, and so on.

What about narrative coherence? Postmodernists scoff, but a writer of suspense fiction and scholarship had better be committed to coherence. My scavenger hunt into various muckraker texts is all very well for mini-demonstrations of narrative taxonomy. But in terms of narrative as mapped by White, Brooks, and others, can one read a muckraker text as one might a novel? My own worn, interlined copy of *The Jungle* lay at hand, invitingly familiar from courses regularly taught in American fiction and in turn-of-the-century American literature—in my "Blockbuster" course too. *The Jungle* could be discussed according to the insights of literary studies, and I'd have the advantage of familiarity with its key scenes, having written a few pages on the novel in a study of literature and technology.

But perhaps *The Jungle* was too familiar, which is precisely the reason to turn elsewhere. In the Boston University Library in the early 1980s, I had pulled down a volume on Standard Oil by Ida M. Tarbell, her name then only vaguely familiar to me. Tarbell's two-volume book looked intriguing, though at the time my focus was elsewhere, on literature and engineering. Tarbell, I thought, was one of numerous writers certain to gain new attention in the feminist years of recovery of women's writing. "Sensible, capable, and very affectionate," Steffens called her, a peacemaker in the often turbulent *McClure's* New York office (*Autobiography* 392–93). Somewhat reluctantly, I had reshelved her book. That was then. Now in 2002, I got another chance.

Ida Tarbell and *The History of the Standard Oil Company*

> *We are a commercial people. We cannot boast of our arts, our crafts, our cultivation; our boast is in the wealth we produce. As a consequence business success is sanctified.*
>
> *—Ida M. Tarbell,* The History of the Standard Oil Company, *1902–4 (2: 284)**

The History of the Standard Oil Company (1902–4) has the documentary heft of a legal brief or a doctoral dissertation. Thick appendices take up a full third of its back pages—including court transcripts, letters,

---

* All citations are to Ida M. Tarbell, *The History of the Standard Oil Company*, vols. 1 and 2.

8. Ida M. Tarbell featured on a first-class U.S. postage stamp of "Women in Journalism," 2002. The citation credits Tarbell's "landmark trust-busting exposé as well as serialized biographies for *McClure's Magazine*."

contracts, petitions, affidavits, articles of incorporation, charters, and so on. All relate to the so-called "rock-oil" which for centuries had flowed along creek surfaces in northwest Pennsylvania and "burned fiercely when ignited" (1: 4). Initially bottled as a cure-all, the oil became American entrepreneurs' black gold when they grasped the commercial potential writ large in a chemical analysis by Yale's Benjamin Silliman, who in 1855 found that this oil yielded gas, paraffin, lubricating oil—and "as good an illuminant as any the world knew" (1: 7).

The contours of the oil story are well known. By 1858, the newly organized Seneca Oil Company sent "Colonel" Edwin L. Drake to Titusville, "a lumberman's hamlet on Oil Creek," to gather "the tools, engine, and rigging necessary to bore a well" (1: 9). In the next few years, eastern stock companies raised capital to support numerous "ambitious and vigorous" young entrepreneurs who leased land parcels and sunk wells. "In answer to their drill, oil poured forth in floods" (1: 12). Illumination by whale oil and tallow was soon replaced worldwide by refined petroleum, which also found myriad uses as lubricants. "It was the discovery and development of a new raw product, petroleum, which had made this change from wilderness to marketplace," says Tarbell. She echoes Genesis to say, "This product . . . not only peopled a waste place of the earth" but "revolutionized the world's methods of illumination" and also to boast that it "added millions upon millions of dollars to the wealth of the United States" (1: 3–5).

The major agent of this revolution was John D. Rockefeller, the former Cleveland produce dealer who became an oil refiner in 1865 and in 1870 combined his various companies into the Standard Oil Company. Tarbell's *History* presses the argument that Rockefeller, together with his brother William and a small cohort of Standard Oil Company associates, systematically and relentlessly sought to regulate the price of crude and refined oil by controlling the output and, in addition, controlling the pricing and means of transportation of oil.

Tarbell, in sum, worked to prove that Rockefeller's Standard Oil Company was determined, not to compete against, but to destroy, all competition and thereby monopolize a basic commodity and necessity of life at the well, at the refinery, and in the marketplace. As a narrative, Tarbell's *History* must, as Peter Brooks succinctly puts it, demarcate, enclose, establish limits, impose order, all while moving through its "discrete elements—incidents, episodes, actions" (*Reading for the Plot* 4, 5).

Tarbell was aided by a recent study of Standard Oil, Henry Demarest Lloyd's *Wealth Against Commonwealth* (1894), but she rejected its socialist politics. A proponent of capitalist free enterprise, Tarbell intended hers to be an account of Standard Oil's perversion of the free-market system. "As I saw it, it was not capitalism but an open disregard of decent ethical business practices by capitalists which lay at the bottom of the story" (*All in the Day's Work* 204).

Tarbell wanted hers to be the definitive and conclusive history of attempted monopoly. She offers readers her bona fides as a student of the "great mass of sworn testimony," the "large pamphlet literature," and "files of the numerous daily newspapers and monthly reviews" containing "statistics and full reports." Tarbell also conducted first-hand discussions with officers of Standard Oil. Her occasional admission that some information remained inaccessible—for example, that "there is no evidence of which the writer knows" only heightens credibility when struck against this prefatory first-person simple statement: "I have been able to find practically all of the important documents relating to the subject" (1: 103, ix–x). She is the textbook case of the muckraker methods Mark Sullivan sets forth in *Our Times*.

NARRATOR-WITNESS

Crafting her narrative persona as a scrupulous investigator and reporter—as the apparent witness—Tarbell declined to extend personal identity beyond those roles. "The conclusions expressed in this work are my own," she states, personalizing a project whose documentation steers it in the opposite path, to depersonalize it. No reader encounters her autobiographical connection to the oil industry, her upbringing in Rouseville and Titusville, her father's struggle as an independent refiner nor her brother's affiliation with the independent Pure Oil Company, which was one of few companies to survive competition with Standard Oil. Tarbell kept clear of all such disclosure. Was this hypocrisy? Not according to James Phelan, who writes in *Narrative as Rhetoric* that "voice exists as a trait of a speaker, but it need not be the basis for some full portrait of that speaker."*

Stylistically, Tarbell's is a voice of sobriety. Nowhere will readers of *The History of the Standard Oil Company* encounter such operatic air as: " 'Petroleum to-day is . . . carried wherever a wheel can roll or a camel's hoof be planted. . . . It is the light of Bagdad, the City of the Thousand and One Nights.' " Dismissing such style as "dithyrambic" (2: 244–45), Tarbell is even chary with punctuation, using exclamation points sparingly. Her high-impact diction is tactically sparse and seemingly innocent of narrative maneuver, as when she says a few independent refiners escaped Standard Oil's "strangulation" (2: 29).

The Tarbell persona, securing itself as trustworthy and credible, nonetheless promises a "story" and "narrative" with pictorial and dramatic components (2: 270, 274, 487). "The work we have in mind," she wrote in that letter to a young editor, "is a narrative history of the Standard Oil Company . . . a straightforward narrative, as picturesque and dramatic as I can make it" (qtd. in Brady 125). The dramatic and pictorial would appear, for instance, in a kinetic metaphor on excess oil production in 1873: "It seemed as if Nature, outraged that her generosity should be so manipulated, . . . had opened her veins to flood the earth with oil" (1: 125). Or this: "In studying [Mr. Rockefeller's] career, one is frequently reminded of Tom Sawyer's great resolution—never to sully piracy by dishonesty" (2: 24).

Tarbell needed verve to reach an audience that reformist writers in the 1890s had concluded were listless and indifferent, or worse—so resistant that efforts to stir them would be "futile" (2: 255). Citizens of Gilded Age America, one critic of 1899 claimed, increasingly bowed

---

* Phelan adds that voice is "typically a mechanism . . . for influencing its audience's responses and understanding of the characters and events that are the main focus of the narrative" (see ch. 2: 47, 48).

their collective knee to the golden calf of wealth (Regier 52). Tarbell worried that the American public were now "listening in wonder and awe" solely to "the unctuous logic of the Mother of Trusts" (2: 255). Hers was a fight against idolatry, her weapons a battery of facts charged with rhetorical power. "These are not mere affirmations of a hostile critic; they are facts proved by documents and figures" (2: 285).

NUMBERS, CLOCKS, CALENDARS

Readers encounter in the *History* a distinctly important feature of most nonfiction narratives: the use of numbers, clocks, and calendars. These are especially familiar to me, a sometime writer of suspense novels in which the demand for numerical facts is unrelenting. Times of day, amounts of money, the calibre of guns in millimeters—these must be logged constantly. Tarbell's narrative also enlists numbers as a technique of particular importance. Quantities in weights and measures, financial expressions in specie and currency—these index and explain human action (or inaction), motives, conflicts, desires. Dates and hourly times, in addition, create a sequence serving to plot the linear progression with verifiable chronological strictness. This is something all writers of detective fiction must learn to do—we are reminded too of Peter Brooks's remark that the preeminently nineteenth-century genre is the detective story.

Numerical and chronological facts appear to be neutral and incontestable, but they are covertly malleable in serving strategic purposes, as writers, politicians, scientists, and accountants know well. Remember also Steffens's caveat about a public averse to reading figures, by which Steffens largely meant raw data, tables, statistics, and the like. To refute Standard Oil's "slurred-over" numerical facts, Tarbell needed to present her own in accessible form in the narrative. A useful approach to this was voiced by a McClure associate, a British labor writer named Alfred Maurice Low, who said the investigative writer's challenge was to "clothe the statistical skeletons with the living expressions of men" (qtd. in Wilson 135). This makes numerical data the bone structures to be fleshed out and clothed as manifestations of personages. In short, numbers make the man, and by his numbers, a man may be known to his very marrow.

Tarbell's "living expression" of Rockefeller is thus largely revealed in dissection of his statistics. Dates, dollars, and numbers of barrels of oil, for instance, become argument's trellis for Tarbell's account of events of the early 1870s. At that time, she tells us, Standard Oil did not manufacture lubricating oils but supplied stock to the Morehouse and Freeman Company, which in 1871 produced 25,000 barrels of

lubricants and 120,000 boxes of axle grease. Seeking petroleum supplies from Standard Oil, Messrs. Morehouse and Freeman were "encouraged [by Standard] to build a new plant [which] was done at a cost
of $41,000, and a contract was made with the Standard Oil Company
for a daily supply of eighty-five barrels of residuum."

But "in 1874 this supply was cut down to twelve barrels," writes Tarbell, adding that "it was impossible for Mr. Morehouse to supply his
trade on twelve barrels of stock" and that "he begged Mr. Rockefeller
for more," knowing the supply "was there in the Standard Oil works."
Morehouse and his partner "offered to buy 5,000 barrels and store it,
but Mr. Rockefeller was firm. All he could give Mr. Morehouse was
twelve barrels a day." Tarbell quotes Morehouse's testimony before
a congressional committee of 1879: "That meant squeeze [us] out—
buy [our] works. They have got our works and are running them; I
am without anything. They paid about $15,000 for what cost $41,000"
(1: 163–64).

In this account, calendric sequencing and repeated quantification
come to the fore (in construction dollars and barrels of oil sought,
supplied, and denied). The narrative itself appears to recede, sup-
planted by a ledger of supplier-customer costs and output, with the
narrative becoming merely glue holding the numerical facts together.
Yet the narrative has only shifted tactics for the moment, foreground-
ing the numerical in order to prosecute its rhetorical program in stac-
cato facts showing Rockefeller's "consolidation through persuasion,
intimidation, or force" (1: 164; 2: 284).

DOUBLE PLOT

What is at stake in *The History of the Standard Oil Company*? Start with
the reading public believed to be seduced by the pseudo-facts of Standard Oil's "unctuous logic." Abandoning its own interest, Tarbell fears
it has succumbed to the mentality identified by Henry James who, in
The American Scene (1904), said that Americans, above all, wish not to
"mind." Tarbell's mission: to turn "mind" into an active verb. "We, the
people of the United States, and nobody else, must cure whatever is
wrong with the industrial situation" (2: 292). This paraphrase from
Jefferson's *Declaration* must be the public's too.

When she proclaims it, Tarbell has already guided readers through
a double-plotted detective narrative, starting with the familiar, popular American story of pioneering and civilization. Until 1872, northwest Pennsylvania, her own birthplace, "had been little better than
a wilderness," inhabited by lumbermen who seasonally "cut great

swaths of primeval pine and hemlock from its hills, and in the spring floated them down the Allegheny River to Pittsburg [*sic*]." Deforestation was not a sign of environmental calamity but civil progress. "Too rugged and unfriendly for settlement," this remote region in just a dozen years was "transformed into a bustling trade centre, where towns elbowed each other for space, into which three great trunk railroads have built branches, and every foot of whose soil was fought for by capitalists" (1: 3–5).

"Fought for" is key to Tarbell's *History*, whose second plot is staged as a series of oil wars waged between producers and independent refiners, pumpers, and drillers against the Standard Oil Company and its affiliates over some thirty years. The trope of war confers on this narrative a national, epic scope when Tarbell announces in her preface the availability of "trustworthy" documents equivalent to those "for a history of the Civil War or the French Revolution" (1: viii).

War, of course, was a national plot personal to Tarbell's generation, not only the Civil War itself but its postwar aftermath, almost a residual environment to be lived in, breathed, ingested in the way the later twentieth century and opening years of the twenty-first still dwelt in the tortuous, attenuated Vietnam era and the nostalgia of WWII. "Battles and Leaders of the Civil War" was serialized in *The Century* (whose 1884–86 circulation exceeded 200,000), and in the late 1880s, the war became the focus of popular stage plays, including David Belasco's *The Heart of Maryland* (1895) and Clyde Fitch's *Barbara Frietchie* (1899). For Tarbell, the war was its own mentality. Her second project for *McClure's* was a biography of Lincoln. It must have seemed natural, if not inevitable, to frame her chapters thus: "The Oil War of 1872," "The Crisis of 1878," "The Compromise of 1880," "Cutting to Kill," "The War on the Rebate."

The oil war is Napoleonic, her Rockefeller explicitly the general and emperor, an identity chosen with care—and convenience, since Tarbell had also written a popular biography of Napoleon Bonaparte for *McClure's* (1894–96). Like Bonaparte, Tarbell's Rockefeller has a "genius for detail," a "sense of big and vital factors in the oil business," and "a daring in laying hold of them"—in sum, "very much like military genius." She continues, "He saw strategic points like a Napoleon, and he swooped on them with a suddenness of a Napoleon" (II, 241). She Americanizes Rockefeller's Napoleonic feat, encompassing all wartime military effort both North and South: "If one considers what this means one sees that it compares favourably with the great ordnance and mobilising feats of the Civil War" (2: 242).

The oil wars and Napoleonic Rockefeller, however, come late in the

History, whose first plot shows the struggle to create an industry from a wilderness. Tarbell sets the scene of the "oil farms" with pictorial vividness: "the awkward derricks, staring cheap shanties, big tanks with miles and miles of pipe running hither and thither, the oil-soaked ground, blackened and ruined trees, terrible roads" (1: 116). Devastation? Absolutely not. The derricks and blackened trees are signposts not only of struggle but of industrial vitality. In good times, "the crowded oil farms" are alive with "creaking walking beams [which] sawed the air from morning until night" on land "where engines puffed, whistles screamed, great gas jets flared, teams came and went, and men hurried to and fro." Altogether, these are "the common features of the oil farm to which activity gave meaning and dignity" (1: 116).

Readers first grasp the oil fields' bustle, its ingenuity and its frustrations, then shift to the banks of the Allegheny River, vital to oil transport in the industry's early years, however sluggish in summer, "gorged with ice" in winter, and roiling in springtime floods when oil-laden flatboats attempted to float downstream in freshets. Tarbell's description combines sights and smells in a scene better identified with her acquaintance Mark Twain. "Always exciting and perilous and frequently disasterous," the river bank is "a hopeless jam of broken boats and barrels, the whole soaked in petroleum and reeking with gas and profanity" (1: 15).

As the *History* proceeds, many of its crucial events occur in hotel and office meeting rooms or in Saratoga, "that Mecca of American schemers" (1: 146). But Tarbell's most deeply etched sites are the oil fields and the ground and streams traversed by teamsters and flatboatmen, railroad tank cars, and oil pipelines, her key qualitative indicators consistently "meaning and dignity."

The oil fields, moreover, double as respectability's site of civility and domesticity, terms targeted at a readership for whom these traits are touchstones of their own stated values. The "better element" among the oil pioneers hated "indecency" even in the primitive years when they lived in "pine shanties" among "oil derricks built on a muddy flat" (1: 34–35). Tarbell emphasizes that vice, which was borne on flatboats of whiskey hawkers and prostitutes, was literally cut adrift downriver (and later confined to a red-light zone). "Out of this poverty and disorder they had developed in ten years a social organization as good as their commercial," as proven by Titusville's opera house, two newspapers, college-preparatory school, and band (1: 35).

"Why one should love an oil refinery, the outsider may not see," says Tarbell when describing one independent refiner who "walked with pride among its evil-smelling places." But the reader has long been brought inside the "evil-smelling" oil regions to appreciate twinned civil and business pride earned through the nurture and stewardship of enterprise, of "love" and of its manifest "honour" (1: 156). The acrid odor of petroleum is the aroma of the homeplace.*

Yet energy, not domestication, is the driving force of the oil regions. And here, again, Tarbell cultivates a readership accustomed to Emersonian advocacy of American self-reliance, which was reinforced in the various late nineteenth-century state and local celebrations of American pioneering energies (Kammen chs. 5 and 9). Tarbell emphatically endorses the early oil entrepreneurs' spirit of enterprise, energy, and courage, all traits of worthy combatants. "On every rocky farm, in every poor settlement of the regions, was some man whose ear was attuned to Fortune's call, and who had the daring and energy to risk everything he possessed in an oil lease" (1: 12). The active verbs—to risk, to wrestle, to stake, and to strike—index the "courage and dignity" which define the oil regions.

Tarbell hammers one major doctrinaire-guiding principle, namely, that business competition be spirited and, above all, fair. "One would like to feel that it is possible to be a commercial people and yet a race of gentlemen" who are by definition "sportsmanlike" (2: 288). "Manhood" and "fair play" are synonymous in this all-male story of Rooseveltian strenuous life (1: 37). Tarbell's narrative expects its readers to be—indeed, formulates its readers as—committed to a system of ethics in which fairness, that is, honesty in accordance with rules and exemplified in athletic competition, is transparently accessible to all. Both participants and spectators assent to the rectitude of the system.

The oil producers are thereby Tarbell's heroes, men in whom "life ran swift and ruddy and joyous" and who "believed in independent effort—every man for himself and fair play for all." Theirs was civilization's "conquest to be proud of." "Their sense of fair play" had been "the moral code" and "the saving force of the region in the days before law and order had been established" (1: 36, 97, 101).

Tarbell's American plot of pioneering and civilization is, perhaps surprisingly but understandably, Darwinian. Darwin's *Descent of Man* (1870–71) argued the inevitable human extinction via "encroach[ment]

---

* Tarbell's formulation is opposite of Rebecca Harding Davis's 1904 description of the Pennsylvania oil region in her memoir *Bits of Gossip*: "Twenty years later [in c. 1873] I went back to the old farm. The orchards, the yellow wheat fields, the great silent woods, were all swept away. In their stead a vast plain, treeless and grassless, stretched to the horizon. Here and there upon it huge derricks and pyramids of hogsheads of petroleum rose against the sky. The farmhouse was gone; in its stead were the shops and saloons of a busy drunken town.

"My old friends had struck oil; their well was one of the largest in the State. Money poured in on them in streams, in floods. It ceased to mean to them education or comfort or the service of God. It was power, glory. They grew drunk with the thought of it" (70).

upon races and species of men" (Barrett and Freeman 9). More specifically, Tarbell shows a debt to the political sociologist Herbert Spencer, who is best known for his coinage of the key phrase in social Darwinism—"survival of the fittest"—a concept elaborated in his 1893 *The Inadequacy of Natural Selection* and the 1898 *Principles of Biology*.

Tarbell first read Spencer in 1872 in *Popular Science Monthly*, reportedly rejecting his precepts in favor of the Tarbell family ethos of the "brotherhood of man" (*All in the Day's Work* 28). In the name of fair play, however, her *History* advocated a principle of competition in which the strong succeed, the weak fail. "Give the refiners open and regular [shipping] freights, with no favors to any one, and the stronger and better equipped would live, the others die" (1: 88). Yet always this proviso: "give all a chance" (1: 88).

That chance to live or die in fair competition is crucial to her plots, which conjoin American pioneering with industrial development and then segue to the battlefield. Fairness is central to the business ethos of *The History of the Standard Oil Company*. Depriving businessmen of that fair chance is Standard Oil's unforgivable sin. "This huge bulk, blackened by commercial sin" had "violated" the oil regions men's "independent manhood" and "sense of fair play" (2: 231; 1: 97). Tarbell uses the 1900s euphemism for rape when she says the men were "outraged" by the Rockefeller-led violation (1: 97).* The *History* charges business homicide against Rockefeller and Standard Oil and also against those businesses that colluded in destroying competition, notably the railroads, which entered into secret pacts to give Standard alone rebates on every barrel shipped (and fees on competitors' shipments too). This is the "dynamic shaping force of the narrative discourse," the plot as armature of the oil story, supporting and organizing the rest and projecting its beginning-middle-and-end classic structure (see Brooks ch. 1: 11).

The drive to crush competition rather than to compete fairly creates crisis in the oil regions—and in the narrative. Thereafter the plot of industrial-era American pioneering is subsumed by the war plot. It is understood that the oil regions, which represent the best American energy and initiative, must defend against the invasive aggressors. It is understood, too, that the regions must engage militarily, that they will fight in successive campaigns. Tarbell, however, was loathe to confront a faultline in her merging of militarism with her social Darwinism. She insists that the military code of behavior, which is synonymous with

---

* Tarbell quotes but fails to comment on Rockefeller's own social Darwinist statement, reportedly made to a competitor, who recalled hearing Rockefeller telling him, speaking of his and similar companies, " 'There is no hope for any of us. But the weakest must go first.' And we went" (1: 155).

that of gentlemen-sportsmen, must govern a social Darwinist world. But she fails to see the incompatibility of the two governing principles. Inexorably driven by evolutionary force, the insurgent "fittest" would not and could not necessarily submit to a gentlemanly nor military nor athletic field code of conduct.

SOUTH IMPROVEMENT

Crucial to the war plot of the *History*, Tarbell exposes Rockefeller's prime strategy, which originated in 1871 in a business blandly named the South Improvement Company—"the most gigantic and daring conspiracy a free country had ever seen" (1: 94). In 1872, it was "a company unheard of" in the oil regions when producers' freight rates inexplicably soared by as much as three hundred percent (1: 70). "On every lip there was but one word, and that was 'conspiracy.' " The culprit was the mysterious South Improvement Company, which the oil producers soon called the "Monster," "Forty Thieves," and the "Great Anaconda" (1: 71, 72). Though the South Improvement Company was disbanded after three months of intense legislative investigation prompted by the oil regions producers, the company set a structural precedent to be followed repeatedly in the future. Its objective was to crush competition by collusion with the railroads for three purposes: to obtain rebates (refunds of its own shipping costs), to secure drawbacks (payments from the railroads from shipping costs of rivals), and to obtain confidential information about the shipments of competitors by gaining access to their records.

Tarbell's exposé of Rockefeller as prime mover in—the very engine of—the South Improvement scheme depended on her 1901 discovery in the New York Public Library of a scarce pamphlet, *The Rise and Fall of the South Improvement Company* (1873). In it, she found a compilation of documents published by the Oil Producers Union relating to this monopolistic move. This was the sole document linking Rockefeller directly to South Improvement Company, a connection that Rockefeller had denied for thirty years. As Tarbell's biographer says, "Ida could prove that Rockefeller was a linch-pin of an illegal ring whose tactics he transferred to the Standard Oil Company" (Brady 124).

But the South Improvement episode gave Tarbell a linch-pin of sorts for the war plot of the *History*. Battle after battle of the thirty-years' oil wars distills itself to the same battle: Standard Oil replaying the South Improvement Company's aborted scheme. Each Standard Oil subplot in the *History* unfolds with the same culprit and the same mystery solved, meaning that readers repeatedly encounter the standard plot of Standard Oil, whether in its incarnation as trust or holding company, whether chartered in Ohio or New Jersey, whether in 1872, 1889, or 1896. "To-day, as at the start, the purpose of the Standard Oil Company is the purpose of the South Improvement Company" (2: 256).*

ROCKEFELLER AND THE LEGITIMATE GREATNESS
OF THE STANDARD OIL COMPANY

The *History* presents a desultory roster of individually ethical oil men—producers, independent refiners, shippers, and others—who are paragons of "fair-play." They come and go. Tarbell's project, however, has no single protagonist who approaches the monumental stature of John D. Rockefeller, for whom it is "an intellectual necessity to be able to direct the course of any particular gallon of oil from the moment it gushed from the earth until it went into the lamp of a housewife" (2: 31).

This is to say that the *History* focuses upon what Brooks terms the "analytic topography of a person," its antagonist, Rockefeller. The first page bears two key epigraphs, one of which is:

> *"The American Beauty Rose can be produced in its splendor and fragrance only by sacrificing the early buds which grow up around it."*
>
> John D. Rockefeller, Jr., in an address on trusts
> to the students of Brown University

Initially seeming preposterous, the metaphor of Rockefeller's oil company as cultivated rose is not, however, absurd. Tarbell advocates business enterprise in an American land of "commerical people," and the *History* includes a chapter on "The Legitimate Greatness of the Standard Oil Company." In business culture America, Standard Oil is admirably "strong in all great business qualities—in energy, in intelligence, in dauntlessness," all certain to ensure "permanent stability and growth" (2: 231–32). Tarbell tells us that she personally toured a modern Standard Oil factory, which manufactured tin cans for oil sent to Asia and the tropics, and found "the five-gallon can [is] a marvel . . . a marvelous example of economy not only in materials, but in [production] time and in footsteps" (2: 239–41). (Her field-trip exuberance anticipates her own 1917 essay defending, as democratic, the Taylorist efficiency movement.)

Tarbell commends Standard Oil in repeated praises for efficiency,

---

* Says Brooks, "Narrative always makes the implicit claim to be in a state of repetition. . . . It must make use of specific, perceptible repetitions in order to create plot, that is, to show us a significant interconnection of events" (see *Reading for the Plot*, ch. 4: 97–100).

for company employees' loyalty, for corporate internal competitiveness, and for the structure of internal oversight committees: "Anything in the oil world might come under their ken, from a smoking wick in Oshkosh to the competition of Russian oil in China" (2: 232).*

The notion of Standard Oil as an American Beauty rose, then, at first may seem as *outré* as the idea of vast power represented in the figure of the Virgin Mary, but Tarbell is as earnestly straightforward as Henry Adams in the 1907 *Education* when he equated the Virgin with the dynamo.

MACHINE AND SHADOW

Half mastermind, half villain, Tarbell's Rockefeller emerges in figurative language basic to narrative, but disciplined by personality traits that she found central to Rockefeller's character. Her models for this—and for him—were few. One was the bourgeois Benjamin Franklin, revivified in the Horatio Alger, Jr., novels. Employed full-time at age sixteen on modest pay as a clerk-bookkeeper, Rockefeller kept a meticulous record of every expense in a "small ledger" and was "but twenty-three years old when he first went into the oil business," having "already got his feet firmly on the business ladder" and learning that " 'it was a good thing to let the money be my slave and not make myself a slave to money' " (1: 40–43).

There is no evidence that Tarbell found precedent for Rockefeller elsewhere in in American literature or history—or that she would have recognized in Melville's Ahab the corporate CEO megalomania identified in the mid-twentieth century by C. L. R. James in *Mariners, Renegades, and Castaways* (1952). Still some fifty years in the offing were Ayn Rand's unbridled egoists, notably the master architect Howard Roark of *The Fountainhead* (1943). Tarbell had her Napoleon, who was a sort of Rorschach test figure throughout nineteenth-century America, by turns eulogized and demonized. In any case, Napoleon could only get Tarbell part of the way in an American story.

What to do?

Go to Emerson. As she did, finding her own "radiant gist" of an epigraph in his essay "Self-Reliance": "*An institution is the lengthened shadow of one man.*"

This lengthened shadow immediately conjoins Rockefeller with the

---

* Tarbell, in fact, contrasts Standard Oil's admirable "minute economies" to the sometime profligacy of her heroes, the oil regions' producers, who were "notoriously extravagant in the management of their business," sending costly telegrams instead of letters, junking repairable tools, and abandoning wells that were modestly profitable (2: 237; 1: 112–13).

institution of Standard Oil, its operations, its pricing practices, contracts, covert dealings, physical plants from refineries to door-to-door sales wagons, all manifesting themselves in toto as Rockefeller incarnate in the material world.

Tarbell's Rockefeller-as-Standard Oil was in part legitimated by the 1886 U.S. Supreme Court decision in the case of *Santa Clara County v. Southern Pacific Railroad*, in which the Court ruled, under the Fourteenth Amendment, that the business corporation bore the legal status of "person." Large corporations thereafter systematically attempted to exploit images and public relations to bring to life "as a moral 'person'" the "inanimate business corporation," which was widely regarded by the public as coldly soulless (Marchand ch. 1).

Tarbell worked in the opposite direction, relentlessly driving the idea of a soulless Rockefeller and Standard Oil. She represented both in the technological figure of the industrial-era engine, whose fuel and driving power made it a key metaphor for the nineteenth-century psyche (see Brooks ch. 2: 42). Tarbell's chosen image was familiar to large segments of the reading and traveling public, for at the U.S. Centennial Exposition of 1876, held in Philadelphia, the seventy-foot-tall Double Corliss engine had caused a sensation. The fifty-six-ton steam engine, ceremonially started by President Grant and the Emperor Dom Pedro of Brazil, powered all exhibits in Machinery Hall and dwarfed the bonneted ladies and top-hatted gentlemen visitors who stood in awe at its base.

Images of the Corliss engine were reproduced widely. Although William Dean Howells called the machine an expression of American "national genius," Tarbell tapped public visual memory—and her own personal "deep" and lasting impression as a fair-goer. She allied the world's largest steam engine with a modern pact with the devil (see *All in the Day's Work* 43). The imagined moment of Rockefeller's demonic epiphany occurs when he visits the exhibition and "sits watching the smooth, the terrible power of that famous Corliss engine of 1876, an engine which showed to thousands for the first time what great power properly directed means, [and] he realised that something very like it was at work in the oil business—something resistless, silent, perfect in its might—and he sold out to that something" (1: 158). Sold his soul in a machine-age demonic pact, in short, even as he recognized the mammoth Corliss engine as the paradigm for Standard Oil. In Tarbell's *History*, the company becomes the cerebral Rockefeller "great machine," a "machine with a head whose thinking was felt from the seat of power in New York City to the humblest pipe-line patrol on [Pennsylvania's] Oil Creek." Its "head controlled each one of the scattered plants with absolute precision" (2: 31, 233). Tarbell broaches the notion of artificial intelligence in Standard Oil as a "machine pervaded and stimulated by the consciousness of its own power and prosperity" (2: 126). The cerebrally omniscient mechanism is Rockefeller incarnated literally as the *head*quarters of Standard Oil.

How else to represent this man? A prose narrative writer needs figurative variety. Besides, Tarbell can't simply portray Rockefeller as overtly monsterous nor mechanistic, not when she so strongly endorses the "legitimate greatness" of many business practices at Standard Oil.

What to do?

Go back to Emerson's aphorism and exploit its second image: the shadow. In the era of robust masculinity, her Rockefeller is a shadowy, spectral figure. His power would not find expression in the gusto of open competition on the athlete's playing field so admired in the *History*, but secretly, in the shade and semi-darkness. The *History* turns Emerson's shadow into deadly nightshade.

Like a dramatist, Tarbell delays Rockefeller's appearance until the oil regions' pioneering plot is well underway and readers are allied with the hale pioneers and their struggles. At last she cites the city of Cleveland, favored by rail and water transport, as "destined by geographical positon to be a refining center" (1: 38). She cues the one young man of Cleveland who had "remarkable commercial vision—a genius for seeing the possibilities in material things" (1: 40). At last Tarbell introduces the young Rockefeller, who, like many nineteenth-century fictional protagonists (including Horatio Alger's), is a kind of an orphan, self-fashioned despite two brief references to a father. Tarbell's Rockefeller is "one of the early-and-late sort, who saw everything, forgot nothing and never talked" (1: 41).*

Never talked—here is one key identifier for Rockefeller. Beyond reticence, he is the silent presence and power, absorbing all, remembering everything, disclosing nothing, silent like the Corliss engine, but immaterial as a shadow. He "watched and saved and contrived . . . low-voiced, soft-footed, humble" (1: 43). His policy is "silence" and his attitude "sphinx-like" (2: 127). Tarbell continues this theme: "Although Mr. Rockefeller was everywhere, and heard everything, . . . he rarely talked," this "silent, patient, all-seeing man" who, whenever possible, "kept well out of sight" (1: 105, 92; 2: 232). Rockefeller has a mind that, "stopped by a wall, burrows under or creeps around" (1: 99). He is "a brooding, cautious, secretive man" who "studied, as a player at chess, all the possible combinations which might imperil his

---

* As Brooks says, "The parentless protagonist frees an author from struggle with preexisting authorities, allowing him to create afresh all the determinants of plot within his text" (see *Reading for the Plot* ch. 5 and p. 115).

supremacy" (1: 50). To show the stealthy Rockefeller's aversion to open dealings in the light of day, Tarbell describes him "sitting all day in his den, hidden from everybody" and later, at a congressional hearing, incessantly tapping the arm of his chair "with his white fingers" (2: 125, 261).

Tarbell strategically inserts dialogue to give voice to a Rockefeller whose public speech is also shadow. In February 1888, Rockefeller was summoned by the New York State Senate to testify about the nature of the Standard Oil trust. According to the narrative, he arrived with a "wealth of polite phrases—'You are very good,' 'I beg with all respect.' " Then Rockefeller is asked about a company in which he was a principal director:

Q.   Was there such a company?
A.   I have heard of such a company.
Q.   Were you not in it?
A.   I was not. . . .
Q.   Has not some company or companies embraced within this trust enjoyed from railroads more favourable freight rates than those rates accorded to refineries not in the trust?
A.   I do not recall anything of that kind.
Q.   You have heard of such things?
A.   I have heard much in the papers about it.

Rockefeller, says Tarbell, "with an air of eager frankness, told [investigators] nothing he did not wish them to know," indeed providing a lesson in "how not to tell what you know" (2: 132, 133).

Rockefeller's partners are narrative extensions of him, "cold-blooded men . . . who knew how to hold their tongues and wait" (1: 260). He swears his refinery partners and their wives to utmost secrecy and orders all to "conceal" their money, "not to drive fast horses" nor " 'put on style' " (1: 166). Correspondence among them is to be by aliases, accounts kept secret, mail sent to a special postal box. A wry Tarbell comments, "Smugglers and house-breakers never surrounded their operations with more mystery" (1: 166).

But Tarbell herself narratively produces the very characterization she claims merely to record in fidelity to fact. Her recurrent references to Rockefeller's silence, secretiveness, mystery, and so on form the narrative pattern that drives the action and conflict—and is produced systematically by Tarbell, even if verified by the verbatim testimony of Rockefeller in dialogue. Emerson's "lengthened shadow" stretches over thirty years' time, extending inexorably over occupied territory captured in war.

The narrative, in fact, mystifies Rockefeller in order to demystify him. Tarbell enforces the Rockefeller mystique in order to act as sunlight's "evaporation" of this shadowy, pseudo-"transcendent" figure (2: 66). Among businessmen, Tarbell writes, the panoptical Rockefeller had represented "a kind of omniscience, and the feeling of supernaturalism." His ability to locate rivals' shipments seemed to them "uncanny" (2: 65–66, 62). His dealings are conducted as "secret rites," and the businessmen had begun to "dread" the oil magnate and to "invest him with mysterious qualities" because Standard Oil seemed presciently to know their inmost secret, closely held business information (1: 166; 2: 66). "These men," says Tarbell, lay "too supine in Mr. Rockefeller's steel glove even to squirm" (2: 66).

IDA M.

Toward the end of the *History*, Tarbell offers an elegiac scene of an American ruins, first asking, "For who was there to interfere with [Mr. Rockefeller], to dispute his position?":

No one, save that back in Northwestern Pennsylvania, in scrubby little oil towns, around greasy derricks, in dingy shanties, by rusty, deserted oil stills, men have always talked of the iniquity of the railroad rebate, the injustice of restraint of trade, the dangers of monopoly, the right to do an independent business; have always rehearsed with tiresome persistency the evidence by which it has been proved that the Standard Oil Company is a revival of the South Improvement Company. (2: 254–55)

The narrative strikes a nostalgic note here. The scrubby towns and rusty, deserted oil stills are relics of primitive, prewar better days. The ruins of the oil regions are poignant memorials to the ethic of the playing field, which prevailed before this Standard Oil era of "brigandage," "greed," and "unscrupulousness" (2: 231, 232). That ethic, the narrator insists, can be reclaimed by a vigilant civic effort, a concerted public effort to restore a world in which "commerce is a fit pursuit for our young men." In other words, a free-enterprise world of wholesome patriarchy.

The motor of reclamation, however, is Tarbell. She enjoys the moment when the reclusive, reluctant Rockefeller is "dragged into the open" in 1888 when called to testify by the New York state senate (2: 128). But Rockefeller is really dragged into the open by Ida M. Tarbell. Her *History* is mostly the antagonist's story, but the narrator is its protagonist. Tarbell wrote that Rockefeller "had the essential element of all great achievement, a steadfastness to a purpose once conceived which nothing can crush" (1: 99). This statement doubles back to Tarbell, relentless in pursuit over five years' research, uncrushable, utterly steadfast.

The History of the Standard Oil Company is thus a representation of the protagonist's mind. This narrator, exponent of ethics, trumps the seemingly omniscient malefactor. Another analogy with Rockefeller also suggests itself. Just as Standard Oil drilled, pumped, refined, and sold petroleum, so does Tarbell, an industrial-age author in the commercial marketplace, probe for raw data, refine it into narrative, and produce it for sale. In American literature, Melville had set the precedent for this narrative model, his proto-industrial *Moby-Dick* replete with cetological source material transformed into narrative. Like Melville, although immediately responsive to Rockefeller's late nineteenth-century industrial paradigm, Tarbell exhibits raw data to show it processed into product.

Tarbell criticizes the oil regions' men and independent refiners for being "an impatient people, demanding quick results" (1: 256). She laments the collapse of their union, the producers thereafter actors in "the great human tragedies of the Oil Regions." At that point, she regretfully says, "man after man, from hopelessness, from disgust, from ambition, from love of money, gave up the fight for principle which he had waged for seven years" (1: 261). But Ida Tarbell is likewise a native of the oil regions, native born and native speaker. In a history driven along a rhetorical spine of ethical behavior, of "fair play" and "principle," these producers are culpable. Abandoning principle, they surrender and, she implies, show cowardice and hypocrisy.

She, however, redeems them and their best effort. The *History* is utterly patient, sustaining its years-long "fight for principle." If the "great tradition" of the nineteenth-century narrative is its "concern with authority, legitimacy, the conflict of generations, and the transmission of wisdom," then Tarbell pits herself against Rockefeller to expose the oil patriarch as illegitimate (see Brooks, *Reading for the Plot*, ch. 3). Perhaps Tarbell is the matriarch, but more likely the daughter avenging her oil regions father, all its fathers who represent the legitimate paternity of industrial America.

Chapter 4
Muckrakers c. 2000

Burning bridges, naming names, making enemies. . . . Passion gets these books written.

—*Kenneth Klee, "Modern Muckrakers," Book, 2001*

In the fall of 2001, the mail brought a particularly nice surprise: a copy of *Book* magazine, featuring a cover story on "Modern Muckrakers." This quarterly general-interest magazine devoted to the promotion of seasonal new books now showcased a genre that I believed deserved much greater attention and respect. I turned to it immediately.

Book's "Modern Muckrakers" provided a short crash course on the century-long tradition of the narratives occupying my thoughts. It traced the history of the revered founders, Ida Tarbell, Upton Sinclair, Jacob Riis, and Samuel McClure and *McClure's*, and it recounted the moment of Theodore Roosevelt's politicized christening of the group.

With a full-cover photograph of Eric Schlosser, and doubtless timed to coincide with the paperback edition of *Fast Food Nation*, "Modern Muckrakers" also discussed *Nickel and Dimed* and wound down with quotes from Barbara Ehrenreich. In addition, the article paid tribute to several familiar landmark projects, including Rachel Carson's *Silent Spring* and other titles of the second half of the twentieth century, some to be named admiringly by Schlosser in our luncheon interview. "Modern Muckrakers" also highlighted several intriguing new books and books-in-progress on diverse subjects. These included U.S. Cold War nuclear tests on human subjects, hog factory farms, and a pharmaceutical industry betrayal of schizophrenic patients.*

---

* Books profiled included Carolyn Johnson's forthcoming volume on factory hog farming; Ted Conover's *Newjack*, an anthropological account of undercover experience as a prison guard; Christina Hoff Sommers's *The War Against the Boys*; Christopher

"Muckraking sounds messy, and it is," wrote *Book*'s Kenneth Klee, adding that the genre is "backbreaking, troublemaking and—if practiced by a writer with just the right mix of skill, timing, and topic— even earthshaking" (*Book*, September/October 2001, 48). The article also sets forth the "creed of the muckraker," to "dig and dig some more. . . . pile up the proof, believe that if you can simply speak the truth, people—maybe lots of people—*will see it your way*" (48; emphasis added).

That stopped me. "See it your way? Your way?" It wasn't the resonance from the old Burger King slogan that gave me pause, but the unstated assumption underlying these words. The statement suggested a kind of peculiar individual outlook on the part of the muckraker writer, perhaps a personally obsessive idiosyncrasy or eccentricity. Fueled by "polemical fire," said the *Book* article, these writers "spend years, sometimes even decades, reporting and writing a story that won't let go of them" (48, 46). The article, I realized, was troubling because it made these investigative writers sound like borderline fanatics held captive by their obsessions.

True, anybody committed to a long-term big project must be single-minded and driven, whether writing a book or building a boat in the garage. But the statement in "Modern Muckrakers" was treacherous because it implied that critical societal urgency lay—or lies—principally with the muckraker, that the narrative is the outpouring of a singular passion. "Proceed with Passion" is the subhead on the *Book* front cover.

The flaw in this reasoning—the crack running through it—is the implication that the crisis to be exposed to public view is a kind of hobbyhorse solely of the writer. In this line of reasoning, the writer more or less invents and/or owns the subject and finally rigs the spotlight to exhibit it to curious consumers who may be persuaded to buy into it, that is, "maybe lots of people—will see it your way." The muckraker's *your way* is understood to be the new, unusual, strange, or even weird way offered up for sale. It's as though the skewed outlook is really the muckraker's own, as though the crisis exists in the muckraker's mind, not in the world.

Muckraking narrative, in fact, mostly works the other way around, tapping social crises already roiling the public in deep currents. Recall, for instance, that Tarbell's *History of the Standard Oil Company* was prefaced by Henry Demarest Lloyd's well-received *Wealth Against*

Hitchens's *The Trial of Henry Kissinger*; Robert Whitaker's critique of the pharmaceutical industry's schizophrenia drug program, *Mad in America*; and Eileen Welsome's exposé of Cold War radiation experiments on human subjects, *The Plutonium Files*.

Commonwealth (1894), which itself began as a series of *Atlantic Monthly* articles in 1881, indicting Rockefeller and Standard Oil for "business feudalism."

As we saw in the run-up to the 1906 publication of *The Jungle*, moreover, the topic of food, beverage, and medicine contamination and adulteration had been percolating in the public sphere in America for some two decades previous to Sinclair's best-seller. Middle-class people had been increasingly worried about the issue. In industrializing America, their food no longer came from farmers in nearby locales, but on rail cars from distant processing plants. Many were uneasy about this. Magazine articles, public speeches, and a world's fair booth validated their concerns about jeopardy to their families' health. When it appeared, *The Jungle* became a focal point for public issues already in play. Sinclair's timing was perfect because public interest was already stirring. Public consciousness of the crisis was growing. Sinclair's book was the crystallizing event. Seeming to inaugurate a national movement for legislation to ensure pure food and drugs, *The Jungle* really focused an existing movement and sped it forward.

Similarly, in the late twentieth century, food-poisoning outbreaks and meat recalls were highlighted in newspapers and on radio and TV before the publication of *Fast Food Nation*. Indeed, these events became part of Schlosser's database, which he freely acknowledges. Consider, for instance, readers' encounter with his account of the 1993 Jack-in-the-Box scandal in which children on the West Coast of the United States died from eating hamburgers cooked at temperatures too low to kill the toxins in the ground meat shipped to Jack-in-the-Box restaurants from the packing plants. Turning to the review of that episode in Schlosser's pages, many readers are reminded of a national news story within fairly recent memory.* *Fast Food Nation* refreshes that memory—and exponentially extends knowledge of a largely unregulated food system that in recent decades has lapsed dangerously back to the era of *The Jungle*.

Schlosser is the first to admit that his book arrived at a moment when larger segments of the American public already had become concerned about nutrition, health, and food safety. He remarks in the paperback edition of *Fast Food Nation*, "Had the same book been published a decade ago, with the same words in the same order, it probably wouldn't have attracted much attention" (271).

Schlosser's remarks, both in print and in my interview with him,

---

* It must be noted that subsequent to the deaths and illness from Jack-in-the-Box hamburgers, according to Schlosser, the company instituted the most rigorous meat inspection system in the entire fast-food industry.

serve as a reminder that numerous media serve both to preface and reinforce the muckraker narratives produced in book form. These media in effect enhance the narratives. Newspapers, magazines, TV, films, political cartoons, and so on go far to educate the public continuously on numerous issues of social urgency. They help to create the environment for public understanding of—and engagement with—issues crystallized in muckraker narratives. They become a de facto prep school for the public in c.2000, as did their media counterparts a century earlier.

Magazines play a modern part in this today. True, there is no contemporary periodical approaching the popularity of *McClure's*, but *Harper's*, *The New Yorker*, *The Atlantic*, *Rolling Stone*, *Mother Jones*, *The Nation*, and others regularly publish exposés on such topics as prison conditions, the worldwide corporate takeover of public water systems, and military adventurism. Readers of these very pages have been made aware, in addition, of the extent to which major newspapers, especially the *New York Times* and the *Wall Street Journal*, continuously publish investigations into conditions of U.S. work, health, wealth disparities, transportation safety, and so on. These newspaper reports, often many months in preparation, regularly become the basis for TV news broadcasts on subjects central to muckraker narratives. Indeed, some print reporters develop sufficient interest and expertise to write separate books on topics they've covered for their papers, for example the *Wall Street Journal*'s Roger Lowenstein, who wrote the story of a hedge fund that nearly brought down the global financial system in 1998 in *The Rise and Fall of Long-Term Capital Management* (2000).

Magazine exposés are complemented nationwide by investigative reports in the alternative weeklies, often on topics ignored by the daily press. Launched as sixties-era counterculture or underground papers, the weeklies thrive on a mix of irreverent entertainment and investigative reporting. New York's *Village Voice* is the best known of these, but throughout the United States the weeklies contribute a sizable number of exposés in the public interest. Boston's *Phoenix* has disclosed the likelihood of crime rising in the aftermath of state cutbacks of drug detox programs, while the *LA Weekly* has investigated a North Hollywood (NoHo) "Love Canal," an urban renewal project situated by an industrial corridor of auto paint shops spewing airborne toxic fumes. The Nashville *Scene* has exposed favoritism and numerous irregularities in the Metropolitan Nashville Police Department, a topic ignored by the major daily, *The Tennessean*.

Television plays its part in contemporary muckraking too. Prime-time network news hour-long investigative documentaries have become rarities in recent years, but the long-running CBS *60 Minutes* consistently achieves high ratings for investigative projects. *60 Minutes II*, along with such news-magazine programs as NBC's *Dateline* and ABC's *20/20*, raise issues of public concern, from mad-cow disease to SUV roll-overs and Depression-era-like breadlines of citizens unable in 2002 to buy sufficient food on their minimum-wage earnings. Cable channels also present investigative programming, notably Arts and Entertainment's (A&E's) *Investigative Reports*.

Public television (PBS), moreover, in its *POV* (Point of View), *Frontline*, and Bill Moyers's *Now* series broadcasts incisive programs on a range of topics from workplace safety to business crime and racial violence in the United States (The *Frontline* broadcasts, moreover, have a secondary market/audience, as videotape copies are sold cheaply for classroom use, while some viewers tape such programs themselves for wider dissemination among friends, family, and civic and religious groups to which they belong.)

Independent documentary films, many shown on PBS and in major cities, also explore social problems in need of remediation, and these too can have a long afterlife in classroom use. Decades of Frederick Wiseman's films are a case in point. His *Titicut Follies* (1967) exposed the wretched conditions of residents of a public psychiatric hospital in Massachusetts. More recently, Michael Moore's *Roger and Me* (1989) showed the urban decay and desperation following a factory shutdown, which stripped a community of good jobs. Moore's *Bowling for Columbine* (2002) examines the pervasive gun culture in the United States and argues that deep-seated, unspoken fear prompts American firearm violence.

Hollywood movies also serve a muckraker function, their narratives examining such issues as low wages, hazardous workplace conditions, and nuclear and chemical contamination. *Norma Rae* (1979) starred Sally Field as a southern textile-mill worker persuaded to try improving conditions via unionization of her fellow workers. In *Silkwood* (1983), Meryl Streep played the role of an actual Oklahoma nuclear-plant worker who died under suspicious circumstances while en route to give federal health safety officials documents implicating the Kerr-McGee company for life-threatening nuclear safety violations. More recently, Julia Roberts played the title role in *Erin Brockovich* (2000), based on a paralegal who developed the successful pro bono case on behalf of residents of California desert town who were poisoned by water-borne contaminants dumped by a public utility, Pacific Gas and Electric. John Travolta in *A Civil Action* (1998) (adapted from a book by John Hare) played the attorney who represents families of children sickened and killed by cancer when community wells in Woburn, Massachusetts, were contaminated by the W. R. Grace Company.

Cartoons and comic strips, like the line-drawing satires by Thomas Nast and others in the first Gilded Age, also complement and enhance muckraker projects. Consider Garry Trudeau's decades-long sociocultural and political critique in *Doonesbury*, together with Scott Adams's recent excoriation of white-collar corporate America in *Dilbert*, and Tom Tomorrow's (Dan Perkins's) exposé of public susceptibility to Orwellian political doublespeak in *This Modern World*. Popular music is also an agent of cultural critique, from the ghetto cri de coeur of Tupac Shakur to Bruce Springsteen's reprise of Steinbeck's *The Grapes of Wrath*, his "The Ballad of Tom Joad."

These days, of course, the Internet serves as a medium of myriad endeavors from retail shopping to map locations—but investigation into sociocultural problems, from healthcare crises to prison brutality, is just a few clicks away via search-engine assistance. Vast libraries of cached documents—some accurate in contents, others spurious—are readily available to all with computer access. Whole Web sites are fashioned to inform on and solicit support for initiatives on societal problem-solving.

This is all to say that just as in the first Gilded Age, the social efficacy of the new muckraker narratives is contingent to a considerable degree upon complementary media that precede, amplify, and sustain their messages. These media collectively help to establish and maintain what has long been called a climate of opinion.

To return yet once more to *Book*'s 2001 article on "Modern Muckrakers," we find yet another troubling assumption: that each muckraker narrative is an individualistic project, an entity unto itself, a solo act. In literary ways, this is true. Each title carries the signature of a single author. Each narrative is individualized by the style and structure of its writer. Setting aside the differences in topics, any group of students could be asked "identification" questions on anonymous passages from Laurie Garrett's *Betrayal of Trust*, Naomi Klein's *No Logo*, or Joseph Hallinan's *Going Up the River*. The students would recognize each text from the authorial trait that was so mystifying to my creative-writing class at Penn State eons ago when John Barth spoke of individual "voice."

When muckraker narratives are considered as separate entities, however, their interlocking relationships go unnoticed. The custom of book reviewing plays a part in this. Hadn't I myself discovered each of "my" narratives in separate book reviews? By tradition, hadn't each review treated the topic at hand as isolated and self-contained? Isn't this "natural"?

Yes, but the single-book, single-author treatment of muckraker narratives gives readers tunnel vision. The cross-referencing—or cross-pollination—of their projects remains hidden. The very idea of author-topic individualism ghetto-izes the single book and blocks the broader societal view that these projects all share. The isolation of one text from another blocks reflection on what possible relation, for instance, meat processing and the fast-food industry have to do with low-wage work. Or corporate branding with public health. Or prisons with any of these.

Building a shelf of "modern muckraker" books, however, I soon found the links. So would any reader. From one volume to the next, one jots "cf." or "compare" in margins across the separate narratives. In her critique of public health's "collapse," Laurie Garrett could be Naomi Klein's coauthor in the refences to social costs of "the competitive sprint for global economic power," and to the public-health activists so "enraged over pharmaceutical pricing and health care access inequities" that they joined the 1999 public protests against the World Trade Organization in Seattle (*Betrayal of Trust* 548, 570).

What's more, the plight of low-wage workers—typified by the sick and injured house cleaner "Holly" in *Nickel and Dimed*, and by "Kenny," the disabled, fired Monfort meat packinghouse worker in *Fast Food Nation*—both figure in *Betrayal of Trust*'s warning that public health in the United States had reached a crisis stage: "the government's safety net—Medicaid and Medicare—didn't reach to protect a third of Americans living below the poverty line." Holly and Kenny typify workers trapped in an era of the "profit-making paradigm," when, writes Garrett, "with each passing day more and more Americans put off vital health care needs, clogged public hospital emergency rooms, or went bankrupt trying to pay their medical bills" (549). To learn further in Hallinan's *Going Up the River* that prisons are a $37.8-billion industry, and central to it corporate brands of the multinationals, is to find a link with *No Logo*'s exposé of big-brand monopolies. Cross-connections multiply into a web of related issues. To read these books together is to be reminded once again of Edward Said's remark on "independent intellectuals who actually form an incipient community."

To revisit *Book*'s "Modern Muckrakers" article yet again, one sees something else: that keen interest in a given book's topic is no guarantee of attention to a writer's narrative skill and talent (or, if one will, strategies and moves). Emphasis, instead, is on the extractable message. As we saw, the newspaper book reviewers had praised the new muckraker narratives as "eloquent," "vivid," "good reading," and so on. But they focused mainly on the take-away message of each: raise the minimum wage to a living wage; get serious about the life-and-death matter of meat inspection; rebuild the public-health system as a crucial function of national security; face up to the social consequences of incarcerating two million citizens; discover that branded space destroys public life.

Such statements of theme are vitally important for fact-based narrative, of course, but the thematic impact on readers depends on talented writing and narrative skill. These traits, however, are given short shrift in discussions of muckrakers' books. Reviewers' token gestures toward narrative sophistication probably go back to the literature versus journalism split. Attention to narrative design is de rigueur for literature but not on the reviewers' "required" list for journalism.

Analysis of the *McClure's* narratives nonetheless points a new direction for evaluation of modern muckrakers. Tarbell, Baker, Steffens, and others show the kinds of insight to be gained from disclosure of narrative design. Such possibilities are explored in the series of interviews that follow, based loosely on the *Paris Review*'s Writers-at-Work series. The interviews probe the background of these writers, their development, their methods, and their slant on the kinds of work they do. It may or may not be surprising to learn that while they have long considered themselves readers, none concentrated on literary study in school, but focused instead on economics, history, and the biological sciences. Only one, Hallinan, majored in journalism. Four of the five, however, emphasize the influence of a remarkable high-school English teacher in directing their careers.

Their commitment to traditional narrative—as Peter Brooks would say, to the fact-based detective story—renews this form. While the later twentieth-century modernists and postmodernists may harbor "suspicion toward plot," as Brooks says, the muckrakers commit themselves to the genre in which plot survives and thrives.* Just as Tarbell, Baker, Steffens, and Sinclair give up the secrets of their narratives, however, so must their heirs of the succeeding century. Each interview here accompanies a brief discussion of the particular title—*Nickel and Dimed*, *Fast Food Nation*, *No Logo*, *Betrayal of Trust*, and *Going Up the River*.

---

* Says Brooks, "With the advent of Modernism came an era of suspicion toward plot, engendered perhaps by an overelaboration of and overdependence on plots in the nineteenth century. If we cannot do without plots, we nonetheless feel uneasy about them, and feel obligated to show up their arbitrariness, to parody their mechanisms while admitting our dependence on them" (*Reading for the Plot* 7).

9. Barbara Ehrenreich, 2001. Credit Sigrid Estrada. Used by permission.

Barbara Ehrenreich, *Nickel and Dimed: On (Not) Getting By in America*

We will always need people to clean our streets, empty our bedpans and build our buildings. Computers can't do the most fundamental jobs at the core of our economy. There are a lot of dirty jobs, jobs requiring hard physical work, that someone's going to have to do.

—*Kate Bronfenbrenner, Cornell University, quoted in* New York Times, *September 1, 2002*

It is wrong, in a land of plenty, to ask people to work full time for pay that is not enough to feed, clothe, and house them. And yet we do it all the time.

—*Bob Herbert,* New York Times, *September 16, 2002*

"People who work should not be poor."
—*Aspen Institute Domestic Strategy Group, Covenant Principle, August 2002*

Over the Labor Day weekend 2002, the media reported two new assessments of work in the United States. Both were grim. "More unemployment, stagnating wages and jobs, deeper debt and less security," predicted the Washington-based Economic Policy Institute's eighth biennial *The State of Working America 2002/2003*. Within a day, the Aspen Institute issued a parallel dire warning. Without changes in business practice and public policy, the institute warned, the widening "gap in earnings between workers at the bottom and those at the top . . . [will] expand even further." Also approaching Labor Day 2002, A&E (Arts and Entertainment) Television presented a two-hour *Investigative Report* entitled *Wage Slaves: Not Getting by in America*. This was remarkable because in recent years minimum-wage workers had been represented abstractly as a sinking line on a graph. Now, TV called public attention to a group of actual workers—a home health aide, a receptionist, a school cafeteria worker, and a limo driver—for what one newspaper reviewer called "the vitally serious point, that the nation's lowest-paid workers . . . earn barely enough to live on" (*New York Times*, August 26, 2002: B5).

Many viewers of A&E's *Wage Slaves* realized that the program was prompted by a best-selling book authored by one of its on-camera commentators, Barbara Ehrenreich. *Nickel and Dimed: On (Not) Getting By in America*, a riveting portrait of life as a modern low-wage worker, had risen high on the *New York Times* nonfiction best-seller list almost from its 2001 publication. A well-known social critic, Ehrenreich chronicled her own struggle to stay solvent and decently housed while working a string of three minimum-wage jobs—as a waitress in a south Florida chain restaurant, as a house cleaner in Maine, and as a Wal-Mart worker in Minneapolis. Because one low-wage job was insufficient to meet bare expenses, Ehrenreich also took a double-up job, as millions are forced to do. In Maine, she worked seven days per week, spending weekends as a nursing-home kitchen and dining-room worker. Through it all, Ehrenreich kept a journal, took notes, and shaped her experience into a narrative that first appeared as an article in *Harper's*, then as the expanded book-length *Nickel and Dimed*.

"Immersion journalism," Ehrenreich's term for her project, may recall George Orwell's (Eric Arthur Blair's) *The Road to Wigan Pier* (1937), a personally sympathetic study of the wretched lives of Depression-era miners and their families in an impoverished Lancaster coal town. *Nickel and Dimed*, however, has American antecedents in the muck-raking era of *McClure's*. At the turn of the twentieth century, Samuel McClure commissioned a young writer, Josiah Flynt Willard, a nephew of the temperance-movement leader Frances Willard, to write a series of articles on criminal underworld conditions in several American cities for *McClure's*. An educated New Englander, Flynt (who dropped Willard and used "Cigarette" as his underworld sobriquet) had sub-merged himself in what he dubbed the "Under-World." He surfaced to report on criminal culture and its symbiotic relation to the police and politicians. Flynt's "True Stories from the Under-World," pub-lished in *McClure's* from August to October 1900, presaged Steffens's *Shame of the Cities* and opened a tradition of American undercover journalism.*

Flynt had set the immersion journalists' precedent, telling a startled middle-class reading public about a world they did not know existed, even though they lived in its midst and were touched by it. From first-hand experience, he explained an entire subculture of robbers and thieves—called "guns"—in numerous U.S. cities and states, whose "under-world" included territorial networks, social hierarchies, favors exchanged, governing rules, telegraphically swift communications, and a colorful crime lexicon still in play in the detective noir era of Raymond Chandler.

Flynt's stories had demonstrated the authority of the undercover narrative to jolt the middle class out of its earnest, obtuse pieties and insularity—and thereby to lay a groundwork for social change. As McClure wrote, "These studies were made . . . in the hope that they will aid the movement now in progress to better the government of our cities" (qtd. in Lyons 179). Said McClure of Flynt's writing, "The char-acters are real, and the incidents have all occurred at various times and places." "These stories," McClure emphasized in his editorial headnote, "are not fiction in the ordinary sense," but of "a class con-cerning which the great mass of people knows nothing" (*McClure's*, August 1900:356; see Filler 68–79; Harold S. Wilson 123–26).

One century later, *Nickel and Dimed* also was initiated at the urging of a magazine editor, *Harper's* Lewis Lapham, who heard Barbara Ehrenreich say that "someone" ought to go "out there" and try to

---

* These stories were coauthored with Francis Walton, since Flynt at this time was a journeyman writer. Students of American literature will also recall Jack London's un-dercover report on the poverty and crime of East End London, *The People of the Abyss* (1903), and his subsequent writing on working-class revolutionaries in *The War of the Classes* (1905), *Revolution* (1910), and *The Human Drift* (1917).

"make it on $6 or $7 an hour." Like a recruiting poster come to life, Lapham reportedly gave Ehrenreich a half-smile and replied, "You." By 1998, the legacy of Flynt and others had become so traditional that Ehrenreich could call her project an "old-fashioned kind of journalism" (1).* Like Flynt, she protected the confidentiality of her sources but informed the public of an invisible "class" about which "the great mass of people knows nothing." Like him, she would cover a large territory, from the South to New England and the upper Mid-west. She would find, as had he, a similarity of conditions everywhere in an "under-world."

Ehrenreich's introduction presents her ground rules: to avoid jobs utilizing her education or journalistic skills; to take the highest-paying job offered and try to hold it; and to find the cheapest accommodations affording "an acceptable level of safety and privacy" (4). Ruling out homelessness or sleeping in shelters and allowing herself a Rent-A-Wreck rental car in each location, Ehrenreich decided to identify herself to employers as "a divorced homemaker reentering the workforce after many years" (5). "I wore my usual clothes . . . and my usual hairstyle and makeup" (7).

The idea, she says, "was to spend a month in each setting and see whether I could find a job and earn, in that time, the money to pay a second month's rent" (6). As a white woman, she sought work in areas of the country in which her ethnicity would not make her conspicuous in a working class comprised mainly of people of color. She wanted to learn, "How does anyone live on the wages available to the unskilled?" (1). "Maybe when I got into the project," she hypothesized, "I would discover some hidden economies in the world of the low-wage worker" who "may have found some tricks as yet unknown to me" (4).

She found no tricks. On the contrary, Ehrenreich found that "you could work hard—harder than you ever thought possible—and still find yourself sinking ever deeper into poverty and debt" (220). America's

* Perhaps the best-known such project is John Howard Griffin's *Black Like Me* (1961), the account of a white man who in 1959 underwent medical treatment to darken his skin to travel as a Negro through Louisiana, Mississippi, Alabama, and Georgia, reporting firsthand on racist encounters in the racially segregated South. *Black Like Me* is credited with building public support for the developing Civil Rights movement.

More recently, in 1992, ABC's TV newsmagazine *PrimeTime* sent two associate producers undercover to work at Food Lion supermarkets in North and South Carolina, where they used hidden cameras to film unsanitary conditions in the meat and deli departments—the relabeling of outdated meat and the mixing of fresh with outdated ground meat. Food Lion successfully sued Capital Cities (ABC), not contesting the truth of the televised report but arguing that the reporting techniques were illegal and that the ABC workers had been hired based on false résumés. The 1997 jury verdict awarding Food Lion $5.5 million in punitive damages was later reversed on appeal.

working poor, Ehrenreich found out firsthand, neglected their own children to care for the children of others. They kept the homes of their employers "shiny and perfect" while living in substandard housing in an era of soaring rents. In an era when "shareholder" had replaced "citizen" as the identity of America's affluent population, the working poor, Ehrenreich found, "endured privation so that inflation will be low and stock prices high" (221).

As narrator, however, Ehrenreich puts herself in a complex situation. With a working-class family background, she nonetheless is *in* but not *of* the class whose work and life experience she will report:

Most obviously, I was only visiting a world that others inhabit full-time, often for most of their lives. With all the real-life assets I've built up in middle age—bank account, IRA, health insurance, multiroom home—waiting indulgently in the background, there was no way I was going to "experience poverty" or find out how it "really feels" to be a long-term wage worker. My aim here was much more straightforward and objective—just to see whether I could match my income to expenses, as the poor truly attempt to do every day. Besides, I've had enough unchosen encounters with poverty in my lifetime to know it's not a place you would want to visit for touristic purposes; it just smells too much like fear. (6)

Neither visitor nor tourist, this narrator will not cultivate low-wage life as a self-dramatizing getaway to the exotic. Ehrenreich knows better than to go "slumming." Throughout *Nickel and Dimed*, she reminds readers repeatedly that her lifetime of healthcare, good nutrition, and gym workouts make her better able than her coworkers to withstand the physically punishing work and its marathon hours. She will not pretend to suspend disbelief in the bourgeois institutions undergirding her foray into the subculture of low-wage work.

Ehrenreich remarks in our interview that her footnotes constitute a second, short "expository" book within *Nickel and Dimed*. With her numerous books rooted in the social sciences, Ehrenreich signals her authorial allegiance in running citations from U.S. government reports, corporate documents, studies conducted by policy institutes and nongovernmental agencies, and so forth.* This data-based exposition doubtless originates in Ehrenreich's training in science. The former scientist's "revelation," however, was that personal, emotional responses were also "data" to be analyzed and reported. *Nickel and Dimed*

---

* Footnote statistics are drawn from federal legislation, such as the Fair Labor Standards Act; reports to Congress, such as "Rental Housing Assistance: The Worsening Crisis" (2000); in addition to findings from not-for-profit citizens' groups, such as the National Coalition for the Homeless; plus scholarly studies (*Workers in a Lean World*, 1997) and newspaper reports (*Toronto Star* and *Washington Post*).

is an account of individual experience silhouetted with corroborating demographic statistics. These both amplify and typify Barbara's on-the-job experiences. A minimum-wage Everywoman emerges like a hologram.* In compilation of factual data, Ehrenreich continues the tradition of the first Gilded Age muckrakers for whom facts were the sine qua non of narrative argument. As with Tarbell, Steffens, and the others, Ehrenreich deploys facts that will not be subject to dispute but will elicit unanimity of response with a larger objective of civil action.

Barbara Ehrenreich has written eight books, including the best-selling *Blood Rites: The Worst Years of Our Lives* and *Fear of Falling: The Inner Life of the Middle Class*, which was nominated for a National Book Critics Circle award. A former Guggenheim Fellow, she is a frequent contributor to *Harper's Magazine*, *The Nation*, *New York Times Magazine*, and *Time*. This interview took place in Charlottesville, Virginia, on June 23, 2002.

INTERVIEW WITH BARBARA EHRENREICH

CT: Let me start with what I think of as the beginning. It sounds like you more or less skipped college and got a Ph.D. in microbiology. Is that right?

BE: No, no, I wasn't any kind of prodigy. I went to college at Reed in Portland, Oregon, and majored in chemistry and then switched into physics, and then went to Rockefeller University and ended up in cell biology, so it was experimental, it was lab research; and it was manual labor, highly skilled manual labor.

CT: Everybody must want to know, How did you move over into writing?

BE: Well, at the same time that I was doing this graduate work, I had been sucked into the antiwar movement and was beginning to question why I wanted to be a scientist. How much was it my father wanting me to be a scientist because he had not continued to be one? What was going on? And I decided I wanted to be an activist. I got my Ph.D. and went to work on things that were more socially urgent.

CT: So activism to you meant the written word?

BE: No, I was working first with a group called Health Policy Advisory Center, which sounds very innocuous, but really we were pretty radical. And we worked to get better healthcare for poor

* For the male version of Ehrenreich's account of "scraping by" (5), minus footnote documentation, see Iain Levison's *A Working Stiff's Manifesto: A Memoir* (2002).

neighborhoods in New York City. And I wound up doing a lot of writing and research. We had a newsletter. We would do studies and reports. Actually, I also had written something with my then-husband. We had gone to Europe in 1968 and wrote a book for Monthly Review Press about the student movements.

CT: [19]68—the year of European student protest.

BE: But I still wasn't thinking of myself as a writer. It was more through these political interests.

CT: Were you a reader as a kid? What did you read?

BE: I count myself lucky that young-adult books hadn't been invented yet, so I had to read the, quote, classics. This meant Sir Walter Scott in childhood, and then as a teenager, I got heavily into Dostoevsky and Conrad, and then in my later teens discovered Sartre and Camus. But I come from a matrilineal line of novel addicts. My mother just read constantly, mostly fiction—my sister, my daughter. And we don't generally read trash.

CT: Literature and science are both in your biography. Anybody would notice the presence of science in *Nickel and Dimed*. It's interlarded throughout—the "spirit of science," the "albinism" of Maine, the "biology of nutrition." In what ways do you think that scientific training contributes to your work as a writer?

BE: It made me unafraid to learn new things. If you could get through some of the highly technical courses I got through, and they were pretty hard for me, you know you're not going to be scared off. I just know whatever it is, I can research it. I can get some facility in it pretty quickly. But further back, as a kid, I wrote diaries. I still have a whole stack of these things from about age fifteen to early twenties, just different random sheets of paper.

CT: *Pensées*?

BE: Yes, very deep *pensées*. Nothing trivial. [*Laughs.*]

CT: So, let's fast-forward a little bit. You're unafraid to learn new things, and you're starting to write for publication.

BE: Well, as a graduate student, I published papers in the research I was doing. And the good thing about that experience, looking back, although stylistically it's a nightmare to use passive voice and so on, is that it was training in just getting organized. There was no fluff, no literary quality to anything, but it was just how do you organize the facts and take a reader along in this very disciplined, structured way. I think that was good training.

CT: You wrote a novel, *Kipper's Game*. What did you get out of that? Was it a self-education in a different kind of writing?

BE: It was fun sometimes and agony other times. Have you written fiction?

CT: Three published mystery novels and more on the way, so I'm a kind of fiction addict. What I'm trying to press toward is the way in which *Nickel and Dimed* shows the benefit of that kind of work.

BE: That's interesting you say that because my wonderful editor, Sara Bershtel, said the same thing, that the novel was great practice in moving people from room to room, that kind of thing. . . .

CT: Including momentum of the story? Because it is very much a story of how Barbara journeys through a low-wage world. And the other characters have to be vividly realized in a few strokes. You're continuously limning new characters.

BE: I was also protecting their identities. Some fascinating things about some characters were left out so as not to identify them.

CT: You made the strategic decision in *Nickel and Dimed*, at some point, to put the hard facts, the data, into footnotes. Did you decide on that at the beginning?

BE: That came from *Harper's*. The first chapter in slightly shorter form was published in *Harper's* as an article. My editor said that if you want to put in bunches of facts, use this footnote format. And I thought "great," because it puts another book in there, but of course a very short expository one.

CT: That seems to me incredibly important. I pressed Joseph Hallinan on the issue of when and how and what facts he inserted in *Going Up the River: Travels in a Prison Nation*. He said it's a very hard problem. To have high impact, you can't deluge your reader with facts. You have to cull that one fact you think will be memorable. One such fact in his book is the six thousand trees cut down to make way for a prison in rural Virginia.

BE: On a mountain top.

CT: That's only one of a whole welter of facts that he had available. In, say, your *Fear of Falling*, there's a lot of data that makes its way pervasively through the text, but *Nickel and Dimed,* a first-person narrative, might become weighed down or stalled were you to pause to tell us what this or that study says.

BE: It was a big relief not to do that. I'd be in these low-wage work situations, and very curious about something, but not able to research it in a normal journalistic way until I got back home, and then I'd do all of this research.

CT: Right. And add footnotes to amplify on—contextualize—what you were living.

        There's a great deal of book-club adoption of *Nickel and Dimed*, and I would argue it's because it tells such a good story.

Would you talk a bit about developing your persona for this book? You come in as first person, and you're Barbara, but you're also creating a Barbara for the reader. There are biographical facts that make their way through—that your forebears were miners in a Butte, Montana, copper mine; you learned to wash dishes at age six; your father had Alzheimer's—these kinds of biographical facts pop through like little time-released moments. At the same time, you can't rant or plead for adoration or pity. This is a complex persona you have to create to sustain the credibility of the whole project, because if you crash, the message goes with that crash.

Was it just natural to disperse biographical information here and there, intermittently, almost desultorily? Do you think you're just so experienced as a writer at this point that you have an intuitive feel for striking the right tone?

BE: When I started this, I didn't know what I was going to write. I mean, my first assignment with *Harper's* was just to see if I could make enough money on a minimum-wage job to pay one month's rent, then see if I could make the next month's rent within a month. And I said, "What am I going to write?" I'll keep records of my expenses, but what else? I didn't even know about the content, what was going to be interesting, what was going to become a magazine article. I thought it would be just a little financial report. So, naturally, keeping a diary, I mean a journal—

CT: What do you mean "naturally?"

BE: That's what I had to do. Where did I look for apartments? Where did I interview for jobs? What was I told? How easy was it to get the job? And, I thought, "Well, I should write about the work itself, too," which was surprisingly hard in every case.

And it was a little revelation, in that first month in Florida, when I realized that what I was feeling was maybe some data too. You know, my responses to things were data also, and I should take careful note if I felt—feelings of incompetence and the really terrible feeling when you begin a job, and you are the stupid one. But that proved to be relevant.

BE: Each of these three work stories in *Nickel and Dimed*, it seems to me, has that moment when you undergo a kind of initiation rite or an induction, and the reader experiences it with you. In the Maine section, I think it's when the Alzheimer's patient spills the milk on you. The reader undergoes that experience too. So you realized your responses to such incidents were important data, and they needed to be reported.

BE: I hadn't in the beginning. I thought of this as a subjective component. And it evolved into immersion journalism. I would
note in my journal: "I woke up in the middle of the night worrying about how I screwed up in the restaurant."

CT: So, you're saying that this book project evolved. The *Harper's*
article was the inception, and then from there you agreed to
undertake this larger—

BE: The article got a lot of attention, and so my book editor Sara
Bershtel said, "Do a few more, and we'll have a book." I
thought, oh yeah, do a few more—easy enough for you to say.
My big fear when I turned it in to her was that she would say,
"We need another—"

CT: Three are plenty to map America's low-wage territory. I think
it's crucial to this book and to much investigative writing that
the writer speaks on behalf of others who cannot speak for
themselves. This representation of those who are marginal, de-
prived, poor, has a long history—Dickens, Orwell, Rebecca
Harding Davis's ironworkers. You say you haven't read the
early twentieth-century muckrakers, but you're speaking for
other people. Does that seem like a particular responsibility?

BE: I do think of myself as speaking for them, but there's a distance
maintained throughout.

CT: Absolutely right. You are scrupulous about that distance. At the
same time, yours is the in-the-trenches report on work conditions of people who are, you could say, too burdened to come
up for air and speak about their own work conditions. You have
to establish a certain authority to issue this report.

BE: I'm conscious of that. I've created a Web site, nickelanddimed
.net, to post some of the incredible letters I get, life stories from
low-wage workers. I got this twenty-page letter last night from a
woman. There's another woman who wrote me ten letters, each
of them about four pages long, and they are just telling her
whole story. So, I post them. If nothing else, the Web site gives
people the sense that they're not the only ones having these
difficulties. And they are very well written. People are good
writers. A lot of well-educated people find themselves in these
situations, too.

CT: Like letters to Eleanor Roosevelt during the Depression. [Ehren-
reich nods.]
       Let me ask you something about a characteristic of the narra-
tive. You have the story of Barbara and the three jobs, the three
places. You also have embedded at certain points little essays,
like mini-essays. Like the one on the Maine revival tent, in

which you point out that the Sermon on the Mount indicates Christ was a precocious socialist. It's wonderful.

BE: That's one of my favorites. And some people think it's *anti-Christian*. It's totally *for Jesus*.

CT: Do such little essays just happen? Does an insight strike, and you just type it up and find a little nest for it?

BE: They're just from reflecting on the experience, just spending time alone in motel rooms and that experience.

CT: Let's talk about your two identities in the narrative. There's Barbara, the working stiff, and then Barbara, the interpreter, the intellectual. Is there any challenge to keeping those two parts of yourself going, with momentum and continuity?

BE: The part that was hard to maintain was my former self, my real self. I was really shocked at how quickly I got into each work situation. Maybe I have no personality structure. I'm just a blob. But I'd get into a situation and quickly find it defining my thoughts, my dreams, what I woke up in the morning thinking. And I had taken books with me for the research I was working on, but I never opened one.

CT: How could you? You were working all day.

BE: There wasn't any time. All that began to drift away.

CT: Had you worked any of those jobs before?

BE: Waitressing. That's the one.

CT: Is it possible that *Nickel and Dimed*, which of course is a best-seller, is part of the current media zeitgeist of reality TV—the *1900 House* on PBS that was a British house where a family lived in it as if it were 1900, and the *Survivor* series? And I wonder whether you feel that your project fits the "reality" moment.

BE: I think so. It's not an attempt to feel like the working poor, but think of it as a survivor narrative. Definitely.

CT: There's a lot of humor in the book. Is that deliberate?

BE: I sometimes get a little irritated when people say, It was smart of you to put that humor in there. It's not something you inject. The absurdity is in the world. I have to report it.

CT: But it is one dimension of literary versatility. For instance, there's a certain scene in the Key West restaurant when you are overcome by the "the perfect storm," a convergence of demanding, impatient customers, too few servers on duty, hardly any cooks at work. It's hilarious in a darkly comic way, the clientele satirically skewered as you represent yourself nearing collapse ("all I know is that my legs have lost interest in the venture and have announced their intention to fold").

At the critical moment, you simply walk out, leaving a scene which is treated in the text as high burlesque. You then enter a poignant scene in which, as you write, "the thick tropical night parts to let me pass," after which you recount a feeling of self-abnegation and failure, not relief and not freedom. Finally, you quickly provide a coda to the whole episode, tying up loose ends about coworkers. Within a few pages, in sum, we find radical shifts in literary style, technique, tone. It's admirably adroit handling, done well so that readers keep confidence in your authorial control. Did you work hard at editing to achieve this?

BE: No. The whole book was written very quickly. (I shouldn't confess this.) But you see, I had the journals; I had the raw notes.

CT: Please say more about the writing process.

BE: Every day I would write in it for an hour and a half or two hours. I would just handwrite it. If I got home late, if I had a shift that went to like 11 P.M., I was not going to start typing. I would just make very sketchy things, handwritten. Remember this. Remember that. It was like another job. I took as much as thirty pages of typed notes for each city. And I would immediately go home [to Florida] and start turning that into a chapter. I was driven. I couldn't waste a minute. I started writing the first chapter when I was still in the trailer [near Key West] because I wanted to still smell those smells and feel those hurts, whatever they were. So, you know, the problem then became how to massage the sentence, give it shape, eliminate the many things to make it more into a story.

CT: Did you write each story before you embarked on the next job?

BE: Yes.

CT: OK. So you did take time out. Interesting, because the narrative is so continuous. You leave Florida, head up to Maine, check out the albino culture, seek some shelter, then head on to Minneapolis. It's seamless. But there's a kind of defiance in your tone, sort of, "they won't get me." Though intermittently, your courage fails. Is that verbatim? Reporting the data of your responses?

BE: I would go up and down. I do want to say something about the writing though: I really enjoyed the phase of going from the journal to the chapters. I had never written in first-person at any great length, maybe some essays in the past, but never anything like this. First-person, present tense—it was really fun. So it zipped along.

But I also realized that the great thing about the first-person thing, about having the first-person stance, is that I could be funny about miserable things. You see, I can't laugh when I'm talking about some woman who's having to skip meals to feed her children. If I'm not the one who's incurring these things, I just find myself becoming lugubrious. When it was other people, I couldn't do it. So that revealed something to me—that it's hard to write out of people's human misery without naturally being lugubrious about it. But when writing about my own problems, temporary problems in this book, there's no stopping me.

CT: Well, there's one quality that a writer about human misery has been stripped of in the late twentieth century, and that is sentimentality. Dickens could go full-bore. So could the nineteenth-century sentimental American writers such as Harriet Beecher Stowe. These writers outsold Hawthorne and he called them a mob of scribbling woman. Mostly women writers, they could indulge in the sentimental.

BE: I can do that.

CT: Well, no, you can't nowadays. People might be able to read a nineteenth-century sentimental novel, and of course, romance fiction is where it can go—Danielle Steele maybe, but it can't into investigative writing about the miseries of people who aren't making it, so you're stripped of that whole kind of world view. You don't have that. You can crack hard jokes about yourself—

BE: I can be self-deprecating and sarcastic and all those things, but I couldn't do that about real people's lives.

CT: You said elsewhere, in an interview with Robert Birnbaum for *Narrative Thread*, "There's a lot of good writing. What there's less of is having something really important to say. I'm not as impressed by great writing as I was when I started out as a freelance writer. . . . Now more important is the question, What is there to say? What's the story?" Would you follow up on that just a little bit?

BE: Yes. It was about six or seven years ago. I was asked to review Richard Ford's novel *Independence Day*. It's beautifully written. He's an amazing writer. But what was it about?

CT: Is it the problem of what is called workshop fiction?

BE: Yeah, I think so. It's the experience of reading this 400-page book and being amazed at the technology of the sentences and paragraphs, and then thinking, "What was it about? Two days in the life of a realtor?" So, I thought about this. A few times I've taught a course on essay writing at Berkeley's Graduate School of Journalism [at the University of California], and I decided to call my course "Having Something to Say" and putting all the emphasis on what you do before you sit down at the computer and actually compose something. That's what they haven't thought about. All the students are colorful writers who use great turns of phrase. But the hard part is, So what's your idea?

In our discussion, Ehrenreich fretted a bit about her final chapter, "Evaluation," fearing that it might read more like an expository essay than an integral part of her story. She needn't have worried. "Evaluation" is just that—a stock-taking of her own experience and its significance in an America of gross wage disparities, lack of affordable housing and health care, no pension or insurance for millions, costly (and often subpar) transportation, and a workplace of constant surveillance and degrading invasion of privacy. All these form a familiar litany of modern America's societal hobbling, its self-inflicted "death by a thousand cuts." "Evaluation" works, however, because of the adroit balance Ehrenreich strikes between narrator-Barbara and character-Barbara.

Barbara Ehrenreich is the protagonist of a story that is part memoir, part report. She implies a reprise of the personalized 1960s-era New Journalism of Tom Wolfe, Norman Mailer, and Hunter S. Thompson. Yet she throttles back too. "No Marxist rants," Ehrenreich promises at the outset, revealing her left-leaning politics but vowing to avoid preaching. She will "censor the profanities that are . . . part of [her] normal speech." "Four-letter words" are "forbidden" (4, 167, 8). But what will constitute "normal speech" in *Nickel and Dimed*, in which "Barbara" doubles both as narrator and as central character? The speech code vow is humorous but opens a serious point. How will reportage and memoir coexist? How will Ehrenreich both show and tell her story?

Consider the moment when the author gets a job at a Portland, Maine, cleaning service. In a Dickensian twist, she dubs it The Maids, a business dedicated, we learn, not to household hygiene but only to its polished appearance. In the scene below, the newly hired Barbara prepares to view orientation videos on rules and equipment ("dusting, bathrooms, kitchen and vacuuming—each starring an attractive, possibly Hispanic young woman who moves about serenely in obedience to the male voiceover" [73]):

While I wait in the inner room, where the phone is and Tammy [the office manager] is at her desk, to be issued a uniform, I hear her tell a potential customer on the phone that The Maids charges $25 per person-hour. The company gets $25 and we get $6.65 for each hour we work? I think I may have misheard, but a few minutes later I hear her say the same thing to another inquirer. So the only advantage of working here as opposed to freelancing is that you don't need a clientele or even a car. You can arrive straight from welfare, or, in my case, the bus station—fresh off the boat. (73)

This informational passage lets readers discover for themselves the grossly distorted wage-profit ratio. Edged in irony, this is the voice of on-site information. The narrator may hold strong views but mostly subordinates them to the task of exposition of facts.

Barbara-the-character, however, lets loose her feelings in a broadly satirical barrage that reinforces *Nickel and Dimed* as civic melodrama, a narrative of a Manichaean social world split between forces of light and darkness. As a Maids cleaning "team" member, she describes the moment when a pitifully frail, sick (and possibly pregnant) coworker, Holly, admits to being too weak to clean. Character-Barbara responds:

> For the first time in my life as a maid I have a purpose more compelling than trying to meet the aesthetic standards of the New England bourgeoisie. I will do the work of two people, if necessary three. The next house belongs to a woman known to Holly and Marge as a "friggin' bitch," who turns out to be Martha Stewart or at least a very dedicated acolyte thereof. Everything about it enrages me, and some of it would be irritating even if I were just dropping by for cocktails, and not toiling alongside this pale, undernourished child: the brass plaque on the door announcing the date of construction (mid-eighteenth century), the wet bar with its ostentatious alignment of single-malt Scotches, the four-poster king-sized bed with canopy, the Jacuzzi so big you have to climb stairs to get into it and probably safe enough for diving when filled. (97–98)

Here the "enraged" Barbara is revolted by McMansion-era showcase ostentation for whose upkeep the owners bear no personal responsibility. "That's not your [bathroom] marble 'bleeding,' " a furious Barbara-as-character yearns to tell the $1-million-condo owner who is appalled by discoloration of bathroom fixtures. The bloodshed is, rather, of "the world-wide working class" whose labor undergirds this gross luxury and whose bodies are pain-managed by Excedrin, Advil, and occasionally alcohol (89, 90). This enraged, socially excoriating Barbara is the character within the narrative, her scalding denunciation civic melodrama's "high emotionalism and stark ethical conflict" (Brooks, *Melodramatic Imagination*, 20, 12).

Nickel and Dimed sustains the sense of social urgency—of civic melodrama—in a follow-up scene of cleaning the New England house, as we learn that a row of decorative hanging copper pots in the kitchen—"deployed to catch stray beams of sunlight or reflect the owners' no doubt expensively buffed and peeled faces"—must be taken down and burnished "with the owner's special polish":

The final pot is unexpectedly heavy . . . and as I grasp it from my crouching position on the countertop, it slips from my hand and comes crashing down into a fishbowl cunningly furnished with marbles. Fish fly, marbles skitter all over the floor, and water . . . soaks everything, including a stack of cookbooks containing *Cucina Simpatica*, a number of works set in Provence, and yes, Martha Stewart herself. . . . My punishment is seeing Holly's face, when she rushes into the kitchen to see what the crash was, completely polarized with fear. (98)

The real casualty of this fiasco, we realize, is not Barbara, but Holly, the victim of her poverty and especially of her entrapment in a terrifying social order whose grip strangles her. It is the two Barbaras together who drive home this raw point. It is the two Barbaras who cry "shame!" at the book-buying readers who have the time to read *Nickel and Dimed* in part because they—no, we—hire others to clean our homes and serve us, wait on us. These low-wage workers, finds Ehrenreich, truly define the term service economy. *Nickel and Dimed* thus renews the civic melodrama of the first Gilded Age. Its goal in c.2000 is to "recognize and confront evil, to combat and expel it, to purge the social order" (Brooks 11).

In June 1894, two years after the Homestead steel strike was quashed, *McClure's* published Hamlin Garland's report from industrial, manufacturing America: "Homestead and Its Perilous Trades: Impressions of a Visit." The Carnegie Steel workers' homes, Garland wrote, were "dingy rows" of "tenement houses," their streets "horrible" (3). In infernal images, Garland described the working conditions of men who produced steel girders and rails for trains and trolleys. The workers were "lean, pale, and grimy," though actively "swift and splendid" as tigers, lest they die in showers of molten metal (4, 6). "It's a dog's life," says one, describing twelve-hour shifts, summer's unbearable heat, and an average hourly wage barely supporting life on a day-to-day basis (8).

The service economy of postindustrial America is Ehrenreich's territory. There are no cauldrons of molten steel, no streets of "yellow mud" where "groups of pale, lean men slouch in faded garments" (Garland 3). But seeing these contemporary low-wage workers—really seeing them—remains a problem. If the uniformed maids are invisible, their counterparts in other low-wage jobs are equally unseen. *Nickel and Dimed* finds that "thanks to consignment stores and Wal-Mart—the poor are able to disguise themselves as members of the more comfortable classes" (216). The poor, in short, are often invisible because they themselves are undercover, passing as middle class. *Nickel and Dimed* outs them and narratively makes the case for a living-wage standard in the United States. Ehrenreich's narrative message is beginning to ricochet around the country. *Nickel and Dimed* is being read by book clubs and assigned in schools. In the spring of 2001, Harvard undergraduates occupied the university administration building in a successful "Justice-for-Janitors" campaign resulting in a three-year contract with living wage and benefit provisions. Nashville's *Tennessean* editorialized in September 2002, "They deserve a higher minimum wage, vigorous workplace safety laws and access to affordable health-care coverage. More than anything, they deserve a corporate culture that is not willing to sacrifice people in its pursuit of profits."

Let *Nickel and Dimed* have the final word here, expressed in a metaphor that Ehrenreich saved for last, a metaphor meant to be hard-hitting in a country that prides itself on generosity and philanthropic action. In America, the "working poor," says Ehrenreich, "are in fact the major philanthropists of our society. . . . To be a member of the working poor is to be an anonymous donor, a nameless beneficiary, to everyone else" (221).

*   *   *

Eric Schlosser, *Fast Food Nation: The Dark Side of the All-American Meal*

> *"Feedlot Perils Outpace Regulation, Sierra Club Says"*
> *"McDonald's Fat Debate Goes On"*
> *"Court Lessens Federal Power to Shut Down Meat Plants"*
> *"Studies Suggest Meats Carry Resistant Bacteria"*
> *"Sara Lee Recalls Meats"*
> *"Sara Lee Pleads Guilty in Listeria Case"*
> *"Meatpackers' Profits Hinge on Pool of Immigrant Labor"*
> *"19 Million Pounds of Meat Recalled After 19 Fall Ill: ConAgra Is the Source—U.S. Says Much of Tainted Beef Has Been Eaten."*
> *"Random Testing for E. Coli Is Set for Meatpacking Sites"*
> *"Cargill Expands Beef Recall, Shuts Down Plant Amid E. Coli Fears"*
> *"Meat Safety at Risk"*
>
> —Headlines, New York Times *and* Detroit Free Press, *August 2001–February 2003*

> *Today the U.S. government can demand the nationwide recall of defective softball bats, sneakers, stuffed animals, and foam-rubber toy cows. But it cannot order a meatpacking company to remove contaminated, potentially lethal ground beef from fast food kitchens and supermarket shelves. The unusual power of the large meatpacking firms has been sustained by their close ties and sizable donations to Republican members of Congress. It has also been made possible by a widespread lack of awareness about how many Americans suffer from food poisoning every year and how these illnesses actually spread.*
>
> —Eric Schlosser, Fast Food Nation, *2001*

10. Eric Schlosser, 2001. Courtesy HarperCollins.

Months after my Vanderbilt "Blockbuster" students had read Upton Sinclair's *The Jungle*, I played another class an audiotape of a radio broadcast interview with Eric Schlosser, the author of *Fast Food Nation*. Simultaneously, the class saw the 1978 Frederick Wiseman documentary film *Meat*, shown with the sound off, like a silent movie.

The students listened to Schlosser's scathing critique of America's fast-food culture while onscreen the beef cattle moved toward slaughter. Schlosser calmly discussed fast food's nutritional deficiencies and the deplorable working conditions in meat-packing plants as the students watched carcasses butchered and vats of trimmings ground into hamburger and pressed into patties that were boxed, then frozen and loaded onto tractor trailers heading for the nation's interstate highways.

Only after class did I recognize my reinforcement of the viewpoint that was so dismaying to Upton Sinclair a century earlier, when he complained that he'd aimed for the public's heart and instead hit the stomach. *Meat*, I realized, warped the students' response. The crisis of mistreated workers was of greatest importance to Sinclair, as it clearly was to Schlosser. I had emphasized this point weeks earlier in class. Now, however, I had unconsciously shifted the students' attention to the meat. I, the instructor, had reinforced the narrow reading, the meat reading.* Indeed, the newspaper headlines above indicate the extent to which, in public discourse, the focus remains on the meat.

Fast Food Nation, true to the tradition of muckraker narratives, supports its story with an armature of facts—of production, of pathology, of chronology. The text is braced from first to last with factual data. Ehrenreich compacts the demographic facts in footnotes in *Nickel and Dimed*, but Schlosser's *Fast Food Nation* deploys its facts in the narrative, calling attention, for instance, to the fact that "every day in the United States, roughly 200,000 people are sickened by a foodborne disease, 900 are hospitalized, and fourteen die" (195). Schlosser points out that the major source of food poisoning nowadays is not, as in the past, someone's picnic potato salad, but the "rise of huge feedlots, slaughterhouses, and hamburger grinders." "The meat-packing system that arose to supply the nation's fast food chains . . . has proved to be an extremely efficient system for spreading disease" (196). Figurative language is here too, like the unnamed government health official's comparison of the modern feedlot to "a crowded European city during the Middle Ages, when people dumped their chamber pots out the window, raw sewage ran in the streets, and epidemics raged" (201).

---

* I also tried explaining (unsuccessfully, I suspect) to my students that Wiseman's *Meat* was shot in a packinghouse operated under union labor, with health and safety conditions far superior to those they heard Schlosser describe.

Schlosser writes, "A tiny uncooked particle of hamburger meat can contain enough of the [*E. coli* 0157: H7] pathogen to kill you" (201). How so? Because "food tainted by these organisms has most likely come in contact with an [apparently healthy but] infected animal's stomach contents or manure, during slaughter or subsequent processing."

Fast Food Nation has much to say about "What's in the Meat," notably the "virulent and potentially lethal" pathogens *Escherichia coli* 0157: H7, *Salmonella*, *Staphylococcus aureus*, and *Clostridium perfringens*. Schlosser also names *Listeria monocytogenes*, which kills one out of five of its victims. (It was *Listeria* that, according to the 2001 *Detroit Free Press* headline story, killed fifteen people, caused six miscarriages, and seriously sickened eighty people from contaminated deli meat and hot dogs made at the Sara Lee Corporation's Bil Mar Foods plant near Grand Rapids, Michigan [August 30, 2001].)

"The medical literature on the causes of food poisoning is full of euphemisms and dry scientific terms," Schlosser writes, navigating official terms that he finds either dull or evasive. Because the Latin names for the deadly organisms sound more euphemistic than formidable, he suddenly changes rhetorical tactic. The social urgency of microbial contamination calls for a radical rhetorical move: an Anglo-Saxon expletive. There is "a simple explanation for why eating a hamburger can now make you seriously ill," he says. "There is shit in the meat" (197).

Fast Food Nation is a geographically expansive narrative that branches in several directions. It includes biographies of self-made American entrepreneurs in the food and restaurant business, such as Carl Karcher of the Southern California Carl's Jr. restaurants, which is a chain originating in the young Karcher's purchase of a hot-dog cart at the beginning of World War II, developing later as family restaurants, then as fast-food outlets.

As promised, *Fast Food Nation* also gives readers the "dark" side, including the invasion of foods high in sugar and fat into public schools and thereby its contribution to the growing rates of obesity and predisposition to diabetes in children nationwide. The narrative recounts the development over the past quarter century of an increasingly ruthless, dangerous, and centralized meat processing industry that is insulated from regulation by political influence. Continuously it records the hellish working conditions and low wages of those earning their living in food production and distribution, very few of whom enjoy insurance or healthcare benefits, almost none of whom enjoy workplace protections afforded by a labor-union contract.

The cast of characters in *Fast Food Nation* is large and wide-ranging. Apart from the entrepreneurs (including Ray Kroc, of McDonald's, who is paralleled with Walt Disney), we meet a Colorado former pro hockey player–turned–Little Caesars pizza franchisee who tries his best to treat employees fairly while surviving in a fiercely competitive franchise food environment. We also meet high schoolers whose hourly wages at McDonald's or Taco Bell underwrite the costs of their automobiles and shorten the odds these young people will ever seek any higher education. (Some, at age fifteen, work twelve-hour, late-night shifts, which violates the Fair Labor Standards Act.) We learn from lawsuits, both won and pending, that because fast-food chain managers are rewarded for keeping costs low, some coerce employees to work "off the clock" rather than pay them overtime (a practice of which former employees have accused Wal-Mart, embroiling the company in a number of lawsuits).

We also meet the Western beef cattle rancher Hank, who represents many ranchers facing the loss of independence, as he and others like him become meat-industry sharecroppers in a production system long established in chicken farming. We meet meat cutters ankle-deep in blood and feces in packing plants located in remote high plains deserts, far away from areas where collective bargaining is likely to occur because of high turnover and an immigrant workforce terrified by the threat of job loss. In those places, we see workers who are maimed and even killed with impunity, many of them illegal immigrants from Mexico. Overall, we learn that from the 1970s, the federal government stood aside as the industry consolidated into a new beef trust consisting of four major packers who control eighty-four percent of the nation's cattle: ConAgra, IBP, Excel, and National Beef. "Market concentration in the beef industry is now at the highest level since record-keeping began in the early twentieth century" (138).

Readers of *Fast Food Nation* find a textbook case of Mark Sullivan's criterion for muckrakers of a century ago: "they put out their product as *fact*, and asked the public to accept it and test it as such." Schlosser's self-avowed "sincere passion for accuracy led [him] to document every assertion in this book," he says, naming the project's fact checkers. The afterword of the paperback edition states that although *Fast Food Nation* had been "strongly attacked" by politically conservative publications and by the McDonald's Corporation, "thus far its critics have failed to cite any errors in the text" (276).

The rhetoric of *Fast Food Nation* is modeled on Ray Stannard Baker's ethos of the "complete picture, the truth, vividly and dispassionately set forth." Baker's 1894 strategically low-key portrait of the hungry, penniless family of the striking Swedish Pullman Company worker anticipates Schlosser's passionate dispassion in presentation of meat-packing workers in High Plains towns. Schlosser, like Baker, presents

himself as a disinterested scribe: "The workers I met wanted their stories to be told. They wanted people to know about what is happening
right now" (186). Some of these workers, like Baker's Swede, speak
no English, so the narration presumes translation but implies a uni-
versality transcending language barriers.

Schlosser, however, frames their stories with narrative telling detail,
such as this: "the voices and faces of these workers are indelibly with
me, as is the sight of their hands, the light brown skin criss-crossed
with white scars." Readers are thereby reminded of *Fast Food Nation*'s
stated fact, that the death and injury rates of packinghouse workers
are the highest of any occupational group, making packinghouses the
most dangerous workplaces in America. The individual workers typify
groups "linked by common elements." The elements prove common
not only to blue-collar workers but also to those in high-rise towers and
office parks: "the same struggle to receive proper medical care, the
same fear of speaking out, the same underlying corporate indifference"
(186). Each worker is individual yet typical, typical yet individual:

Raoul was born in Zapoteca, Mexico, and did construction work in Anaheim
[California] before moving to Colorado. He speaks no English. After hearing a
Monfort ad on a Spanish-speaking radio station, he applied for a job at the
Greeley [Colorado] plant. One day Raoul reached into a processing machine
to remove a piece of meat. The machine accidentally went on. Raoul's arm got
stuck, and it took workers twenty minutes to get it out. The machine had to be
taken apart. An ambulance brought Raoul to the hospital, where a deep gash
in his shoulder was sewn shut. A tendon had been severed. After getting
stitches and a strong prescription painkiller, he was driven back to the slaughterhouse and put back on the production line. Bandaged, groggy, and in pain,
one arm tied in a sling, Raoul spent the rest of the day wiping blood off card-
board boxes with his good hand. (186–87)

The short declarative sentences, the understatement of the horrific
injury, and the cool rhetorical evisceration of the company that mis-
treats the hurt worker—these make up the studied "dispassion" of the
narrator and locate us firmly in the realm of civic melodrama, a
drama of moral life split sharply into a polarized good and evil operat-
ing as real forces in the world. Raoul's story proves to be the baguette
prefacing the featured bio of a modern-day version of Jurgis Rudkis,
protagonist of *The Jungle*. Kenny Dobbins is a loyal packinghouse
worker whose body—from his skeletal-muscular system to his immune
system, to his respiratory system and his heart—is permanently damaged by work-related injuries that tally the careless indifference of his
employer, Monfort. In a state of total disability in his mid-forties,
Kenny says, "They used me to the point where I had no body parts to
give" (190). Schlosser's voice maintains its dispassion: "His anger at

Monfort, his feelings of betrayal, are of truly biblical proportions" (190).

Eric Schlosser is a correspondent for the *Atlantic Monthly* magazine, in which he has published feature-length articles on U.S. prisons ("The Prison-Industrial Complex"), on marijuana and the drug wars ("Reefer Madness"), on the families of murder victims ("A Grief Like No Other"), and on immigrant farm labor ("In the Strawberry Fields"). "Reefer Madness" won a National Magazine Award, and *Fast Food Nation: The Dark Side of the All-American Meal* became a *New York Times* best-seller from its 2001 publication. This interview took place in New York City on September 13, 2002.

INTERVIEW WITH ERIC SCHLOSSER

CT: Let me get this straight: your predecessors are the investigative writers of the 1960s–70s, not the first-generation muckrakers?

ES: In the [19]60s and [19]70s, when people like Bob Woodward and Carl Bernstein and I guess Norman Mailer were doing all kinds of investigative pieces. If you look at *Silent Spring*, it started off a whole new round of this sort of writing.

CT: I agree that late 60s–early 70s, writing was very important. Francis Fitzgerald's *Fire on the Lake*, David Halberstam's *The Best and the Brightest*, and Theodore White's books on presidential campaigns, William Greider's books too—those are important projects, and if I were doing a study of investigative narratives over the longer term, they would most certainly be included. But I am speaking now of the two Gilded Ages, the second one spanning the last 25 years or so. And I'm thinking we're back to social barbarism.

ES: Back to *The Jungle*.

CT: Back to *The Jungle*, exactly. And that's where I stake my claim, from the images of that era of the robber barons to Enron, from Jacob Riis's tubercular children up to Laurie Garrett's portrait of the AIDS era.

ES: As an historical analogy (my background is in American history), you're right on the mark, a common theme between the 1890s and the 1990s and the kind of writing that both have inspired. So that's an historical analogy.

But from a literary point of view I feel that the kind of work that you're describing has continued to be produced. The kind of muckraking or investigative journalism that occurred in the first decade of the twentieth century was back in in the [19]60s and [19]70s. It wasn't up against the extreme disparities in wealth and [the] poor and the return of social Darwinism and the constant economic concentration—all of those things which today really look like the turn of the last century.

CT: I agree, and I'm glad to have this on the record. But I think your key statement is that that work was not up against such a socioculturally extreme regime.

ES: In the case of the Vietnam War writing though, it was up against something different but equally ominous, if not more threatening as a journalist. The threat to put LSD on [journalist] Jack Anderson's steering wheel was something that was seriously considered.

CT: You're raising the issue of the social power and authority of an investigative journalist. I wonder whether the powers-that-be, to borrow Halberstam's term, regard investigative journalists as a serious threat to their special interests. I'm not sure they do. Naomi Klein says that she was threatened with a lawsuit by a company called *No Logo*, which then dropped the threat and offered to go into business with her. Have you been threatened? Has anybody threatened to sue you?

ES: I have not been overtly threatened with a lawsuit. I have had it made clear to me that all of my public comments that can be obtained through transcripts are going onto computer chips. That message was given to me by a meat-packing person was a way of saying that the libel laws apply to what you say as well as what you write.

I would argue with your contention that these powers-that-be don't care. I think they care enormously, and again the analogy that's really strong is the relationship between this current group of writers and books and the social conditions that are so similar to the 1890s and the conditions that produced those books. That analogy is great. I would argue that this tradition has continued and one place that's continued it, in its own very powerful way, is *60 Minutes*. *60 Minutes* has been fearless in the way that they take on very powerful corporate interests. Those companies do not want *60 Minutes* anywhere near them, and when *60 Minutes* does a segment on these companies, it has an effect. It doesn't necessarily change the world, but—Maybe I'm being delusionally optimistic about the power of journalism and the word, but I would argue against any kind of [Herbert] Marcusian argument that this is just being co-opted and is another commodity. I mean, you could talk about how Rupert Murdoch is publishing *No Logo* or whatever, but at the same time it changes culture.

CT: I'm not making that argument about appropriation. I'm questioning whether the writers—you, Ehrenreich, Klein—are perceived as an effective challenge to the existing social and corporate-political arrangement.

ES: I don't know about that. Here's the much more interesting question to me. I would argue that this sort of work has always been done, but: Why is it now being read? That's what's significant. To me, it's not a question of whether Barbara Ehrenreich's book is going to change social policy on the working poor. What's interesting to me is that millions of people are interested in Barbara Ehrenreich's concern for the working poor, whereas they might not have been ten years ago. And in no way am I diminishing her work. It travels back from her work. But why are people interested in these books now?

CT: OK. Let me pose this question. I realize in talking to Barbara, I asked the wrong question. I asked, "What got you interested in this subject?" That question implies on the part of the writer a personal interest, perhaps even an eccentricity, an individual interest that's confined to that writer, perhaps to that writer alone. The bigger question is, How is it that certain social and cultural conditions have become so urgent that you, as a writer, were drawn to it and devoted two, three, however many years, of constant work to this topic to bring the message forward to the best of your investigative and literary abilities? I think that is the better question.

ES: To the degree that other people are interested in the same thing, it means that you're not eccentric. A journalist who finds a subject because he or she thinks it's important and other people think it's important too is, in a way, connected to the moment.

That doesn't mean you have a superior insight. It just means that, consciously or unconsciously, you care about what other people care about too. The problem has been that the mainstream media has overwhelmingly ignored subjects that ordinary people care about, and ordinary people *would* care about. And you combine that with the political changes and the economic changes, and people are now really interested in these things. When the writer addresses them, it doesn't take twisting their arm to get them to hear it.

Especially when you think about what I wrote about in *Fast Food Nation*, it seems like the most obvious thing that people would read. It's true that publishers were not jumping over one another to publish a book on the subject. But at the same time, now in retrospect, what we eat, what's in the food we eat, the implications of how we produce it—that just seems like "of course, people should care about that." In my mind, it doesn't take Einstein to figure out doing this book.

CT: Maybe the venue of the book itself has particular relevance at this time. I taught a course that featured what I called "block-busters," books that had changed public thinking.

ES: In a course in the English department?

CT: English department. I mean another ridiculous barrier that's persisted over a long time is a distinction between literature and journalism. They're separated by a Chinese wall.

ES: Didn't that come down in the [19]60s with Tom Wolfe and John McPhee?

CT: What has happened, at least in literary study, is that exceptions are made for a few people, i.e., John McPhee gets an honorary pass as a literary figure. Similarly Wolfe. But on the whole the wall still stands, at least within the mentality of literary studies. One can ask, Whose interest is served by maintaining it? I think the wall blocks literary attention to writers such as yourself.

ES: But I would argue that same wall has created certain kinds of fiction. The same mentality that creates a wall between fiction and nonfiction, which to me is absurd and irrelevant, is one that has promoted a certain kind of fiction over other types of fiction that are much more socially and culturally engaged. I mean, there are periods of our history when our fiction has involved much more than upper-middle-class emotional crises. These are worth writing about, but not to the exclusion of writing about everything else. I mean, anything's a valid subject. But when that's *all* that is being written about, it's a reflection of the academy.

CT: Academic genre barriers. I would like to get on the record your background as a reader-writer. Were you a reader as a kid?

ES: Yeah, but I can't remember titles.

CT: Hardy boys?

ES: Baseball books, sports autobiographies. I was very sports crazy. But I also read children's versions of, you know, Mark Twain, stuff like that. But I was not by any means a precocious child reader. I read the newspaper at an early age. My childhood—

CT: You grew up in New York?

ES: New York and Los Angeles, and my childhood was formed by the [19]60s because I was a kid during all of those tumultuous events that were going on. So I didn't live through them, participate in them first-hand, but they were part of reading the paper as a kid.

CT: And you had important papers in those two cities.

ES: And also the awareness of the Vietnam War because, you know, older brothers and friends, or camp counselors, or people like that, older figures were subject to the military draft lottery. I remember when Martin Luther King [Jr.] and Bobby Kennedy were assassinated. So there was a lot of news when I was a little kid.

CT: Sounds like you had a sense of the immediacy of public events, public affairs.

ES: Which was a major topic of conversation when I was in high school. Interests which could be viewed as eccentric interests were to me, just real interest in: What's happening? Who's it happening to? Why? Things like that. Once I got to college, I felt more and more alienated from the Reagan/Bush generation, even though Reagan was my president.

CT: Your college years—is that when you started taking your own writing seriously?

ES: Really in high school.

CT: Is there something you wrote that brought you alive to that possibility?

ES: It was just a great teacher. An English teacher in high school, when I really was thinking about being a playwright or a fiction writer or an investigative journalist. I was reading all kinds of things, such as Seymour Milman's investigative books on the military-industrial complex. They were really interesting, provocative works of nonfiction. To me, as an aspiring playwright who loved the theatre, there was not a hierarchy of fiction/nonfiction.

I was interested in what playwrights in the Sixties were doing. A lot of the [19]60s theatre was so experimental, so collaborative, and not text-driven, although a lot of Sixties theatre is now forgotten. You could argue that McPhee and Wolfe and Norman Mailer were doing the real art. But I never felt that one was higher, better, etcetera than another.

CT: And you went into a history major. Isn't that right? At Princeton. And therefore, by majoring in history you weren't subjected to an indoctrination about literary hierarchy.

ES: I resisted it. I had a grandfather who was an extraordinary person, very brilliant person. I was extremely close to him, and from a very early age he drummed into me the absurdity of categories of knowledge. He was a painter, and he was also a Renaissance fellow and also interested in so many diverse texts, and so the hierarchies and the divisions between areas of learning were

arbitrary and ridiculous. And so for me, studying history, thinking of getting a graduate degree in history—

CT: You did a graduate degree?

ES: I have a graduate degree in history, and I thought about teaching history, but I never thought about being an historian. I didn't
study history to become a historical novelist. I would personally
discourage aspiring writers from studying writing as a major as
an undergraduate. You could study history or science. That's my
own bias.

CT: OK. You're on record.

ES: You need to be engaged with the world whether that's through
your studies or through your active personal engagement in the
world. That will benefit you as a writer, not a degree in writing.

CT: Let me ask you about working with McPhee, about your development as a writer in your college years and later on. Was he
your main guide?

ES: I took a course with him. At that point I still wanted to be a playwright. I was writing plays that were *almost* produced, not quite
produced. I began to write short stories and novels. And I worked
for a film company and was a story editor at a film company. I
tried to write a screenplay and was a member of the Screenwriters
Guild, and I began writing nonfiction again because even though
I had the beginnings of a career in film, it was not going to take.
This was before the whole independent-film world took off.

    I had friends who were writing nonfiction, and they encour-
aged me to try, and I was able to try to do it because I remembered this McPhee course. And I remembered certain things
that we had done in the course and certain things that he had
taught. And so I wrote an essay and sent it to *The Atlantic*, which
turned it down because it was similar to another they had assigned. I didn't really start to write nonfiction and try to do it
seriously until my early 30s, and the first piece that I published
was in *The Atlantic*, and that's pretty much where I published after that. So it's a very atypical career path.

CT: It's atypical, but I would make the point that all that other writing that you had done was the foundation for your nonfiction
writing. The skills you exhibit in *Fast Food Nation* and in the
pieces in *The Atlantic* and *Rolling Stone* show a foundation of narrative skill that had to come from somewhere.

ES: I don't know how direct the linkage. I probably spent the most
time with dialogue as an aspiring playwright, but if you look at
my nonfiction, there is very little direct quotation, and I've chosen a style that is not pages and pages of listening to people talk.

But getting back to McPhee, the things that were so crucial from his course, that all his students learned, and are critical to any kind of writing, is the primary, fundamental importance of structure. However you go about it, whether you start with a structure and work around it, or whether you write and write and write, and then impose the structure on what you've done, you have to be aware of the structure of your writing.

So that was a fundamental thing. Another was a devotion to craft. I'm not saying that any of us who publish anything have achieved what McPhee has achieved, but the idea is this: as a writer you are a craftsperson the same way a woodworker is. There are tools, there are techniques, and there are things that require integrity to do. (And there are things that are just cheap and tacky and shoddy.) And in McPhee's work, there is incredible craftsmanship and integrity, not just in the structures, but in the individual sentences.

McPhee would ask, "Why are you using this punctuation?" And basically that meant caring about the punctuation, caring about every word. And the other thing that he was just huge on, which is applicable directly to this kind of reporting, is total immersion. Total immersion not so that you can show everyone how much you know about it, but total immersion so that your work is the tip of the iceberg of what you know. Everything that you *don't* put in the piece, everything you leave out, informs everything you leave in.

It's the idea of not doing an interview with anyone until you already know the subject and you already know about them and have the opportunity to nurture a conversation, as opposed to just showing up, not knowing the subject, not knowing anything, and being nonattentive. So, in some ways those ideas are applicable to any kind of writing, but I think they are most applicable to this sort of writing.

CT: This leads to another related issue to me, which is, I'll call it, "The Care and Feeding of the Reader." You had mentioned about *Fast Food Nation* what I think any thoughtful reader of the book must notice. That is, that the reader has to be educated and attracted before confronting some of the most disturbing aspects of the subject. So that long before we meet Kenny, the worker who donates his body to the meat-packing industry, which reciprocates by firing him and cutting off all benefits, and before we go down the line up to our knees in blood and viscera and lethal *E. coli*—long before that, we are treated to a kind of celebratory profile of our culture. We meet the guy who represents the best of American can-do, of bootstrap work at the hot-dog stand, leading to his chain of restaurants all through Southern California. Nationally, he hooks up to the *Hardee's* chain, and that logo star is smiling at all of America. So we're welcomed into this world, although in any given sentence, you've got a dark shadow falling. There'll be a word, there'll be a phrase, and it's like tympani sounding in the background.

Then later, hold on because I really want your response to this, I'm going to give you two examples from *Fast Food Nation*, where you made a deliberate word choice. One, in this account of Kenny and his physical abuse until his body is destroyed: his lungs, his bones, his muscles, because of the tasks Monfort imposes on him. And we're deep in his horrific history, and you use the word "unpleasant" as Kenny is asked to do increasingly "unpleasant" tasks. That, of course, is a word that gives us a moment of oasis from the relentless workplace destruction of this man. Later on, when you're talking about the Jack-In-the-Box food contamination and the death of children, you say about one child who dies that finally part of his brain was "liquified."

Now, between "unpleasant" and this little boy whose brain is "liquified," there's a vast array of terms with different emotional and intellectual connotations, so that my question is, Do you have your reader in mind? Is it a strategic design within the structure, and would you talk about that?

ES: Whether the book works for the reader or not—and there are some readers for whom it doesn't work—it's all deliberate. The sequence of paragraphs is deliberate. From the first chapter through the last paragraph is a deliberate sequence. And it's a narrative, but not a narrative in which you're following some family or protagonist. In a weird way, this sounds so pretentious, but the book is about these people. So, the meat-packing worker chapter or the food safety chapter—ideally the book is bringing us closer and closer to the truth. It's one thing to have abstract empathy for the workers of different backgrounds, but eventually it all comes back to you. So that's the sequence of the chapters in that case. I can't remember enough about the sentences that you just mentioned to say that there was some design. But it's not arbitrary at all.

CT: You run a risk, if you don't handle it right, of driving readers away. You run the risk also of emerging as a ranter, a polemicist. The minute readers sense an ax to grind, they flee.

ES: You don't need to rant. There's no need to rant. Reality speaks for itself. I guess allowing the subject to speak for itself is also a

McPhee technique. The writer is not interposing himself between the subject and the reader. The question for me is, Is there a fundamental integrity? It doesn't matter whether it's a novelist or a playwright or a nonfiction writer. You know why and what they are doing and you know what's motivating that effort. And some people are amazing and largely unrecognized, like Ted Conover [author of *Newjack*], and some people full of shit and successful beyond belief. That's my little philosophical—[*Schlosser breaks off.*]

CT: Anyway, *Fast Food Nation*—

ES: Americans constantly hear that things got better, better, better. You talk about *The Jungle* coming out in 1906, and this public cry for pure-food legislation. It took thirty to forty years of union organizing and strikebreakers and pitting one minority against another minority, and people getting bloodied and hurt. It took decades for people to come to a point where they had a decent job, and a really good job by the early [to] mid-1960s. A meat-packing worker was on a par with an auto worker in terms of benefits, job security, seniority. He would have a middle-class life on the basis of this: your spouse need not work, and your children could either go to college or they could go work in the plant with you. And that's what usually happened. So the idea that this part of history that spans sixty years has vanished in twenty is a terrible situation.

When I go to college campuses, I'm talking to kids, and I'm looking at people who were born in 1984. So if they're going to get this knowledge, it's going to come from a person. It's not going to come from any kind of life experience of their own.

CT: Or it'll come from a text. From *Fast Food Nation*.

The reception of *Fast Food Nation* speaks volumes about the challenge of the investigative narrative in its relation to the reading public, or publics. In our discussion, Schlosser has emphasized the writer's own requirements—of structure, of craftsmanship, and of deep-seated knowledge of the subject. He has insisted that the writer's subject is connected to a moment in which, "consciously or unconsciously," the writer "care[s] about what other people care about."

We both want to think so. But I have neglected to pose to Schlosser the problem of reader-writer mismatch. I failed, that is, to introduce the notion of selective reader responses, of readers as "interpretive communities," as Stanley Fish put it in *Is There a Text in This Class?* (1980). Readers of *Fast Food Nation*, as of any book, could be grouped according to the values and assumptions and preoccupations that they bring to the text. Their own mental baggage, it is now understood, inevitably directs and conditions the act of reading. Certain critics, notably Wolfgang Iser, have called attention to the text's inevitable "gaps" that the readers "creatively" fill, despite efforts on the part of texts and their designers—the authors—to guide and control the act of reading.

A kind of tug-of-war is implied here. The writer develops a narrative structure intended deliberately to shape the responses of the intended reader. In muckraker narratives, civic education and activism are authorial objectives. Yet the reader brings to the book a backlog of beliefs, priorities, and predispositions—in short, a whole worldview that serves as screen and filter. We saw this problem arise when Lincoln Steffens sought to change middle-class, white Anglo readers' biases against the "alien sinister races" of immigrants whom these readers had blamed for political corruption. Some things on the page will get through; others are dammed.

Readers' worldviews come from sources too numerous to name here, though class, gender, and ethnoracial identities all figure in.

Schlosser would probably agree. His campus lectures to college students, he indicates, are history lessons by which young people might open themselves to new viewpoints. I have said that *Fast Food Nation* is just such an instrument. Yet Eric Schlosser's conclusion on the post-1960s disappearance of the working-class middle class goes far to explain why the workers' stories haven't received much attention in reviews of *Fast Food Nation*. The 2002 paperback edition, for instance, is prefaced by glowing excerpts from thirty-nine reviews of the book. Only three name working conditions as significant. Schlosser's narrative skill is acknowledged in these blurbs and his exhaustive research into every area of the topic praised, as are his wit and "flair for dazzling scene-setting and an arsenal of startling facts," as the *Los Angeles Times* put it. "Eric Schlosser may be the Upton Sinclair for this age of mad cow disease," said the *L.A. Times*. Said the *Baltimore Sun*, "This is a book about America's stomach."

How can this be? In the twenty-first century, how can *Fast Food Nation* become another *The Jungle*, the readers pouncing on the meat story to the gross neglect of the narrative of working conditions in America. How is it that the book's reviewers, an educated lot, have failed to help shape readers' response to the civic melodrama of hellish working conditions? How, in fact, have the reviewers' own tastes been shaped?

Suppose these reviewers, like many of Schlosser's readers, have studied another well-known narrative combining the slaughterhouse and its workers. *Moby-Dick* (1851) features several chapters on whale slaughter and butchering, as Melville invites readers to consider the terms of their own red-meat diets—to the "meat-market of a Saturday night," to the "gourmand dining off that roast beef," to the mate Stubb's delectable dinner of grilled whale steak (406, 407, 404).

Melville precedes Schlosser by one and one-half centuries, but he too had specified the danger and risk of the slaughtering-butchering work of whale-oil production for lighting and lubrication in the pre-petroleum era. For instance, the thin hemp whale-line, which is tied to the harpoon to be thrust into the unsuspecting whale, must be coiled in perfect "minute spiralizations" free of any tangle or kink. Failure to take this "utmost precaution" can mean the loss of a crewman's arm, leg, or "entire body" when the harpooned whale dives deep.

A second line from an additional whale boat is sometimes needed, the second boat hovering nearby "to assist its consort," lest the first boat "be dragged down . . . into the profundity of the sea," that is, "doomed" (385, 386). "This arrangement," says Melville, "is indispensable for common safety's sake" (385). The work is terribly dangerous, the pitching boat more perilous than the comparable earthly industrial scene of "manifold whizzings of a steam-engine in full play, when every flying beam, and shaft, and wheel, is grazing you" (387). For mutual self-protection, however, the crew follow safety procedures, which Melville specifies in detail.

Do classroom teachers of American literature ask students to pay attention to working conditions on this factory ship, the *Pequod*, and thereby help educate students—future book reviewers and readers—about the importance of the topic in their citizenly lives? In the last twenty years, as the union contract workplace safety protections (and middle-class pay scales) disappeared, have we resorted to this American classic to frame classroom discussions of the workplace in canonical American literature?

No. We leap eagerly, instead, to Melville's philosophical musing that "all men live enveloped in whale-lines," that "all are born with halters round their necks" and realize the "silent, subtle, ever-present perils of life" only when "caught in the swift, sudden turn of death" (387). These are the phrases that are underscored in our classroom desk copies, these the metaphysical statements we call to students' attention. These, we emphasize, are the so-called enduring truths, or conundrums of the human condition worldwide across millennia. Perhaps, additionally, we might link these statements to the act of writing itself and claim that Melville was meditating on his own literary peril. Or we venture a psychoanalytic suggestion of birth crisis as the umbilical lifeline becomes death's noose.

None of these approaches, however, focuses on labor, its risks, the protocols for "common safety's sake." None, that is, encourages citizenly obligation to take responsibility for worksite conditions. They appeal instead to a community of readers predisposed to expect a high-minded "classic" text, classicism itself understood to exclude direct social engagement. After all, our college and university students are not and never will be slaughterhouse or fast food workers.

Five years following the publication of *The Jungle*, the American Academy of Political and Social Science published a volume entitled *Risks in Modern Industry* (1911). It is a compilation of statements by a wide range of officials voicing differing viewpoints on a topic that all participants agreed needed urgent attention in the United States: the high rates of industrial-era injury and death of workers. The Secretary of Commerce and Labor weighed in, as did a consulting engineer, a vice president of the American Federation of Labor, an assistant district attorney of New York, a Unitarian minister, a member of the executive committee of the American Red Cross, and the general secretary of the National Consumers' League.

Given their positions, their statements were to some degree predictable. The Secretary of Commerce and Labor voiced the business goal to minimize waste with a minimum of governmental regulation, while the labor union leader promoted workers' health. The district attorney emphasized mutual responsibility of management and workers for meeting provisions of the new worker compensation law in his state, New York, while the Red Cross spokeswoman highlighted the need to prevent workplace disasters.

The pages of *Risks in Modern Industry*, however, are rife with convergent statements on "accidents . . . out of proportion," on "the number of men and women annually killed and maimed in the industrial occupations of America . . . greater than in the bloodiest battles of history," on victims' "dependents who suffer the direct and terrible consequences of the family of a wage earner . . . carried lifeless into his home" (72, 74, 76). They speak of the "enormous" social and economic costs, of the new possibility for "elementary justice," and of the fact that the very term "disaster" refers not only to "pestilence, famine, fire, and floods" but to the "calamity" of industrial accidents in which a half-million people are estimated to be annually killed or injured in the United States (American Academy of Political and Social Science 84, 86, 90, 91).

Slaughterhouse workers were not singled out for attention in the 1911 volume, nor in its 1926 successor *Industrial Safety*, whose title accentuated the gains made over fifteen years in worker protection via an organized safety movement.* Heavy industry—notably steel, coal, and railroads—took precedence, and no food-processing industry was named. The trend toward worker protection, however, was clear. A fast-food nation was then decades in the offing, as was the rise—and subsequent decline—of unionized work in the United States. As Schlosser states toward the close of *Fast Food Nation*, "Over the past twenty-five years the United States has swung too far in one direction, weakening the regulations that safeguard workers, consumers, and the environment. An economic system promising freedom has too often become a means of denying it, as the narrow dictates of the market gain precedence over more important democratic values" (261).

Workplace conditions in the downsizing era of the new Gilded Age, however, may tend to aggregate workers, if not into a uniform collar, at least into proximity and mutual regard. Those at the desk may come to see kindred spirits, at least distant relations, across the fast-food counter to the boning knife. "There is nothing inevitable about the fast food nation that surrounds us," Schlosser writes (260). In a spirit of optimism, he adds that "people can be fed without being fattened or deceived" and that "this new century may bring an impatience with conformity, a refusal to be kept in the dark, less greed, more compassion, less speed, more common sense, a sense of humor about brand essences and loyalties, a view of food as more than just fuel. Things don't have to be the way they are" (afterword, 288).

*   *   *

Naomi Klein, *No Logo: Taking Aim at the Brand Bullies*

> The station wagons arrived at noon, a long shining line that coursed through the west campus. . . . The roofs . . . were loaded down with carefully secured suitcases full of light and heavy clothing; with boxes of blankets, boots and shoes, stationery and books, sheets, pillows, quilts; with rolled-up rugs and sleeping bags; with bicycles, skis, rucksacks, English and Western saddles, inflated rafts. As cars slowed to a crawl and stopped, students sprang out and raced to the rear doors to begin removing the

---

* "By the second decade of the twentieth century an unlikely alliance of reformers, radicals, feminists, unionists, and machine politicians had placed the social needs of working people squarely on the nation's political agenda. In 1912 alone, thirty-eight states passed child labor laws and twenty-eight states (mostly northern and western) set maximum hours for women workers; . . . by 1915, workmen's compensation laws were on the books in thirty-five states" (*Who Built America* 2: 211).

Industrial Safety includes chapters on the organization of safety councils, on the economic benefits of worker safety, on the enforcement of safety codes, and on safety features of the workplace and equipment, for example, flooring, lighting, and eye protection.

11. Naomi Klein, 2002. Photograph courtesy The Herald/Gordon Terris. c. SMG Newspapers Ltd.

> *objects inside; the stereo sets, radios, personal computers; small refrigerators and table ranges; the cartons of phonograph records and cassettes; the hairdryers and styling irons; the tennis rackets, soccer balls, hockey and lacrosse sticks, bows and arrows; the controlled substances, the birth control pills and devices; the junk food still in shopping bags—onion-and-garlic chips, nacho thins, peanut creme patties, Waffelos and Kabooms, fruit chews and toffee popcorn; the Dum-Dum pops, the Mystic mints.*
> —*Don DeLillo*, White Noise, *1985*

Beginning *White Noise* with a description of typical American students arriving at college with their awesome array of possessions, the novelist Don DeLillo prompts this classroom exercise: read the name of each generic item aloud, then ask students to provide brand names. "Clothing," I call out. The response is immediate and vigorous.

"Gap!" "Diesel!" "Tommy Hilfiger!"

"Boots and shoes?"

"Timberland!" "Nike!" "Reebok!" "Adidas!"

"Luggage?"

"Samsonite!"

Students who don't ordinarily speak up in class vie eagerly with classmates to fill in the brand blanks. Levis, North Face, JanSport, Wilson, Sony, Panasonic, Dell, Mac, Nabisco, and so on ad infinitum. It's five minutes of big-brand glossalalia.

It's also a teachable moment as I segue to the follow-up query from civic life. "Let's try a version of this with our representatives in Washington, D.C.," I say. "How about cabinet secretaries? Treasury? Interior? Health and Human Services? Home-state Senators? House of Representatives? Judiciary?"

Silence falls. Embarrassed giggles erupt. In recent years, a good many students have told me they "hate" politics, and I can hardly blame them for ignoring officials whom the *New York Times*'s Bill Keller calls "a collection of the spineless led by the cynical, constantly lap-dancing for special-interest cash to finance the permanent campaign" (November 2, 2002: A27). I hasten to assure the class that my intention is not humiliation but a civics quiz meant to expose the extent of branding in our brains as we prepare to discuss *White Noise* as a novel of American consumer culture. Ignorant of the U.S. Senators, we know the brands the way musicians know notes.

Naomi Klein's *No Logo: Taking Aim at the Brand Bullies* (2000) dissects this new age of branding to its deepest and furthest global ramifications. Brand-name colonization of the mind is only part of its provenance. Tracing the ways in which brands have replaced products, *No Logo* links the corporate branding of civic or public space—a parallel colonization campaign—with sweatshop labor in the Global South. It also locates a direct relation to the degradation of jobs in the United States and elsewhere in the West. It shows the ways in which race and poverty are exploited for profit, as the corporate "suits" stalk inner-city blacks for trend-setting "cool" fashion ideas, which are marketed to suburban whites but also back to poor blacks who crave them as status markers. A prize-winning best-seller in Canada and Europe and translated into a dozen languages, *No Logo* exposes the contemporary socioeconomic structures of a postindustrial North America and Western Europe, in which the so-called global village operates largely by human exploitation, by the curtailment of citizenly human rights, and by corporate and governmental censorship. Klein's project expands civic melodrama from the nation-state to the globe. *No Logo* reveals "an intense emotional and ethical drama" in a material world where "what one lives for and by is seen in terms of, and as determined by, the most fundamental psychic relations and cosmic ethical forces" (Brooks, *The Melodramatic Imagination*, 12–13).

The morally contending forces of light and darkness, equally crucial to the civic melodrama of the first Gilded Age and to the second, require *No Logo*'s mapping of a growing resistance to this new economy and its (anti)social arrangements. Klein writes, "The title *No Logo* is not meant to be read as a literal slogan (as in No More Logos!), or a post-logo logo. . . . Rather, it is an attempt to capture an anticorporate attitude I see emerging among many young activists."

Klein's project originated during research on university campuses in the mid-1990s, when she met students who were increasingly uneasy about the incursions into their schools by private corporations—for example, ads encroaching in the cafeterias and bathrooms, school districts and colleges-universities inking deals with soft-drink and athletic-wear firms. In those years, she finds, the humanities faculties, including the much-vaunted "tenured radicals," were too preoccupied with "merits of the canon," identity politics, and the culture wars to notice that "their campuses were being sold out from under their feet" (103–5).

Klein learned, in fact, that when universities signed contracts with such firms as Reebok, Nike, or Coca-Cola, nondisparagement clauses prohibited members of the university communities from criticizing their corporate practices. Some students, Klein found, nonetheless were concerned about corporate interests taking precedence over educational ones, including free-speech rights. They worried too about the ethical practices of some of the corporations now "entangled" with their schools, "practices far away, in countries like Burma, Indonesia and Nigeria" (xviii–xix, 96–97).

As a journalist, Klein heard similar concerns expressed by activists across the United States, the United Kingdom, and elsewhere. "There was the McLibel Trial in London, a case of two British environmentalists who turned a libel suit McDonald's had launched against them into a global cyberplatform that put the ubiquitous food franchise on trial. There was the explosion of protest and activity targeting Shell Oil after the shocking hanging of Nigerian author and anti-Shell activist Ken Saro-Wiwa" (xix).

One premise of *No Logo* is that the authority of powerful, gargantuan corporations now exceeds governments', including the democracies'. The multinational corporations, Klein writes, "are also the most powerful political forces of our time" (339). The crux of her argument is that the "corporate obsession with brand identity is waging a war on public and individual space: on public institutions such as schools, on youthful identities, on the concept of nationality and on the possibilities for unmarked space" (5).

Readers of *No Logo* get lessons in economics and history. Decades ago, Klein explains, corporations had focused proudly on the manufacture of their products, as I well know from my Pittsburgh grade-school tour of the Heinz plant, when we got souvenir pickle pins for our jerseys and pinafores. Brand names, from Wrigley to Chrysler to

Hershey, were then product-based badges of honor. Brand extension existed in desultory places, say in Chicago's Wrigley Field or New York's Chrysler Building, landmarks that promoted respect for companies and their founding patriarchs as they stimulated desires to chew Doublemint or drive a Chrysler New Yorker. The ball park and skyscraper reverted to the products, to the cars and the gum. In this older paradigm, the products were sold via advertising and marketing.

In the 1980s, however, this fundament of American manufacturing changed radically. "Overnight," Klein explains, " 'Brands, not products!' became the rallying cry for a marketing renaissance led by a new breed of companies that saw themselves as 'meaning brokers' instead of product producers." In the new model, she explains, "the product always takes a back seat to the real product," which was "the brand." "In its truest and most advanced incarnations," Klein states, branding "is about corporate transcendence" (21).

As "flaky" as Klein admits this sounds, her research into marketing literature shows that products are no longer presented as commodities but as "concepts: the brand as experience, as lifestyle" (21). Nike's Phil Knight thus rejects the notion that his business is shoes and casual clothing, instead proclaiming Nike to be a health and fitness company. And Starbucks, according to *Advertising Age*, offers customers not just coffee drinks, but " 'immersion . . . in a cultured refuge,' " which the company expresses in four C's: coffee, community, camaraderie, and connection (112, 135). In short, the brand now beckons consumers to enter into a "lived reality" (29). These newest logos replace plastic shells and golden arches with a glowing, healthy "New Age sheen" (131).

This branded "lifestyle" is totalizing, and thus radically different from people's connections to older product-based companies. Klein writes, "Corporate sponsors and the culture they brand have fused together to create a third culture: a self-enclosed universe of brand-name people, brand-name products and brand-name media" (60). *No Logo* says this "is the meaning of a lifestyle brand: you can live your whole life inside it" (148). This is the vexing issue in Klein's civic melodrama—that the dark world seduces by apparent light.

Klein understands the attraction of the "branded worlds," reflecting that "it has something to do with the genuine thrill of utopianism, or the illusion of it." "Why wouldn't these creations be seductive?" she asks in all sincerity, adding that for younger people like herself, "these private branded worlds are aesthetically and creatively thrilling." She sympathizes with the "emotional power" of nostalgic longing captured in "the marriage of work and play at the Nike World Campus, the luxurious intellectualism of the Barnes & Noble superstores or the wilderness fantasy of the Roots Lodge." She warns against dismissal of these as mere crass commercialism: "for better or worse, these are privatized public utopias" (157–58).

This era of corporate branding, *No Logo* argues, was made possible by privatization and deregulation policies in the United States, Canada, Britain, and elsewhere, notably under the political leadership of Ronald Reagan, Brian Mulroney, and Margaret Thatcher. "Corporate taxes were dramatically lowered, a move that eroded the tax base and gradually starved out the public sector. . . . [while] there was almost no vocabulary to speak passionately about the value of a non-commercialized public sphere" (30). "As government spending dwindled," Klein points out, "schools, museums and broadcasters were desperate to make up their budget shortfalls and thus ripe for partnerships with private corporations" (30). In the mid-1980s, "sponsorship took off as a stand-in for public funds" (34).

No Logo explains how well-meaning corporate sponsorship combining philanthropy with public relations degenerates into brand takeovers (of events, of places, of celebrities who sometimes become brands in their own right, for example, Tiger Woods). Klein states the public peril: "When any space is bought, even if only temporarily, it changes to fit its sponsors. And the more previously public spaces are sold to corporations or branded by them, the more we as citizens are forced to play by the corporate rules to access our own culture" (185). Shopping malls may be the new American Main Street, but they are private property where freedom of speech and assembly legally take a distant second place to private property rights.

At the same time, a kind of civic enervation occurs as community and other groups increasingly believe they cannot possibly stage their own events without corporate support. A society whose media, streets, and retail spaces are controlled by multinational corporate interests, *No Logo* says, results in "corporate space as a fascist state where we all salute the logo" (187). Put in other terms: "every company with a powerful brand is attempting to develop a relationship with consumers that resonates so completely with their sense of self that they will aspire, or at least consent, to be serfs under these feudal landlords" (149).

The powerful brands, however, have been built upon the "involuntary philanthropy" (to borrow Barbara Ehrenreich's term) of hundreds of thousands of wretchedly paid workers in the Global South. U.S. plant closings have been inversely linked to an upsurge of industrial factory growth in Asia, Central and South America, and the Caribbean, where labor is cheap and health and safety regulations nonexistent. No longer do the big-brand companies own their manufacturing facilities but instead contract (or outsource) production through shifting networks of subcontractors who operate factories that can be moved overnight to any spot on the planet where human beings can be hired to work for less or least.*

The U.S. public has been told by the media and business press that this state of things marks a progressive evolution of late capitalism. As the United States and western Europe move forward into a high-tech service economy, the message goes, it is natural that the less developed parts of the world now take their turn as manufacturers. These messengers imply, yet dare not say outright, that it is equally "natural" for these new industrial workers to relive the early, brutal manufacturing history of Britain and the United States. Thus the Mexican factory maquiladora workers across the Rio Grande or the textile workers in Sri Lanka or Pakistan toil under conditions reminiscent of the United States and English nineteenth century. Theirs are the kinds of workplaces that today's students read about—and deplore in a historically easy sympathy—in Dickens's *Hard Times* and Rebecca Harding Davis's *Life in the Iron-Mills*.

No Logo offers a first-person tour of a south Asian free-trade zone where manufacture and product assembly of big-brand items now takes place. As a journalist, Klein presents an on-site report from Cavite, a 682-acre walled city housing 207 factories in a Philippine EPZ (Enterprise Processing Zone), a "tax-free economy, sealed off from the local government of both town and province—a miniature military state inside a democracy" (204).

In Cavite, as in similar sites across Southeast Asia (and Latin America), young women work twelve- to fourteen-hour days, "sent off to sweatshop factories the way a previous generation of young men were sent off to war" (214). Klein exposes as a mere feel-good myth the notion that these factory jobs are stepping stones to worker prosperity, since currency devaluations of the late 1990s made these jobs a life's losing game of Chutes and Ladders, with each rung up the prelude to a sudden steep plunge. While the corporations "are treated to an all-expenses-paid 'tax holiday' during which they pay no income tax and no property tax," the host governments of the Enterprise Processing Zones "put their own people on the auction block, . . . allowing workers to be paid less than the real cost of living" and providing "the services of a military willing and able to crush labor unrest" (206).

Without health-care benefits, job security, or overtime pay then, young women workers jam six to a six-by-eight concrete bunker dorm room, earning wages barely paying for vendor-cart noodles and fried rice. They "cannot dream of affording the consumer goods

* As this is written, the *New York Times* reports that from 2000 to 2002, 287,000 manufacturing jobs have exited Mexico, where wages in the maquiladoras average $2.00–$2.50 hourly. The jobs have migrated to China, where hourly wages begin at 35 cents per hour (November 5, 2002: W1, W7).

they produce" (210). At one factory where the assembling of IBM computer monitors takes place, Klein learned, "the 'bonus' for working hours of overtime isn't a higher hourly wage but donuts and a pen" (211). Supervisors vigilantly thwart efforts at unionization to secure worker rights, and dissidents have been murdered. The sewn and assembled products of this labor bear the brands of, among others, Nike, Reebok, Ellen Tracy, Sassoon, Gap, Liz Claiborne, Aztek, Apple, IBM, Zenith, Panasonic, General Electric, General Motors, Fruit of the Loom, Tommy Hilfiger, Guess?, Polo Ralph Lauren, Banana Republic, Victoria's Secret, Old Navy, Jones New York, Calvin Klein, Wal-Mart, J. C. Penney, Target, Sears, and Nordstrom. (An appendix in *No Logo* charts the companies/labels, the factories, and the hourly wages [ranging from thirteen to thirty-five cents], to the hours per week [60 to 96], the workweek being six or seven days.)

Yet Cavite, like all such sites, is nonetheless fraught with the angst of insecurity. "The factories are cheaply constructed and tossed together on land that is rented, not owned" because "the jobs that flew here from the North could fly away again just as quickly" (206). The context is one of pervasive fear: "the governments are afraid of losing their foreign factories; the factories are afraid of losing their brand-name buyers; and the workers are afraid of losing their unstable jobs" (206).

No Logo exposes the information split by which the much-vaunted Global Village operates. "Despite the marketing-based rhetoric of One Worldism," Klein writes, "the planet remains sharply divided between producers and consumers, and the enormous profits raked in by the superbrands are premised upon these worlds remaining as separate from each other as possible" (346). This system, Klein finds, functions on ignorance in each realm. The producers are unaware of the retail market value of the products they make and/or assemble at pennies-per-hour wages. The consumers, in turn, are "sheltered from the production lives of the brands they buy" (347). *No Logo* joins the efforts of activist groups to "expose the riches of the branded world to the tucked-away sites of production and [to] bring back the squalor of production to the doorstep of the blinkered consumer" (347).

Yet *No Logo* argues that the new world of work in the West—including the United States—is disturbingly analogous to the Global South. "Zone workers in many parts of Asia, the Caribbean and Central America have more in common with office-temp workers in North America and Europe than they do with factory workers in those Northern countries" (218). Klein explores the extent to which, in the United States and Canada, good jobs have become McJobs: "it seems as if more and more of the twenty-something-going-on-thirty-something clerks working for the superbrands are looking around—at the counters in front of them where they serve Sumatran coffee, and at the best-selling books, and made-in-China sweaters—and are acknowledging that, for better or worse, some of them aren't going anywhere fast" (236).

Nor are wages indexed to rising living costs. Since the mid-1980s, Klein finds, "large chains such as Wal-Mart, Starbucks and the Gap . . . have been lowering workplace standards in the service sector, fueling their marketing budgets, imperialistic expansions and high concept 're-tail experiences' by lowballing their clerks on wages and hours" (236). Just as the big-brand multinationals have "freed themselves of the bur-den of providing employees with a living wage" in places like Cavite, so "in the food court and at the superstore, they have managed a similar trick" (237). Part-time positions (and unpaid internships) in the United States, she finds, "are used as a loophole to keep wages down and to avoid benefits and overtime; 'flexibility' becomes a code for 'no promises' " (242). The 1990s notion of everyworker as "Free Agent" (as in the slogan "Be Your Own CEO," promoted in such magazines as *Fast Company*), is discredited in the face of a very different, no-benefits job reality, which is dubbed in ironic self-contradiction "permatemping."

Naomi Klein, a Canadian, is a columnist for the *Globe and Mail* and the *Nation*. Formerly a writer for the Toronto *Star*, she has contributed to the *New York Times*, the *Village Voice*, *The New Statesman*, and *Newsweek International*. She has lectured at Harvard, Yale, Emory, and New York Universities. *No Logo* won Canada's National Business Book Award in 2001. Klein's second book, *Fences and Windows: Dispatches from the Front Lines of the Globalization Debate*, was published in 2002. We spoke in Toronto on October 31, 2002.

INTERVIEW WITH NAOMI KLEIN

CT: I'll start by asking how you came to see yourself as a writer. I've read other interviews in which you discussed your bio, but this is about you as *writer*.

NK: Well, I still struggle with definitions of writer versus journalist versus activist.

CT: —because the gatekeepers separating those categories have been very active keeping their fences high and strong.

NK: That said, part of what I want to do in life is push my own bar-riers and create space to be more writerly, to have more space for creativity in my own writing.

CT: Can I take you back to childhood? Did you keep a journal? Did you write in diaries?

NK: I was a journal fiend, starting in fourth grade. Actually, after I read *The Diary of Anne Frank,* I decided to keep a diary. So I still have my first diary, which has an ice cream cone on it, and it talks about Anne Frank. That's how I know. I don't really remember. And I wrote a lot of poetry as a teenager, and I filled dozens of journals of angst.

CT: Let's stay back there for a little while. Did family members encourage you to write, and were you much of a reader as a kid?

NK: Yes—in fits and starts. First, I read a lot of books about kids who had survived the Holocaust. Then in grade four, I got really sick, and I spent six months in bed, and I read like crazy, just tearing through books. The first adult book I read was *Catch-22* when I was twelve or thirteen. It got me so depressed that my mother took it from me. She said it was having a bad effect on me. I was becoming really grouchy [*laughter*], and she thought maybe it was over my age limit or something. I was out of my demographic.

So that was definitely my first real grown-up book. I just found it in my parents' library, where I used to find a lot of books. All of Philip Roth's books were down there because my dad's from Newark, New Jersey, so he had all of those. My mother didn't like them. But I read all of them. I also read really crappy books, like all of Judy Blume's books. I just read whatever was in the basement. But after that I got really social and I think there was a long stretch when I became a teenager, pre-teen, where I wrote in my journals about boys. And how much I hated my parents [laughter]. I wrote a lot of poetry on my own, which was mostly teen angst alienation stuff.

Looking back, a lot of the conflict for me was the fact that I grew up in a very political family, but they sent me to very conventional schools, Jewish day schools that were very consumerist. I felt pretty isolated, so I worked it out in writing.

CT: When you say "political family," you must mean leftist, counter-cultural.

NK: Both my parents were activists in the [19]60s. My father's parents were Socialists and union organizers. My grandfather was blacklisted for union organizing at Disney. And when my father was drafted to serve in the Vietnam War, in order to prove his status as a conscientious objector, he would have had to go into his red-diaper baby family history, which he didn't feel able to do. So we came to Canada.

My father worked in public health and my mother worked as a filmmaker doing early feminist film. I was born in Montreal, and then we went back to the States in the early [19]70s, to Rochester, New York, and made a decision after five years to move back to Canada, not as draftdodgers, but basically out of preference. It was a choice between leading a kind of marginal existence of small clinics and small independent film projects in the States, versus being able to really stay true to their values but work in the mainstream of public health care in Canada and in public film at the National Film Board, which was really quite a remarkable institution at that time.

And so my mother made films like *Not a Love Story*, which was really an important film about pornography. She made a lot of films about women and peace, and both parents were involved in the antinuclear movement—that was their main focus when I was a teenager—disarmament. My father was part of Physicians for Social Responsibility and worked with Helen Caldicott, and my mother was making films about women who were part of the peace movement in the Soviet Union. And my brother got immersed in that too. He started a student antinuclear group that had hundreds of chapters across Canada.

So my rebellion was just to say, "I want to go shopping. Leave me alone. You guys are weird." It really was a form of rebellion. I know that it seems like a really conventional route, but actually in my context it was not. I had to fight to be conventional in my house, and it was a source of tremendous conflict. I was always political, but it wasn't in the sense of organizing and joining groups. [*Pause*] I guess I started to think of myself as a researcher and tasted the thrill of the kind of writing that I do now when preparing for my Bat Mitzvah speech.

CT: Really?

NK: When I was twelve. I went to a kind of unconventional synagogue—not by New York standards, but by Montreal standards—a reconstructionist synagogue. We had a really nice rabbi, and he was close to my family. We weren't religious, but my mother wanted me to have a Bat Mitzvah, and she wanted me to go to Jewish school, so she sent me to this Jewish school that was filled with kids who were incredibly racist.

Until then, everything I knew about Judaism my mother had taught me, mainly that you dedicate your life to fighting oppression and racism and slavery. I just took for granted that the struggle that we tell every year at family Seders about Jews escaping from slavery is about a universal struggle whose relevant lesson is: *never again do that to anyone*. I grew up with that. I totally took it for granted. I didn't think of it as political. I just understood that that's what it meant to be Jewish.

And suddenly I found myself in this school with kids whose

Judaism was narrow and self-interested. Let's stick together. Let's militarize the state of Israel. You know, let's create our ghettos and make as much money as we can.

Now this was in a very multicultural part of Montreal, and on one side was a school that was all African-Canadian and Caribbean kids, and on another a Jewish school full of Moroccan kids, because there's a big Moroccan-Jewish community, most of which is French speaking. And there would be all kinds of fights and the word "nigger" was thrown around all the time at my school. It was really quite racist, and to me amazingly shocking, and I was really uncomfortable with it.

So I decided that I was going to give my Bat Mitzvah speech about how bad it is that Jews are racist. I mean, the level of analysis wasn't much more than that. It was just that we, of all people, should not be racist, but we are racist. I had been holding it in for a really long time, so my first draft of the speech was pure rage. It was, "You call the kids down the street 'niggers' and then you all go to Florida and say you want to get black." I remember that one. [*Laughter.*]

I owe a lot to the rabbi who read that draft. No doubt, he was just trying to figure out, "What am I going to do with this girl? She can't do this." And so he suggested that maybe I go and interview some people who work with others on these issues, so that I would know that there is diversity in our community. He made appointments for me to meet with my own school principal and with the Anti-Defamation League. So I went and I interviewed some fairly important people in the Jewish community about this issue, and I got some balance in response. And my mother came with me to all of these things.

CT: This is in Montreal.

NK: Yeah. The message of the speech basically remained the same, but I learned that research can temper that blind rage that makes people turn off. It pressured me to open my own mind about why the community was like this. But it was still quite a strong speech, and it was reprinted in the synagogue bulletin. That was my first published article.

CT: That's important.

NK: It was hugely important, and I really enjoyed the research, and I enjoyed interviewing people.

CT: So this was really a breakthrough experience—many identities started to come together, the researcher, the activist, and the writer.

NK: It was all there. And I had a mother who was always being attacked for not being objective, for being part of a movement. She was part of the women's movement, and her films were consciousness-raising. I remember very clearly when she would screen a film, people would cry, people would walk out, there would be discussion—it was that era. And then she'd get completely torn to bits by the mainstream press for not being a real journalist. So I was prepared for a lot of what I think happened. And, yes, she helped me a lot. I also went to a good high school with a good English department. And I got some cool assignments that sent me to the library to do research, earlier, I think, than most people.

CT: Do you remember one or two of them?

NK: I had a couple of really good English teachers who encouraged me and gave me interesting assignments, one of which was to write an essay [on the topic] "America: Policeman to the World." At this point I guess I was fifteen, and my brother, who was more political than me, said, "Why don't you write about Chile?" I said, "OK, how do I do that?" He took me to the library, and I found you could read *Time* and *Newsweek* magazines from 1973, and I read all of these *Time* magazines from 1973, and I couldn't believe it. And so I wrote a paper about the CIA complicity in the coup against [Chilean President Salvador] Allende, and all the trade links, and that was a huge breakthrough.

   And that's because I went to a good school where they were giving us really good, challenging assignments, which woke me up because I had been such a bad student. I was really an erratic student. I would get 90s in English and 3s in math, and they didn't know what to do with me. And then, in a course on religion and ethics, I wrote an essay [entitled] "Religion: Opiate of the Masses," and I went to the library again, and this was my second really intense library experience. I didn't see it as anything related to my family, but I guess it was. I just found it a very persuasive argument that religion was the greatest deterrent to social change. And I wrote an extremely forceful essay arguing this to my teacher, a priest, and he gave me a 96. Maybe it was a crisis point in his own development.

CT: You're talking very precisely about the seduction of research and how satisfying and gratifying that can be. Part of the process, also, is developing a writing style that is appealing, compelling, finding or inventing phrases that are also gratifying to you, so that writing is not just drudgery but a source of some gratification. How did that come about?

NK: Well, as I said, I was always interested in writing. I saw my-self as a writer before I saw myself as a journalist, and writing for my student newspaper was just a way of writing. In high school I was editor of our poetry journal. But then I started writing about politics, and that was that. But it has always been about reconciling myself to the fact that I do share the values I grew up with. All the writing that I did leading up to *No Logo* was always about trying to reconcile this central tension of being drawn to pop culture and the world that we actually live in. And it meant trying to let go of the kind of moraliz-ing, read-this-because-it's-good-for-you that permeates so much of left literature and left culture. I had such a central conflict in my own life, having, like, the granola parents and not re-jecting their politics—but rejecting the lifestyle and the self-righteousness, and rejecting just the aesthetics of it, you know? [*Laughter.*]

I set this challenge for myself, not consciously, but to find in-tersections, to write at that intersection between the serious and the political and the shiny and the pop culture, because I be-lieve that's the way in, certainly for my generation. And I knew because I was in touch with my own revulsion at leftist aesthet-ics, that I couldn't live with myself if I just created more dreary pamphlets.

CT: [*Laughter.*] All right—

NK: If I could just say, I really do feel that a great many ideas are not taken seriously because they are presented with that self-righteousness. There's a sense that you don't have to make the writing good, you don't have to make the design good, because the argument is so important, and you're so right, you know, that you shouldn't even have to try to persuade or entice or se-duce. To me, it's just the exact opposite. It's exactly because it's important and right, that you need to use every tool in your ar-senal to make it appealing, accessible, personal, timely. Just the idea that you can repeat yourself for 100 years, because you're right and Marx said it—to me, that's crazy and also incredibly self-defeating and self-sabotaging on the part of many, many left intellectualist writers.

CT: But somewhere you developed this appealing style.

NK: I seem to know it intuitively, because I was aware of my inner need to reject the politics that I grew up with—the culture that I grew up with—and to try to reconcile all that with what I was drawn to. You know, my mother made films about pornogra-phy, right, and I'm pretty much in touch with what I believe is a kind of a discourse that tries to make an argument that is right but leaves no space for people's desires.

CT: Let me get specific about your writing "arsenal." There's a couple of phrases that I've marked, almost at random. For instance, you refer to activists subjecting McDonald's to the "corporate equivalent of a colonoscopy." That is hilarious, vivid, accessible, charming, all at once. It brings this medical term crashing into the corporate world. It's got a lot of verve. It's not just for shock value, but finding the word that would stand up to the semantic scrutiny. Where does that skill come from?

NK: [*Chuckles.*] At first I didn't have that specific word. My uncle is a doctor—he's a cardiologist—and I remember asking, What is the most disgusting, most invasive procedure?

I think a lot of this kind of word choice—maybe this is true of Barbara [Ehrenreich] as well because she spent a lot of time writing columns—but for me the biggest influence, the people who made me want to write in newspapers were Barbara and Molly Ivins. I read Ivins because my parents had a subscription to *The Progressive* and to *Mother Jones*, and I would read her columns. I think that made me really interested in the format of the column, because in a column every word counts and you need your punch lines. And you need to use humor, and the dictates of column writing are: you have to grab the reader, you have to give them a couple of good lines and a couple of laughs.

When I started out to write *No Logo*, I was looking at all of those books on economics and on culture, and I felt really strongly those books needed a good dose of column writing. Though my problem with *No Logo* in the first draft was that it was too much like column writing. There were too many lines like "corporate colonoscopy." And my editor said, you know it's one thing to be smart-assed in an 800-word column, but it's another thing to—She wrote a note to me, "Remember that they know that they have a fearsome 400 more pages left with you."

CT: The fearsome 400.

NK: That's a good guideline. And so she really taught me, my editor Louise Dennys really taught me, that a book shouldn't be like one long column, and that you have to use those lines sparingly. But it was definitely the discipline of column writing that gave me a sense of the zinger.

CT: Time-released zinger.

NK: —sarcasm.

CT: Let's backtrack a little bit. How did you get into column writing? How did that evolve? Or happen?

NK: A lot of the writers who I loved most, particularly women writers, were having fun with the genre—like Ivins and Ann Powers
in the *Village Voice*, and Barbara Ehrenreich, and bell hooks.
These were the people I was reading in university. I just
thought that there were a lot of women who were mastering it.
It seemed like a lot more fun than reporting, and a lot more
space to have your personality come through, and I was never
really interested in being a reporter.

So as soon as I got to university [The University of Toronto],
I started writing for the campus newspaper, but as an activist.
So we were involved in some campaigns around the issue of
class size: that we were at an education factory, with each student one of a thousand students per class. I was writing about
women's issues, about campus safety and date rape. There was
never a separation between the issues that I cared the most passionately about and what I wrote. In my second year, I became
editor of my college newspaper, and by my fourth year I was
editor-in-chief of the university newspaper, which is called the
Varsity. Because it's such a big school, it's really a big job, a
25,000-circulation newspaper, which comes out once a week. It
was a big responsibility, a full-time job. So I dropped out of university. The problem was, I spent my fourth year editing the
newspaper.

CT: Yes, any university student heavily into drama, or sports, or the
newspaper—it's a double life, and something has to give.

NK: [*Nods.*] What I liked about journalism, and I think this is true
for the way my mind works, and maybe it had to do with growing up in these [19]70s child-raising experiments—but I had
trouble with the idea that you ought to learn something just because someone tells you to. If something emerged out of my
own curiosity, then I could learn anything to get to what I
needed. I had to teach myself a huge amount of economics to
write *No Logo*. The reason it took me so long is because I had
this really steep learning curve to climb. But if I know *why* I
need to learn something, I can learn anything. That's what I
found with the campus newspaper. If I'm writing a story to find
out something, then anything between me and that goal that I
have to learn, whether it involves math, whether it involves
other things that have scared me my whole life, I can learn it. If
I know why. If there's a goal. But if it's just because somebody
says, Read this because I say so, I would just naturally rebel.

CT: You've given me a lot of time here, but I want to ask you one
question out of *No Logo*. You talk about timeliness of a message,

how sometimes activists are battering their heads against the wall of an issue, and the media doesn't respond, and the public isn't interested, and then comes this moment of interest, some breakthrough. Eric Schlosser, in fact, told me he thought that if he'd written *Fast Food Nation* ten years ago, it wouldn't have made any impact.

NK: Absolutely. In a sense, it's your timing as well. That people are finally ready to see the underside of the economic boom.

CT: That's right. I've learned that it was true a century ago too. Upton Sinclair's *The Jungle* is usually credited with sparking public interest in food, drug, and beverage safety legislation. What I've learned is that there was a twenty-year run-up to that book.

NK: It makes a lot of sense.

CT: It does. And when I mentioned this to Schlosser, he said that accounts for the reception of the book as an anti-food contamination book, rather than a book equally concerned with working conditions. There was no run-up, no prep in relation to human conditions in the workplace. So, fast-forward to now. *No Logo* gets to capitalize on its moment. But it would not be an international best-seller if it weren't a terrific book. I mean it wouldn't be, you wouldn't be, increasingly a household word if this book weren't really well done.

NK: I hope that's true.

CT: Oh, I know it's true. There's no question.

NK: Timing had a huge amount to do with it. I never pretended that the book was saying things that no one had ever said before. I think that what's new in *No Logo* has to do with the connection and feelings, and also providing an entry point for people who are not ready to read books about the world economy in the abstract. But if it can be related to youth culture, it can find an entry point.

CT: Do you think (this is about the message of your book) that—you imply this but you don't really say it explicitly—given the extent of job loss in the United States, do you think that in part the readiness to absorb your book has something to do with affluent Americans sensing at the edges of their vision that the so-called Third World conditions are not unrelated to what's happening in the U.S., i.e., increasingly unstable jobs and the threat of serious economic problems? Is there some way in which there's a mirroring effect going on?

NK: I do think so, and I think that particularly for young people that is something taken for granted because they've never had the steady jobs. And I think a lot of barriers have fallen that kept the previous generation from being able to see conditions else-where and instead to see everything through a protectionist lens.

CT: Maybe you saw the special "Working" section in the *New York Times* a couple of days ago. Eighty-six percent of the people they polled, in all walks of job life, said that for job protection, if they could join a union, they would join one.

NK: I think that we are in one of these moments, and I think, frankly that the timing for *No Logo* [in 1999] in the U.S. wasn't good. I think this is a better time to be making these arguments. I certainly found that elsewhere in the world, there was much much greater receptivity to my arguments than in the United States.

When *No Logo* came out, I think that the U.S. was still com-pletely drunk on the [1990s] boom, and it was almost like talk-ing about death at a wedding to say that things weren't going so well. It would seem kind of impolite and strange, and I saw a shift just from releasing this new book, *Fences and Windows*, in the U.S. versus what it was like when we first came out with *No Logo*. It was a huge uphill battle. I felt vaguely ridiculous even talking about poor working conditions in the U.S. in the year 1999. In any kind of mainstream forum, it felt ridiculous.

That wasn't true in activist circles. People were interested in talking about Seattle. They were interested in talking about the global movement. I think that in countries that still have a stronger labor culture, for instance, Italy, there's a national dis-cussion going on about the casualization of labor and what it means. There you have general strikes about an issue that only appears to affect a tiny sector of the population because people understand that the issue also affects them in a fundamental way.

In the U.S. and even here in Canada, it's so easy to compart-mentalize. Well, that *only* affects garbage workers. That *only* affects teachers. That *only* affects nurses. We in the U.S. and Canada never really have that broader understanding of societal impact, except with the UPS strike, where there was, Wait a minute, this is about part-time America. That was a very rare moment. It's so hard to sustain those moments in the U.S. because the media is such a disaster.

CT: Our media is endangering our public by trivializing some issues and failing to report others. Also the individualist ethos streaks through our culture and sometimes is a major stumbling block to constructive social action. A colleague of mine at Vanderbilt calls it narcissism.

NK: I think we see these moments where there is a real desire to look past that, but they seem to disappear because the momentum needed to build it is actively suppressed. You can start to feel vaguely absurd. What does it mean to have a best-selling book about branding, fast-food culture, minimum-wage jobs? You sell a lot of books, you go to lots of auditoriums where people agree with you, and there are protests, there are consciousness-raisings. We are living in times where we keep winning the argument and we're losing all the wars. Right? So what does it mean to win an argument?

CT: I like to think that we are still in the prep-school phase and that the drumbeat has to be heard more fully throughout the middle class. *No Logo*, as you say, it could well have been just slightly mistimed in its publication release. *Nickel and Dimed* and *Fast Food Nation* are being read by book clubs all around the United States. This is a phase of public education.

NK: I'm not belittling the impact of the books, but we can't talk about them without acknowledging the crisis that we're facing in our democracy and with our media. Protests of 300,000 people are being ignored or invisibilized.

CT: In the United States, the federal government was equally bad at the turn of the twentieth century. The Senate was a cabal run by the monopolistic trusts. What is different is the media. *McClure's Magazine* grabbed the middle-class, affluent voting public. We don't have that now. And the media, I think, is the most worrisome part.

NK: Democracy so weak and our media so conflicted.

As a writer, as Klein's conversation shows, she strongly rejects the role of preacher, public scold, or "dreary" pamphleteer whom she associates with the traditional political left. No "granola" life for her, nor for her readers. She deliberately writes, as she puts it, "at that intersection between the serious and the political and the shiny and the pop culture." As a newspaper columnist, moreover, she's learned to dispense a couple of laughs in each outing, often through wordplay. Her *No Logo* narrative, in Klein's own terms, owes its readers conviviality and high spirits even as it serves up hard facts.

As the daughter and granddaughter in a "very political family" engaged in 1960s-era peace and disarmament activism, Naomi Klein suggests a familial interest in the various activist initiatives discussed in *No Logo*. On day trips, she "shadows" several "culture jammers" and "adbusters" who have modified big-brand billboards in a backlash against the megabrand ubiquity and the chains' dictation of cultural norms. Self-identified as an activist (accepting the family mantle),

Klein locates numerous resistance projects around the issues central to *No Logo*. She discusses the anti-sweatshop movement, which is active on hundreds of college and university campuses (and features the United Students Against Sweatshops and two cognate organizations, the Worker Rights Consortium and the Fair Labor Organization, the latter begun by Nike's Phil Knight in response to protests against Nike's practices).

Readers of *No Logo* learn also of the reclaim-the-streets movement, which stages acts of civil disobedience in street festivals occurring seemingly spontaneously (actually, with careful planning). "Rather than filling the space left by commerce with advertising parodies, the RTSers attempt to fill it with an alternative vision of what society might look like in the absence of commercial control" (313). Readers learn, in addition, of the union organizing occurring globally as factory workers learn the extent of their exploitation. The Internet, *No Logo* shows, has linked activists worldwide and shredded the information barrier between Global South producers and consumers in the West. It is crucial that Klein document these resistance movements, for they are the active oppositional force for social change in the civic melodrama.

Klein's tone stops just short of flippant. We've heard this in her vocabulary: the seemingly "flaky" marketers, the consumer "serfs under feudal landlords" the ironizing of the business, which proves that a "multinational chain can be an outspoken and controversial player, even while making millions on bubble bath and body lotion" (113).

No Logo freshens vernacular terms and clichés, and it interweaves pop culture with unusual juxtapositionings—as we saw with Klein's reference to the London McDonald's trial as a "corporate colonoscopy." The Tommy Hilfiger logo is "full-frontal branding," while "Nike, king of the superbrands, is like an inflated Pac-Man, so driven to consume it does so not out of malice but out of jaw-clenching reflex" (29, 56). Corporate cultures are "so tight and cloistered they appear to be a cross between a fraternity house, religious cult and sanitarium" (16). Today's standards are "logomaniacal" (15). Ours is the "Age of the Brandasaurus" (59). (Restraint on my part is in order here, lest piled-up examples make *No Logo* seem like nonstop wisecracks, which we heard Klein say she rationed carefully over the 446-page text.) But *No Logo*, true to civic melodrama, reaches for full expressivity. "The desire to express seems a fundamental characteristic of the melodramatic mode." The narrative reaches to "states of being beyond the immediate context of the narrative . . . to charge it with intenser significances, . . . to go beyond the surface of the real to the truer, hidden reality" (Brooks, *Melodramatic Imagination*, 2, 4).

Klein's, in fact, is the very wit that could be found in the precincts of

ad agencies and marketing firms. Her narrative voice critiques branding from *within* the sensibility of its own culture. She admits this, arguing that the acceptance of important ideas requires presentation that
is "appealing, accessible, personal, timely." Packaging is crucial for the
message, and the more important the message, the more persuasive,
enticing, and seductive its format must be. Anything less risks self-
defeat and self-sabotage.

Klein claims credentials from the branded world. In ironic self-
mockery she recounts her own years in logowear ("I was in Grade 4
when skintight designer jeans were the be-all and end-all, and my
friends and I spent a lot of time checking out each other's butt for logos" [27]). Later, she was "one of those students who took a while to
wake up to the slow branding of university life," immersed instead in
"a loosely defined set of grievances lodged against the media, the curriculum, and the English language." Caustically, she remarks that
"finding out what was going on in the boardrooms and labs would
have required a lot of legwork, and, frankly, we were busy" (107).

This self-deprecation and insider identity are crucial to Klein's authority and her companionable relationship with readers. *No Logo* lets
us picture Klein herself at the ad agency table in a brainstorming ses-
sion on behalf of a big-brand client. What James Phelan says of the
narrator of Thackeray's acidic *Vanity Fair* applies to Klein, that she "is
someone who knows and feels comfortable in the circuit of that class"
(*Narrative as Rhetoric* 51). Klein's voice, when compared to the first-
generation muckrakers', most closely approximates Lincoln Steffens's.
He, too, cracked in deadly serious flippancy: "It is idiotic, this devotion to a machine that is used to take our sovereignty from us" (*Shame
of the Cities* 9). No matter that Klein has not read Steffens or his cohort;
she exposes big-brand politics as he had the cities' and states' graft. As
Steffens consorted with pols and businessmen, Klein is pointedly in
and of the culture she critiques. Its savvy is hers, and she has grown
up in its historical moment. Throughout *No Logo*, Klein ironizes her
past—childhood, school days, teens, and undergraduate years—as
prelude to the global command of *No Logo*. At one time a devotee of
the branded world, Klein flees that faux Eden with its sweatshop underground and turns prosecutor.

Klein is not nostalgic. "There is little point, in this stage of our sponsored history," she says, "in pining for either a mythic brand-free past
or some commercial-free future" (39). The future to which *No Logo* is
committed is globally democratic, the route to it a deconstruction of
empire in its contemporary corporate practices.

* * *

Laurie Garrett, *Betrayal of Trust: The Collapse of Global Public Health*

> *It is a measure of just how serious disease specialists view an epidemic of neglect sweeping US hospitals—the failure by doctors, nurses, and other health-care workers to remove bacteria from their hands.*

—Boston Globe, *October 1, 2002*

> *Having failed to prevent enormous human suffering already experienced in Africa, the international community has the opportunity to support India's efforts to stem its AIDS crisis before it's too late.*

—*Bill Gates,* New York Times, *November 9, 2002*

> *The U.S. Centers for Disease Control and Prevention, as expected, tightened its definition of severe acute respiratory syndrome. . . . The U.S. has the sixth-largest number of cases among the 27 countries and territories reporting SARS. Using suspected cases, it had ranked third, behind China and Hong Kong. The CDC said it will now track and report both suspected and probable causes of the disease.*

—Wall Street Journal, *April 2003*

> *U.S. Intelligence officials believe that four countries besides the U.S. possess stockpiles of the small pox virus. . . . The Central Intelligence Agency conclude[s] that Iraq, Russia, France, and North Korea are likely to possess stocks of smallpox.*

—Wall Street Journal, *November 6, 2002*

> *Nearly 800 people sought help at hospitals in four southwest Russian provinces by late today after sanitation problems at a regional milk-processing factory apparently set off an outbreak of bacterial dysentery.*

—New York Times, *November 8, 2002*

A dysentery outbreak in Russia, the failure of hospital healthcare workers to wash their hands, an announced initiative to increase AIDS-prevention strategies in India, a disclosure that four nations are stockpiling a deadly virus, a new definition of a syndrome known as SARS (severe acute respiratory syndrome)—these seem like separable topics, linked solely under the most general purview of health. Laurie Garrett, however, unites these and a formidable range of related health-care topics in *Betrayal of Trust: The Collapse of Global Public Health* (2000). Garrett's book spans the globe in an era when, in the U.S. school curriculum, the subject of geography is at best a distant memory.

Garrett teaches readers, nonetheless, a sobering geography lesson

12. Laurie Garrett. Courtesy The Lavin Agency.

for a planet that has shrunk in size by international shipping and air travel, a planet of increasing human interdependence in which a microbial outbreak in a village thousands of miles away from major population centers poses almost immediate lethal risk to huge numbers of people distant continents away. Garrett also brings the dreadful sociopolitics—or Realpolitik—of weaponized microbes into a discussion of the global "collapse" of public health and the public's new vulnerability to attack by hostile nations or terrorist groups. *Betrayal of Trust*, like *No Logo*, strives to show its readers the necessity of thinking globally. The modern de facto linkage of disparate regions of the Earth requires, Garrett argues, global neighborly attitudes and efficient public-health systems functioning in the interest of sheer human survival.

Betrayal of Trust is a sequel of sorts to Garrett's earlier *The Coming Plague: Newly Emerging Diseases in a World Out of Balance* (1994), which revealed conditions favorable to disease outbreaks and their spread: the worldwide overuse of antibiotics, contaminated water, and chronic wars, which displace whole populations and turn them into migrants. Garrett's message in *The Coming Plague* gained currency from the widely publicized Ebola virus outbreaks in Africa, the Hantavirus deaths in the United States, and especially the worldwide plague of HIV/AIDS. Readers of *The Coming Plague*, writes Garrett, "deluged" her with "demands for solutions" to the health crises. This immunologist-turned-science journalist has no set of pat answers, but her diagnosis of the "collapse" of public-health systems worldwide deliberately provides the context for constructive action (3). This muckraker narrative proves that the time for rebuilding public health structures is critical, urgent and probably short.

The Web site for the U.S. Centers for Disease Control and Prevention posts a definition of public health formulated in 1920 by the MIT-educated, soon-to-be president of the American Public Health Association. Charles-Edward Amory Winslow called public health "the science and art of preventing disease and promoting health and efficiency through organized community effort." The irony of public health, as Garrett observes, is that at its most effective, it goes unnoticed by the public: preventable disease does not break out, nor is the public's health measurably impaired or jeopardized. Out of sight, out of mind. A second, definitional problem, according to *Betrayal of Trust*, is the current middle-class misconception of public health as medicine for poor people, a kind of welfare program for those without a health-care plan.

Direct lineage to Garrett from the muckrakers of the first Gilded Age, moreover, seems uncertain. She cites Jacob Riis's *How the Other*

Half Lives for vivid portrayal of " 'Lung Block,' " and she provides horrific tuberculosis statistics for this one New York tenement block occupied by 4,000 people in 1890. Riis, however, is unusual among the muckrakers, because the generation of Ida Tarbell and her colleagues did not expose malfeasance in public-health programs. The pure food and drug legislation spurred by *The Jungle* addressed only one province of public health. The pages of *McClure's* (as of the 1900s *Collier's* or *Cosmopolitan*) are spare of public-health exposés.

And for good reason. As Garrett says, by the turn of the twentieth century, effective U.S. public-health initiatives were well underway. The very sight of lower Manhattan as observed from the Brooklyn Bridge, says Garrett, is a reminder of the high mid-nineteenth-century mortality figures from epidemics of cholera, smallpox, and yellow fever—but also of the scientists already working on rudimentary public-health compilations of those who succumbed during various outbreaks. It was in New York City as "the global trading post" that "at the dawn of the twentieth century bands of sanitarians, germ theory zealots, and progressive political leaders created the world's first public health infrastructure" (2).

The first-generation muckrakers, then, were beneficiaries of decades-long, nineteenth-century public-health activism. Their focus—on governmental corruption, monopoly trusts, labor strife, and so on—could exclude public health because it needed no civic exposure. By the late nineteenth century, Garrett explains, the American middle class had accepted the germ theory of disease, and their germ "phobia" and determination to rid their world of harmful microbes thus "fueled support for grand public health schemes" (206). The middle class, she adds, "was the interest group that would put into practice public measures based on the notion that 'cleanliness is next to Godliness' " (284).

That very slogan was repeated almost daily in households of my childhood, where the room "fresheners" were Clorox and Fels Naptha soap, where spring and fall seasons were marked by top-to-bottom cleaning as disciplined as a military campaign. Back then, my own case of scarlet fever brought a public health "quarantine" sign posted on the front door, and before first-graders of my generation could enroll in school, we were required to show certificates proving our vaccination against smallpox. Back then, too, polio lurked, and the public was warned to avoid crowds. Each summer outing to a public pool started with anguish on aquatic pleasure versus dangers of a disease that sent survivors to wheelchairs, leg braces, or an iron lung.

But word of an older public-health crisis also circulated in my family. In Pittsburgh, my great-aunt Josephine Hepp, a young professional contralto in the 1910s, had sung at the funerals of victims of the

1918–19 global flu pandemic, which killed between twenty and forty million persons worldwide. Aunt Jo's lifelong financial independence was rooted in the lucrative, though life-threatening, songs she sang at the funerals of "Spanish flu" victims all over Pittsburgh.

The example of those flu funerals, I now see, helps to account for the global reach of *Betrayal of Trust* and its urgency. Garrett tutors readers not only in nineteenth- and earlier twentieth-century pandemics but in a pre-national, pre-Columbian "era of profound globalization," the 1300s, when "stowaways" included "fleas, rats, and *yersinia*," the Black Death bacteria, which "within eighteen months was claiming millions of lives all over the Old World" (546). "Wherever globalized trade went," says Garrett, "disease hitchhikers cotraveled, taking their tolls on Incas, Aztecs, Maoris, Polynesians, Russians, Laotions, French, and Moroccans. . . . Even such slow-motion fourteenth-century globalization came at a cost" (546).

Given this, one understands why Garrett's acknowledged forebears were not the first-generation muckrakers largely concerned with conditions inside U.S. national borders. Garrett claims kinship, instead, with Walt Whitman, the American writer who combined global outlook with historical imagination. In *Salut Au Monde!* Whitman wrote of "plague-swarms in Madras, Nankin, Kaubul, Cairo!" (147), but that single line is not Garrett's hook to fellowship. From her Brooklyn home, when not traveling "on some distant continent," Garrett crosses the Brooklyn Bridge on foot at least once daily, and says her "imagination invariably rolls backwards in time, to the mid-nineteenth-century days": "And I can see the great Brooklyn journalist Walt Whitman leaping from ship to ship as he crosses the East River from his *Brooklyn Eagle* offices" (1).

Garrett, as proud journalist, claims kinship with the Whitman who worked as reporter for the Brooklyn *Daily Eagle* (1846–48). Her camaraderie extends beyond investigative journalism to ally with the American Literatus who sets the planetary precedent for the global structuring of *Betrayal of Trust*. Whitman, the "poet of Mannahatta," of "the New World," of individual states ("Ohio, Indiana, Iowa, Wisconsin"), of men and women, "red aborigenes" and the free and enslaved "negro," is also poet of "the vast terraqueous globe given and giving all, / Europe to Asia, Africa join'd, and they to the New World." These lines from *Passage to India* lie at the root of Garrett's project. They insist that whatever the boundaries human beings may impose—whether geophysical or national, racial, gender based, what-have-you—all are superceded by the writer's pan-global mandate (Whitman 15, 17, 48, 416). Whatever demarcations serve to categorize and order human thought and behavior must be abrogated by the writer in the greater interest, literally speaking, of worldliness. Garrett's linkage to Whitman makes this fundamental statement: the whole globe is the writer's domain.

Garrett boasts that she never took a course in writing, but the narrative skills evident in *Betrayal of Trust* are those of the authors of big, sprawling novels: a large, multinational cast of characters, including historical luminaries, past and present public-health officials, politicians and military personnel, hospital patients, ordinary citizens, and street people. The locales shift fast, from Minneapolis to Japan, from Iraq to Atlanta. Flashbacks and fast-forwards must be handled adroitly. For readers' grasp of issues, back stories must be provided, though not at such length that the whole project loses momentum. And *Betrayal of Trust* must never lose sight of its mission—as Garrett would say in our interview, "to take the elements out of very complex human issues and wrap them into a story." These "elements," above all, are public-health facts, numerical and all others.

Like Whitman, Garrett adopts a personalized omniscient point of view. But while *Leaves of Grass* is tagged frequently with "Walt" graffiti, the only "I" in Garrett's project is her get-acquainted "I" in the introduction. The pronoun then disappears, as she insists journalistic ethics dictate that it must. Garrett reports on-site at firsthand from the world's most jeopardized, damaged, dangerous, and toxic places (including nuclear "hot" zones). But readers must seek her out in the surrogate guise of "the visitor." Yes, she confirms in our discussion, she is indeed the "visitor" in 1994 plague-ridden Surat, India, who is described in *Betrayal of Trust* as the lone figure who alights from the train, which is being mobbed by terrified locals desperate to flee their home city. Yes, she is also the "visitor" in post-USSR Russia, where the health-care system is "a vision of despair and disease. . . . spiraling into chaos," the populace in "despair and gloom on a mass scale" as "people came to appreciate that their futures were in the hands of gangsters" and "the gap between rich and poor reached levels not seen since the days of the czars" (123, 165).

This eyewitness "visitor" serves the narrative as the human face of public-health failure throughout the contemporary world. In Russia and Siberia, the "visitor" describes in detail incidents in which she witnesses "the rampant alcoholism . . . fueled by elegant cognac, run-of-the-mill vodka, and, more often, cheap rotgut moonshine." Its victims include the "new" capitalism's triumphant gangsters gulping cognac while terrorizing servers—actually attacking them with forks and knives in an elegant Moscow hotel dining room. They are also the

Siberian jobless former state workers living downwind from high-rise garbage heaps in holes dug in the ground, their spokesman proclaiming to her, "We never, never could imagine that we would end up here" (131–33).

The "visitor," as readers realize, also has in common with Whitman—and the muckrakers—a sharp eye for telling detail. She duly reports, for instance, from the "Alienation Zone" encircling the Chernobyl nuclear power plant, where the April 1986 disaster "ranked as the largest civilian nuclear contamination event in history" (144). Close to the reactor site, she observes the "ghost towns" from which more than one hundred thousand former residents "fled for their lives, never returning to pull the sheets off their clotheslines: eleven years later shreds of fabric flapped in the wind, offering anthropological clues to the lives once lived here" (145–46). Such specifics also vivify the report from the devastated Siberian industrial city of Norilsk, which is rich in coal and sits atop more than one-third of the planet's nickel reserves. Its chimneys "belch out 2,041,000 metric tons of airborne particulates" (155). On landing in a land- and cityscape of "charcoal veneer," "three alarming sensations took hold: a metallic taste in the mouth, . . . a painful burning in the back of the throat, . . . and an almost constant tearing from eyes unused to the grit that quickly collected on eyelashes, crusting on the lids" (154). Garrett describes a Sunday evening public promenade in which families stroll, the adults in mink and sable coats, some walking purebred dogs as they "produce a *crunch, crunch, crunch* cacaphony, treading upon industrial waste. Their fur coats and pets blacken as they go" (155).

Parallel to rampant alcoholism in the former Soviet Union, Garrett reports, are unprecedented levels of tuberculosis and drug addiction. Readers learn that HIV/AIDS has increased along with the *narkomania* among young men such as Artur and Oleg, whom Garrett confirms she accompanied on a nighttime drug foray in Odessa.

Her Odessa episode with the two typifies Garrett's on-site reportage. She first climbs up ten stories of urine-splashed stairs at dusk with the two young men to buy paint remover solvent from a Gypsy, then takes a car ride and walks the cratered alleyways between cinder-block buildings whose walls are punched with "hand-size holes designed for passage of drugs and cash." Here a second Gypsy sells her companions rough opium stems and dried bulbs, after which they retreat to the home of Oleg's widowed mother and grandmother ("Don't worry, Babushka, nothing bad will happen," says Oleg) for the dangerous, flammable chemical process of extracting enough injectable opiate "to get two addicts high" at a cost of "about $10 and three hours of dangerous labor" (206–10). The mothers and babushkas and health-care professionals of Russia, Georgia, and the Ukraine are justifiably distraught with worry, says Garrett, who tallies the critical shortage of medical supplies, treatment protocols, or socioeconomic hope for legions of such young people.

Theirs are futures foreshortened by AIDS, alcohol, suicide, industrial contamination of the environment, and tuberculosis. Garrett-as-visitor—as witness—thus also appears at the bedside of Konstantin, "an emaciated, bedridden thirty-nine-year-old former Soviet soldier" who "lies dying at the Moscow Tuberculosis Research Center" because "drug-resistant TB has invaded his lungs, liver, kidneys, and heart." He represents the region's raging epidemic of tuberculosis, which has spread especially in former Soviet bloc prisons. (Konstantin, an army veteran and former Communist Party member, had been imprisoned for dissidence.) "Despite a bath of warm sunlight spread across his hospital bed Konstantin wears a wool knit cap and two sweaters, lies under layers of blankets, and still shivers. His colorless face and sunken eyes betray Konstantin's peril" (184).

What of the visitor's, Garrett's peril? Emphatically, she says in our interview, Garrett refuses as a journalist to "go underground," mainly so that she's not suspected of spying. Hers is, nonetheless, a form of personal journalism, which carries safety risks. Repeatedly, she puts herself in harm's way not only to get facts but to confirm them through firsthand experience. Garrett demonstrates the investigative methods that the confrere of the *McClure's* group, Mark Sullivan, listed in 1927 as basic to the muckrakers: the lengthy preparation, the firsthand knowledge, the scrutiny of documents, and the discussions "with everybody who had important, first-hand information." Garrett allies with Whitman at the outset of her book, but the methods in evidence throughout *Betrayal of Trust* show its parentage in the first-generation muckraker narratives. The book is a textbook example of the narrative of disclosure.

All Garrett's anecdotes are therefore grounded in fact: that "after the fall of the USSR per capita consumption [of alcohol] jumped by 600 percent," and that adult alcoholism is correlated with "another terrible trend," which is "child abuse and abandonment," resulting in "a massive, orphaned subpopulation that lived by its wits on the streets of the snowy nation. . . . the male alcohol poisoning death rate in Russia was about 200 times that of the United States" (136, 167, 138). The text states that following the Chernobyl accident, the incidence of thyroid cancer in children "was by 1998 52 times higher than it was before the accident" and that "the incidence in Belarus, which bore the brunt of the fallout, was 113 times above its 1986 level" (149). In addition to the airborne particulates from Norilsk, Garrett writes, "the area's mining and processing operation produced 28 million tons of solid waste, at least 10 million of which was toxic by Russian government standards. . . . Though precise, analyzed statistics were hard to come by, it was clear that the pervasive pollution was linked to internationally high rates of miscarriage, lung cancers, various forms of chronic respiratory diseases" (155).

The "Biowar" section of *Betrayal of Trust* circles the narrative back from the Cold War, in some ways showing the two superpowers as mirrored paranoids. (This section is especially pointed in the aftermath of the 2001 anthrax attacks in the United States.) As the United States strove to weaponize microbes, so did the USSR. Garrett drops "visitor" in favor of "this reporter" to describe the first entrance of a U.S. journalist into VECTOR, the former USSR's Biopreparat, a top-secret Siberian "complex of a hundred large concrete-and-steel buildings, surrounded by an eight-foot-tall concrete wall" and three rows of "wires that once electrocuted unwanted guests" (505). Now, in 1996, "the USSR's premier virus weapon facility, had a seedy, has-been look to it," with cracked sidewalks and broken windows, the Russian soldiers assigned to guard wearing "tattered uniforms" (505). Some fifty thousand scientists and technicians had worked here to develop and weaponize "Ebola, Lassa, smallpox, monkeypox, tick-borne encephalitis, killer influenza strains, Marburg, HIV, hepatitis A, B, C, and E, Japanese encephalitis, and dozens of other human killer viruses" (505). Says Garrett, "And there were dozens of different strains of smallpox—140 of them were natural, wild strains. Some were hand-crafted by the bioengineers of VECTOR, giving them greater powers of infectivity, virulence, transmissibility" (505).

Estimates are, says Garrett, that "some seventy thousand scientists and technicians were employed in [Soviet biowar programs] before 1992. But by 1997 most were no longer to be found toiling in the laboratories, bioweapons factories, or test sites" (507). The haunting, unanswerable question: "Where did they go?"

A science writer for *Newsday* since 1988, Laurie Garrett has won all the major prizes in journalism—the Pulitzer Prize, the George C. Polk Award, and the George Foster Peabody Broadcasting Award. She has been honored three times by the Overseas Press Club of America and has contributed to *Esquire*, *Vanity Fair*, the *Los Angeles Times*, and *Foreign Affairs*. She lectures widely to professional groups and to university and college audiences, and her book *The Coming Plague* was a national best-seller in 1995. This interview took place on September 13, 2002, in New York City.

INTERVIEW WITH LAURIE GARRETT

CT: You've been savaged, you say, by the British reviewers for com-mitting the "sin" of narrative in what they believe ought to be straightforward exposition?

LG: Yeah. In the review of *The Coming Plague*, a couple of reviewers— I think one was the *Financial Times* or the London *Times*—trashed *The Coming Plague* for having a penchant for inserting narra-tive. I thought that was very amusing. In the American reviews, it's the narrative that keeps the reviewer from seeing it as a pedantic argument, and instead pulls them in so that they buy the argument along the way.

CT: But you're telling stories. This requires a high level of writing skill and narrative skill. Let's go to your bio. I know you're a multigenerational Los Angelino. You studied science at the University of California, Santa Cruz. Then you went to Berke-ley for graduate studies. At some point you began working for radio station KPFA. As far as I can see, you weren't a writer.

LG: I never studied writing in my life. My mother was a writer.

CT: Talk about that, please.

LG: My mother went to UCLA in the mid-1930s and became a writer for women's fashion magazines.

CT: —a world possible for a woman at that time.

LG: She became the West Coast editor of *Mademoiselle*, which in those days was a very big magazine, huge. So without going into the whole sort of *Pentimento* story, à la Lillian Hellman, she had a similar thing. Her roommate from UCLA was Hungarian and had gone back to Hungary, and then in [19]38 sent her a cable, "Come quickly. I need your help." So she wrangled an assign-ment from *Mademoiselle* to go handle the launch of—I guess it was the spring fashions in Paris, and then ended up taking her friend out of Hungary, and then covering Germany in [19]39 during the blitz.

CT: So she stayed over there and kept—

LG: Until American females were ordered to return to America. And then the steamship she was supposed to be on was bombed, and they actually ran her obituary in *Mademoiselle*, but it turned out she had changed ships. When she came back, she did the classic American female thing of the period. She got married, had kids, and stopped her entire career.

Years later, after four children, she started struggling to get back into her writing again, and was really determined. She wrote for things like *Photoplay* because we lived in L.A. And then she wrote screenplays, and for television she wrote for *Gunsmoke* and *Wyatt Earp*.

CT: So you're growing up in this milieu. You're a little kid and you're watching your mother write, and you're sort of hanging around, and you learn that she's not just typing, she's creating.

LG: What I learned is that it's really hard. I'd see her writing and throwing things away, and writing and scribbling, and just tearing it up and throwing it out. I also learned that even when you think it's done, nobody buys it. So, I had a really honest sense of that.

And then I'm the third of four kids, and there was a big gap between the first two kids and us, and so my siblings were considerably older than I, and they were constantly telling me to read things and write things that I never would have been doing in school.

CT: What kind of things? Does this include novels?

LG: I remember distinctly the experience of reading *Manchild in the Promised Land*. I was eleven years old. And then when I was in either junior high or high school, [Eldridge Cleaver's] *Soul on Ice* came out. Meanwhile, my older brother had gone to Stanford and was in political theory, so he made me read *Das Kapital*.

CT: The older kids were your tutors.

LG: Yeah, and then meanwhile my mother was absolutely fanatical about literature, and she had very good relations with the History department at Occidental College, and she did history feature writing in the *L.A. Times* in their old Sunday magazine called *West*. And she would take something current about that time in the news and tell the story of the same thing 100 years ago in Los Angeles. And, of course, to Los Angelinos, it was a big deal because most Los Angelinos have no sense of the history of the place. They just think that one day there was Hollywood and before then there was nothing. And she was always writing poems about L.A.'s Union Hotel. Billy the Kid had a shoot-out at that hotel.

CT: So she was bringing the history to the present.

LG: She was a very good storyteller. Let me look back for a minute. Verbally, she told me stories. My bedtime stories as a small child—I don't remember her ever reading a children's book to me. What I remember is: "Mommy, Mommy, tell me about the time the Nazis almost trapped you in Berlin."

CT: And that must have given you, if not a global perspective, a perspective beyond the borders of the U.S.

LG: Oh, yes. Given that my parents were Republicans and they were in Pasadena, a suburban community, we were a remarkably worldly and political family. All of my siblings have ended up in careers that require a lot of writing and a lot of traveling. One of the family rituals contributing to this was Sunday dinners, when we all ate together, and everybody was supposed to be good on any topic. So my little brother, who was six years old, if he wanted to say, "I like Eisenhower because—," we all had to listen to why he liked Eisenhower. In the process, we learned a lot of discipline on how you construct an argument, how you set forth your position. If anybody tried to BS, one of the siblings would definitely get you.

CT: So there's was a combination both of stories and argumentation, and of course that's the crucial double component in nonfiction investigative writing.

LG: [*Nods.*] The other thing is, although I never ever took a writing class, I had a fantastic English program in high school, when I was privileged to be in the Honors Club. I mean, when I think about the quality of the writing, I still sometimes hear certain high-school teachers say to me when I start to write: "Laurie, Laurie: do this."

I grew up in the days when you diagrammed sentences.

CT: I did too.

LG: I actually think it was a good thing. But I also learned a lot from radio broadcasting. Whenever you do broadcast documentaries, you are telling a story. You've got to have an incredible amount of story, and you try to use characters whom you tape very, very effectively. That definitely helped me.

Frankly, when I came to *Newsday*, I was terrified because I was used to writing broadcast material, and there were ways in which I approached sentence structure that were, frankly, agrammatical, but perfect for broadcasting. Because for broadcasting, you can sound like you're sitting there in the living room, telling a story. Your listener will be there with you. Your tone shouldn't sound like you're reading a text. I think the radio work helped me in a strange way when I came to the newspaper, because I ended up having acquired a style exactly as in conversation, and I knew how to take the elements out of very complex human issues and wrap them into a story.

CT: And how did newspaper reporting affect your writing?

LG: You know, it's funny, at the time I came to *Newsday*, we had both New York *Newsday*, and *Newsday* on Long Island, and they were almost like two separate warring entities, and I was one of only two or three reporters who went back and forth between the two, which is extremely difficult politically. And the editor-in-chief of the New York edition was a guy named Don, and he was very classically New "Yawk," "What's up?" "Put some tits on the cover—it'll sell." One day I said to him, "I'm trying to find my voice on this paper because I don't really know who I'm writing for." And he completely misunderstood my whole point, but ended up saying something useful anyway, and he said, "Short, declarative sentences. That's all we want, just short, declarative sentences."

CT: Well, you have a few of those. You have those one-line paragraphs that are really zingers, and they are very carefully chosen for high impact.

LG: They are. When they work, they work, but when they don't, it's embarrassing.

CT: They're sparingly used, and therefore, you no doubt consider placement very carefully. Maybe "Don" helped, and the terrific high-school teacher, and family life. But to go back—you went off to Santa Cruz to study science?

LG: My mother died of cancer when I was nineteen. She reached out to me with a bony hand and said, "Find a cure for cancer so no one else ever has to go through this." So I had a small assignment in science. I studied biology so I could cure cancer, and that was my humble goal. And then I ended up going to grad. school in immunology. As for learning to write, when I teach J-school [journalism] classes, I tell the students—

CT: Columbia?

LG: Yeah, but I've taught at Berkeley as well, and I do a lot of visiting lectureships at various universities around the country. I always tell the students that the best way to learn to write is to become mature, when you can put your ego on the backburner and accept every damn criticism and not get defensive about it.

I'm not speaking about a book editor here. When I say, "Look at your editors," I'm talking about writing every day. Before you ever even get to writing a book, you better have had years of being torn apart daily, and I also, of course, think that you have to write every single day. Writing has to be something that is as basic to you as walking and breathing. It just has to be something that pours from you, and that if you go a couple of days without doing it, you anxiously miss it. It's upsetting not to write.

I mean, it's interesting, when 9/11 happened, my first instincts were to run—first, for cover, being in the middle of it in New York City. But then to run to the computer and file to a listserv of friends and associates in New York. If you're serious about writing, it's hard to do better than to go and work at a newspaper, because every single day, an editor—and it might be a different person every day—is going to say to you, "What did you mean by this sentence? I don't understand this. Don't you think it would make more sense if this came before that instead of the order you have it in?"

CT: Let me ask about a technique in *Betrayal of Trust*. You appear in the introduction but then disappear further on. The reader makes your acquaintance as journalist, but then you vanish.

LG: For a couple of reasons. I personally abhor most first-person journalism. I just find it egomaniacal and offensive. Secondly, I find that by taking this sort of vague character who stands for myself, the reader can better imagine themselves in this situation, or in that scene.

CT: Years ago, John Barth said to me, "Never tell more than three-quarters of your story." And that's what he was talking about— the reader having space to enter into it.

LG: I would agree completely.

CT: So that was a conscious decision.

LG: Yes, but often it's hard structurally to explain how I knew these things without having been there. How do I explain it to the reader in an honest way and keep myself out of the episode?

   But I have never indulged in styles of journalism that I think require that I be present for the reader. For example, I would never ever pay a source to do something, and I would never lie about who I was. I always, always, say that I'm a journalist, even if it means risking being jailed trying to cross a border or what have you. I always feel like, especially as an American—since we're hated in much of the world—I'm better off being com-pletely honest. So I don't end up in jail in [pre-war] Baghdad for espionage. And I feel the same way about my sources. I never try to elicit information by pretending that I'm someone else or denying that I'm doing it as a journalist. So, I don't usu-ally find myself in very many situations where I have to contrive myself into the story, because I've been very straightforward with the people I'm covering from the very beginning.

CT: Do you find at this point that your reputation is a kind of cre-dential or entrée?

LG: Yes, but it's also in the way, because people perform more. I'll give you an example. Back when I was working for NPR, I was much younger, and pretty, and wore my miniskirts, and that kind of thing, and I would show up to interview male scientists.

And in those days my beat was all science, so I'd be astrophysics one day and AIDS the next day. I would show up to do interviews with male scientists, and they would all assume that I was of a lesser intelligence because I was a female. And I could always trap them in the interviews, because they would assume I was too stupid to follow what they were saying. But I would know that so-and-so's research paper contradicts this, and I would wait for the right moment, and then I would pounce. They would completely fall apart and stutter. Literally stutter.

CT: So, you used them in those days.

LG: Yeah, if they're going to be sexist pigs, I'm going to use it against them. I remember one particular Nobel laureate, an astrophysicist at Cal Tech. I was interviewing him, and I suddenly felt his hand going up my skirt, and I said, "Dr. X," with the tape rolling, "would you care to tell the listeners where your left hand is right now?"

CT: Now you're better known and you can't do that. You're Laurie Garrett.

LG: The problem now is that people try to show off, and the interview almost always starts with them trying to win me to their position right from the very beginning. The other thing, I'm getting older, so as a woman I'm not attractive to them nowadays. So now it's about a contest of wills.

A lot of female scientists try immediately to win me over in that sort of girl-girl thing: "I love those shoes." I hate it when I walk in to interview an otherwise extremely intelligent woman who's in a position of authority, et cetera, and her first comments have to do with my hair or how I'm dressed. Two guys don't meet each other for the first time and say, "Hey, nice tie" or "I love that haircut. Where'd you get it?" [*Laughter.*]

CT: Let's talk about *Betrayal of Trust.* Do you think the U.S. citizenry is ready to hear your message about public health?

LG: I would say it's just mixed. I think Americans are among the most personally generous people on earth, and they certainly give more on a personal level than, say, their European counterparts, who basically don't understand the concept of charity.

But politically, Americans are completely off the wall. They have no sense of engagement in the world. When you compare, for example, your average Norwegian or your average Brit or your average Italian and their level of engagement in the world to the Americans', it's quite embarrassing. And I would say that if I have a major area of frustration, it's in trying to get Americans to be willing to read about people other than their own neighbors, and realize that that's part of their world, and they have to expand their sense of world.

CT: To see people of the world as their neighbors.

LG: Well, especially if they are people of color. I mean I've had so many speaking engagements where somebody in the audience says, "Yeah, but that's Africa. What do you expect from the Africans?"

CT: We are not very well helped, are we, by our news media these days. Three BBC guys came to talk to me about two weeks ago, and they expressed shock at the news content in the United States, how dangerous it is for Americans to be so uninformed about what's going on.

LG: They're right. It's all about cost-cutting.

CT: I want to ask about a topic specific to public health. We've been reading a lot about the privatization of water with enormous public-health implications—

LG: [*Nods.*] One of the things I do when I'm giving public lectures is to always request that there be water at the table. I will always hit some juncture where I'm trying to explain the difference between how Americans approach public health and how the rest of the world does. And I'll hold up the little commercial water bottle, and I'll say, "This is really absurd when you think about it. Everybody in this room has already paid with their taxes to have tap water that is adequately purified and is safe for you to drink. And if it's not adequate, you can vote the whole health board out of business. You can do a Freedom of Information Act request and see all the chemical and microbial composition of the drinking water. If you're of the middle class, you worry about your children's health.

But if you're an American, you take an individualistic approach, and instead of insisting on analysis of the public tap water, you spend three times drop for drop more than it would cost to put unleaded gasoline in your car to buy this water. And where is this water from? Tap water. This happens to be tap water from France or Maine, but it's tap water. And not only that, in order to sell it in bottled form, they've put more chlorine in it, so it's actually got more chlorinated subcompounds than you would get from tap water.

CT: I want to read a paragraph from [p. 201 of] *Betrayal of Trust* and ask about a related issue on the relations between the middle class and upper class and public health. You're talking in this passage about the late 1860s:

This theme of public health—the need for support from a sizeable middle class—would resonate throughout the future history of America. In the absence of a middle class, the rich simply lived separate and unequal lives, maintaining spacious homes along clean, tree-lined boulevards and raising their families through private systems of health, education, and cultural training. That a city might starve, politically and economically, in the absence of the elite's interest and finances seemed of little but occasional Christian concern to them. And the poor lacked the education, money, and skills to choose and run an effective government.

My question is whether increasingly the American middle class, once again in this twenty-first century, has come to identify itself in what you call an individualistic way and have therefore abandoned their citizenly role in the community support for public health that benefits everybody and is vital to the survival of the whole community across lines of class and income. So I'm really asking you, has there been a kind of class Balkanization in America in which this statement you make about the late nineteenth century becomes applicable to the late twentieth and twenty-first centuries, when the word "public" becomes a pejorative term, whether it's school, beach, public health? It's synonymous with riff-raff, and in consequence it guts the broad-based support of the very healthy community activism we need.

LG: Well, there's a bundle there for you.

CT: Yeah.

LG: Well, later in *Betrayal* I talk about the effect of white flight from the cities, and the rise of suburbia. I think that was the first stage. Today, I would say the real problem is—the threat is a global one—it's no longer restricted by the towns or suburbs. Most Americans are middle class. Most Americans have enough financial wherewithal to deal with this on a personal level, though many would argue that since the collapse in the stock market [in 2000], that's less the case today than it was five years ago.

CT: A lot of people have lost jobs. A million people in 2002 between January and August lost their jobs.

LG: That's right, so that, obviously, decreases the size of the middle class, but they still have middle-class values. And it means that, if you look right now at how our administration is dealing with bioterrorism, Secretary Tommy Thompson [of the Department of Health and Human Services] has been mobilized. He is seeking a budget of 5.9 billion dollars for 2003, 1.75 billion which would be for basic research, more than a billion of which would be steered to local level public health. But he has not requested in that budget any significant amount to go to the World Health Organization. Even as Senator Patrick Leahy yesterday says on the floor of the Senate, "Maybe West Nile virus is the result of biological warfare." Even as Leahy says that, you have to ask the question, If you're concerned about the West Nile virus, why weren't some of our resources given to the Sudan and Uganda, and Somalia and Egypt, where the virus is?

So, I think that where we are now is that Americans are the global upper-middle class and upper class. There are six Americans whose combined new wealth in the 1990s exceeded the combined new wealth of the 43 poorest nations. And I think they are the super rich, plus your Bill Gates, your Warren Buffet, your Wal-Mart family. But as you get down the food chain here in the United States, most Americans have, still, a sense of personal economy and of community, which is very much defined by ten or fifteen best friends in the immediate neighborhood. They have not yet become global citizens. In that sense, the Europeans are correct to be very, very critical of us. I would say, however, the Europeans—the charitable donations from Europe—have been sparse.

CT: You say in *Betrayal* that some people think public health is medicine for poor people. The U.S. has been in a period emphasizing rights, gay rights and ethnic group rights, and so forth. Does this work against public health? There was a period in recent years, for instance, when HIV-positive blood donors were not told about their health crises. And there's a lot of protection of certain groups and their rights. Is this working against public-health initiatives?

LG: Yes, of course, it makes it more difficult and a harder job—the ways in which we could just march in and force a whole community to get vaccinated in the 1920s has not been possible in the late twentieth or early twenty-first century. On the other hand, I don't know very many people in public health who are in favor of abrogating civil liberties in order to implement programs. I think it's quite telling that in this city, in 1991 and [19]92, we had a multidrug-resistant tuberculosis epidemic, and the Commissioner of Health had to go to the State Supreme Court to plead for the right to mandate treatment for patients who refused to be treated and who were spreading tuberculosis.

And now with the bioterrorism, we're seeing a whole review of public health with recommendations for implementation. Most cities and states in the United States can no longer impose quarantines, and yet recently since anthrax, all have reviewed their public-health regulations and gone to their state legislatures to get permission to change this, and in most parts of America they have now been changed to some degree. But when I wrote *Betrayal of Trust*, there were hardly any communities in all of the United States where [a] Department of Health commissioner could impose a quarantine.

CT: And so would you say that post–9/11, the urgency of the protection of public health in all kinds of ways has made it easier for or opened a new possibility for a strengthening of public health?

LG: Yes and no. I've written quite a lot about it in *Newsday*. Yes, there's money there, there's political will there for the first time, public health is getting some respect, local and state politicians are clamoring for public health to do its thing. On the other hand, public health is now closer to the police and the FBI than ever before. A lot of programs are getting sacrificed. What you are seeing right now is that a billion dollars has gone into local public-health interests here to bolster their capacity to respond to bioterrorism, but nobody knows, and only a fool could possibly believe, that Congress is going to keep chucking out this kind of money year after year. The further we get away from the 2002 anthrax outbreak, the less likely Congress will be to give this kind of money out. That means that something has to give.

CT: And the expectations are very politically activated right now.

LG: The nation wants public health to be able to say, "You will never die of any of these diseases." And, of course, there is no way they can say that. The people in charge of the Public Health Association—that's exactly what I told them: "You're all thinking about the amount of money you suddenly have, but you know, with that money comes a level of expectations that frequently you can't meet. You just can't. And you'd better tell your politicians you can't meet it. You guys are in dangerous waters right now."

CT: Let me ask you one last question. How do you stay optimistic in the face of some of the most dire predictions of bioterrorism you write about, of mutant microbes loosed upon the world? How do you maintain a level of energized, upbeat, positive sentiments? How do you do that?

LG: Because I have a voice and a venue. I can try to make a difference. I can draw attention to the facts that I think the public and those in power need to know, and I have seen them read these things, and I have seen resulting events that are positive.

The American middle class and upper classes, Garrett argues, historically have been crucial for public health's success, dating from the post–Civil War decades when the first-generation muckrakers were children. She explains, "American public health . . . improve[d] in tandem with the rise of the urban middle class, which paid taxes, supported cleanliness and public education, recognized and abhorred corruption, and, as home owners, had an investment in their cities" (284). "Undertaken at the behest of the wealthy and middle classes" were "projects of enormous scale, particularly water and sewer works, that would profoundly improve communities' health" (206).

Garrett makes a vital point in relation to the anti-immigrant phobia examined earlier in this discussion of the first-generation muckrakers. The nativist revulsion and hostility toward immigrants, says Garrett, sparked a stunning movement. "Because the middle and upper classes were convinced that the poor—particularly immigrants—were the source of all truly terrible microbial scourges, they were willing to pay the price in higher taxes for *biological*, as opposed to *class*, warfare" (207).

Garrett's comment to me about American urban-suburban boundaries no longer being meaningful in terms of public health reemphasizes that "the threat is a global one." Her concluding focus in *Betrayal of Trust* is the threat of biowar by terrorists and/or rogue nations. A lengthy section of the book, however, concerns the public health crisis in the United States. It finds direct correlation between the upsurge in tuberculosis and sexually transmitted diseases to such trends as for-profit medicine, the slashing of public-health budgets from the Reagan presidential years (resulting in the closing of Public Health Service hospitals and termination of the corps of physicians providing health care in the inner cities). In addition, as Garrett (joining Ehrenreich and Schlosser) says, increasingly unaffordable health-care costs have left more than forty-two million Americans without coverage. Yet the middle-class values of social and financial responsibility, Garrett feels, are still in place and able to be tapped for action, perhaps to hatch the Phoenix of public health from a system now in ashes.

*   *   *

Joseph T. Hallinan, *Going Up the River: Travels in a Prison Nation*

This summer, visitors are doing time in an abandoned prison that is taking on new life as a tourist attraction.

—USA Today, *August 9, 2002*

Huntsville, Texas—The Texas electric chair "Old Sparky," where 361 killers met their deaths in the 20th century, got a new home this week with the opening of the new Texas Prison Museum.

> *The outside of the museum is designed to resemble the outside of the nearby prison in Huntsville, complete with guard tower. . . . The new museum . . . was built by prison labor.*
> —USA Today, *November 15, 2002*

> *One in every thirty-two adults in the United States was behind bars or on probation or parole by the end of last year [2001], according to a government report yesterday that found a record 6.6 million people in the nation's correctional system.*
> —Tennessean, *August 26, 2002*

> *"Study Shows Building Prisons Did Not Prevent Repeat Crimes"*
> —Headline, New York Times, *June 3, 2002*

> *"Too Many Convicts"*
> —Economist *cover story on American prisons, August 10–16, 2002*

From August through November 2002, *USA Today* highlighted one of America's newer tourist attractions: a Texas prison museum featuring an electric chair, which, according to the museum director, has "a nostalgic effect on people." In addition, abandoned prisons in California, Pennsylvania, West Virginia, Idaho, and Ohio have reopened as recreational sites offering tours, murder-mystery nights, and gift-shop handcuff jewelry. Visitors were said to be attracted to the old prisons' architectural features, to the possibility of paranormal encounters with convict ghosts, and to personal experience reliving a chapter of American history.

One irony was the tourists' seeming obliviousness to their own citizen-taxpayer support of the late twentieth-century prison boom, which has made America, as one wit puts it, "stir-crazy." These old prisons are opened as theme parks, not penal institutions, but according to an August 2002 report from the Department of Justice, by the end of 2001, one in thirty-two adults in the United States was behind bars, on parole, or on probation—totaling 6.6 million people in the nation's correctional system. "We've come to rely on the criminal justice system as a way of responding to social problems in a way that's unprecedented," said Marc Mauer of The Sentencing Project, a nonprofit agency that conducts research on criminal-justice policy issues (*Tennessean*, August 26, 2002: 7A).

The numerous American social problems played out in the prison system form the basis of Joseph T. Hallinan's *Going Up the River: Travels in a Prison Nation* (2001). Hallinan's book has arrived just as the

13. Joseph T. Hallinan, 2001. Credit Andrew Hollings. Courtesy Random House.

American public reportedly is rethinking its punitive tough-on-crime stance of the 1980s–90s. The American public appetite for incarceration and especially for the death penalty has been reportedly softened as a result, for instance, of initiatives on medical marijuana and the DNA-test-based release of inmates wrongfully convicted of heinous crimes. Even so, says *The Economist*, the United States is "the world's most aggressive jailer," with nearly one of every eight American men convicted of a felony.* Americans' explicit fear of crime yet remains a bedrock demographic principle. Almost daily, local TV news reinforces public fear by offering a ratings-driven diet of violent crime (motto: "If it bleeds, it leads").

Hallinan's muckraker narrative guides readers on a journey into the contemporary U.S. prison system, which has been dubbed the "celling of America" and the "prison-industrial complex." The topic itself risks resistance from middle-class readers for whom prisons are toxic territory—unlike branded products, fast food, low-wage service work, or public health, all topics of Hallinan's muckraker cohorts.

Reviewers' praise for Hallinan's literary skill did not lessen my own initial resistence to *Going Up the River*. As a writer of mystery fiction, I had skipped the chance to tour a Tennessee prison and sit in a Volunteer State chair known as "Old Sparky." Hollywood images of life behind bars were plenty for me, from the poignant *The Shawshank Redemption* to the horrific *American History X*. Like many academic humanists, I had gravitated more to Michel Foucault's ideas on criminalization as social repression than to the issue of prison politics and actual prison conditions in modern America. As a classroom teacher, I'd assigned sections of Foucault's *Discipline and Punish: The Birth of the Prison* but twice declined opportunities to teach in prisons. (Many years ago, facing a California municipal court sentence for unpaid parking tickets, I decided to pay the fine rather than serve a one-night jail sentence, hearing urgency in the judge's statement, "Believe me, Miss, you do not want to spend even one night in jail.") Touring French prisons of the eighteenth century in the pages of Foucault, I too was arguably a prison tourist. Name an assortment of institutions— schools, hospitals, factories—and prison is by far the scariest. Despite pleasant-sounding prison names like Limestone, Pelican Bay, and Wallens Ridge, Hallinan quotes one guard as saying, "If you're not scared, something's wrong with you" (88, 89, 116–19).

But fear of prisons is not to be confused with fear of *Going Up the River*, which argues that America has become a "prison nation." "When I began my travels," Hallinan says, "I had no idea of the amount of money to be made from prisons" (xiv). He professes shock equal to the reader's own when he says that "a single pay phone inside

* According to *The Economist*, the United States incarceration rate from 1925 to 1973 was nearly constant, averaging 110 persons imprisoned for every 100,100 residents. By 2000, however, the rate had quadrupled, to 478. The incarceration rate for drug offenses was 15 inmates per 100,000 in 1980, but had reached 148 by 1996. "The notion of rehabilitating prisoners went out of vogue in the 1970s, when research seemed to show that prison programmes had no effect on recidivism. New research suggests the opposite" (August 10–16, 2002: 25, 26).

a prison could earn its owner $12,000 a year" and that "a warden, if he played his cards right, could make himself a millionaire" (xiv).

These and other such specifics open the fuller dimensions of the "prison nation," which flourishes not only from fear of crime but from politics, economics, and business interests. In part it has flourished from legislative good intentions gone awry. Congressional efforts in the mid-1980s, for instance, meant to eliminate wide disparities in judicial sentencing led to mandatory sentences for various crimes, including five- and ten-year terms for drug-dealing. "As a practical matter," says Hallinan, "the guidelines eliminated disparity. As a practical matter, they also eliminated mercy. No longer was a judge free to follow his conscience" (43). Hamstrung judges, then, henceforth functioned more as clerks, and by 1991, "more than sixty criminal statutes in the federal code contained mandatory criminal penalties," among them a five-year mandatory sentence for selling "just five grams of crack [cocaine], the approximate weight of two pennies" (44–45). Hallinan notes that most crack-cocaine users were white, but "the majority of those prosecuted for selling crack were black." By 1993, seven years after passage of the first drug laws, "blacks accounted for more than 88 percent of all people convicted in federal court of trafficking in crack cocaine." By 1997, the U.S. Department of Justice released a report stating that the odds of a black man serving a prison sentence in the United States were now one in four (45).*

Prisons, Hallinan argues in his exposé, are now a national jobs program. The population of new felons swelled just at the moment when numerous U.S. communities faced economic collapse from the loss of manufacturing plants and the closure of military bases in Pentagon cost-cutting campaigns. A coincidence worthy of the keenest ironies of the most *noir* filmmaker or novelist arose: prisons and prisoners now replaced factories and military bases as a source of jobs and revenue. Convicts meant paychecks. The late twentieth-century boom in prison construction, Hallinan argues, is a corporate business opportunity and a de facto public-works project to create jobs in areas of the United States that have been flattened economically by the shutdown of factories and military bases. "Across the country," Hallinan writes, "I saw communities that had whipped themselves into hard-line attitudes that seemed to justify the big, expensive prisons built in their towns" (xiii).

The typical prison that Hallinan visits is "justified less by the crime it

* For white men, the odds were "4.4 percent, or about one out of every twenty-five. For Hispanic men, the odds were one out of every six" (45).

would prevent than the jobs it would create. The Federal Bureau of Prisons been on a twenty-year 'binge' " (158, 205). *Going Up the River* repeatedly finds economically imperiled communities supporting multimillion-dollar prisons whose major function is job creation. These prisons are the new employers of first resort. Hallinan twists an old Hallmark slogan and a title from Thomas Kinsella: financially, "a federal prison is the gift that keeps on giving. . . . Build it and they will come" (178, 159). For "hard-luck" communities, "building a prison was becoming the small-town equivalent of building a football stadium to attract an NFL team" (166).

This fact-based narrative deliberately allows its readers rest-stops between harrowing visits to prisons in Texas, Oklahoma, Iowa, California, New York, Illinois, Georgia, and Pennsylvania. The vexed history of American penology is here (including such flashpoints as the 1971 Attica, New York, prison riot, when forty-three persons died, thirty-nine of them killed by police and guards who stormed the prison after a five-day hostage stand-off). For the present, we learn, today's prison is a world of punishment without rehabilitation, a site in which minimally trained rural white guards "clash" constantly with "inner city inmates" who are incarcerated hundreds of miles from their families and thus doubly isolated. It is a world where gangs rule, drugs and weapons abound, and inmates are shaken down for money and sex, and sometimes assaulted or murdered ("hit") on orders of gang leaders—or guards (88–89).

It is, moreover, a world of horrendously high-risk overcrowding, and also of isolation and sensory deprivation. In California's Security Housing Unit at Pelican Bay, prisoners in windowless white cells stare through perforated metal doors to other white walls. Over time, many become as psychotic as the antarctic castaway in Edgar Allan Poe's *Narrative of Arthur Gordon Pym*. Hallinan carefully chooses the telling details—the prisons' own lurid "radiant gist." For instance, inmates who fling their own feces are known as "chuckers," but the corrections officers are chuckers too. In cells or pods where sounds ricochet unnervingly, inmates who violate the "code of quiet" are "doused with a cup of 'brew,' " whose ingredients are their own "fermented feces and urine" (119).

These specifics do not serve scatological or prurient interests, nor is *Going Up the River* a grisly follow-the-money tale. The recent American prison boom is a complex story of sociopolitics and economics. "People aren't being imprisoned just so someone can make a buck," Hallinan writes. "It's not that pat." The complexities reported in his investigation are sobering: "The prison industry's economic significance is now so vast that it contributes to a political climate in which being tough on crime is on every lip and in every platform. In many states, private prison companies are now major campaign contributors, as are unions for correctional officers. Crime is big business, and the people who earn their living from it can be expected to protect the status quo" (xiii–xiv).

What is that status quo? Both the narrator and the reader enter a prison-nation "corporate America" wonderland, with AT&T alone estimated to gain $1 billion annually from prisoners' long-distance calls. Proctor & Gamble, meanwhile, sells inmates shampoos, deodorants, and other products, annually exhibiting its wares along with the bulletproof vests and prefab cells on display in the exhibition halls at the American Correctional Association meetings. The prison-industry market, we learn, is "estimated to be worth $37.8 billion a year." As if hearing Steffens's warning that the public won't read figures, Hallinan says this sum is "bigger than major league baseball, bigger than the porn industry" (156).

Big enough, moreover, to privatize, notably as Wackenhut and Corrections Corporation of America, whose much-touted cost savings to the public are dubious, but whose investors and executives have profited handsomely. The advent of prisons-for-profit marks a radical turn in citizens' connections to the criminal justice system. Private prisons sever the relation between the public and the transgressive fellow citizens who are incarcerated to pay their debt to society. The transgressors now become a marketplace commodity, while citizens morph into shareholders eyeing the NYSE prices of their CCA or Wackenhut stock. Careers in civil service become business opportunities. "Former wardens or superintendents who had jumped ship to work in the private sector," says Hallinan, have become the "new, previously unimaginable category of individual: the prison millionaire." This individual, he goes on, marks "a turning point in American penology. Never before had it been possible in this country to become rich by incarcerating other people. Now, it is commonplace" (174). One prison in remote western Virginia is typical, "built not because it was needed but because it was wanted—by politicians who thought it would bring them votes, by voters who hoped it would bring them jobs, and by a corrections establishment that no longer believed in correction" (203–4).

Going Up the River nonetheless resists temptation to configure its audience as stockholders or recreational tourists. Its readers, instead, are to be citizen-witnesses on a fact-finding mission. They encounter a travel book that seemingly reprises a proven narrative genre of the American road trip, from *The Grapes of Wrath* to Kerouac's *On the Road*.

Hallinan's project, however, originates in a tradition preceding the travelogue by centuries. *Going Up the River* traces long ancestry back to Early Modern narratives of exploration into terra incognita. These were the accounts by explorers, diplomats, settlers, traders, naturalists, trappers, and others. At the outset of *Going Up the River*, Hallinan presents a narrative persona who is emphatically unfamiliar with the terrain he is preparing to traverse. He is not a guide but an explorer. In a Texas courtroom of the preface, readers encounter the "I" persona preparing for the voyage: "I sat for a week on hard wooden benches in the courtroom . . . and watched as a skinny young prison guard [who] . . . had been lured to prison by prospects of a good working-class job . . . [made] history. . . . as the first guard in Texas history to be convicted of killing an inmate." The narrator goes on, "I began, there in that courtroom, to understand the power of the prison industry" (xi).

This is the voice of the quester at the beginning of knowledge. His account will produce a shaped consciousness and an ideological position, and, according to Mary Louise Pratt, "the journey and the writing about it [will appear] inseparable." Pratt's reflections on Anglo-European travel narratives of a kind of terra incognita, Africa, in the late eighteenth and early nineteenth centuries are helpful here. In service to European nation-state imperialism of the early nineteenth century, Pratt shows, the genre became depersonalized, producing impersonal knowledge or information—until Henry Stanley (author of *How I Found Livingstone*, 1872) revolted against "detachment and decorum" and presented an exposé of his own brutal behavior amid actual indigenous individuals and groups with their own customs and passions. In the mid-nineteenth century, Livingstone offered, according to Pratt, "elements of the new muckraking journalism" (199–221).

Hallinan, unlike Livingstone, is not enmeshed in the prison empire he exposes. He is not an immersion journalist like Barbara Ehrenreich, nor an undercover poseur, like the anthropological Ted Conover, who got a job as a prison guard in Ossining, New York, and produced the narrative *Newjack: Guarding Sing Sing* (2000). Hallinan, instead, is the explorer as emissary from a land of civility to a barbaric state. His terra incognita is the prison system of an established, decadent empire that has compromised—worse, abandoned—codes and values of civility. It is as if this explorer has discovered a New World high-tech Hell.

Like Livingstone, Hallinan repopulates a depersonalized prison territory into zones of human life and activity. He brings to life actual persons—such as inmate Ralph Estrada, who says of his ultramodern "supermax" cell (which is designed to deprive an inmate of human interaction), "It works your brain, man. If you're not really mind-strong, you're gonna go crazy" (115). Quoting a judge who agrees with the prisoner, Hallinan cites the many, many Ralph Estradas in the penal system.

Or take Alva Mae Groves, sent to prison in her mid-seventies along with two of her children, all convicted of nonviolent drug offenses. Selling lucrative crack cocaine from a rural North Carolina dirt road near her family's ramshackle home, Alva Mae had finally joined America's consumer culture after a lifetime of sub-minimum-wage jobs as restaurant cook, field hand, and live-in nurse taking care of people with " 'old-timer's disease' " (59). Says Hallinan, "It will cost the taxpayers of this country about $2.9 million to imprison Alva Mae and her family" (60). The cash figure supports an earlier statement that "virtually everyone [Hallinan] talked to felt prisons were, on some level, a terrible waste of money. Almost no one, for instance, believed that prisons actually rehabilitated anybody. Not the wardens, . . . not the guards; and not, most especially, the inmates. Even rank-and-file Americans had given up on the idea" (xiv).

Before writing *Going Up the River*, Joseph Hallinan wrote about the criminal-justice system for nearly a decade, first for the *Indianapolis Star* and later as a nationally syndicated reporter for the Newhouse News Service. In 1991, Hallinan and his *Star* colleague Susan M. Headden won the Pulitzer Prize for investigative reporting for their series on medical malpractice in Indiana, and in 1998 Hallinan was a Nieman Fellow at Harvard University. He currently writes for the *Wall Street Journal* and is based in Chicago, where he lives with his wife and son. This interview took place in Chicago on June 14, 2002.

INTERVIEW WITH JOSEPH HALLINAN

CT: How did you get to the plan for a book on prisons? You are probably sick of people asking you, but what's the source? You had written, you said, about prisons for four years in newspapers, right?

JH: And off and on, frankly, for much longer than that.

CT: How did that topic get hold of you so obsessively that you committed yourself to a book?

JH: It's perhaps not a very politically correct tale, but when I was in high school in South Carolina, I was a member of the [Kiwanis-sponsored] Key Club. One of the do-gooder things we did is take a tour of a prison, the old prison in South Carolina, CCI. That's Central Correctional Institution, which closed only a few years ago, and was at that time so old that I think Sherman had kept his horses there during the war. That may be apocryphal. I never checked it out. Nonetheless, it was a horrible institution.

They took us to see the electric chair. I mean this place was a dungeon, just incredible, and a fifteen-year-old, white, suburban kid just didn't see stuff like this.

I remember distinctly walking down one of the gangways, basically between cells on a tiered block, and having the inmates all at the bars yelling at us. All these proper, teenage, white suburban boys went down the hall, and one of the guys said, "White boy, we gonna wanna rape your ass."

And that makes an impression when you're fifteen. You never, ever forget that, which is why they take you on these tours. I think now they're called "Scared Straight." I'm sure some of that is put on for dramatic effect, but that was my first introduction to prisons, and I never, ever, ever forgot it, and it sticks with me today. But that was my first introduction. And then working in Indianapolis, I would go to prison quite a good bit. And jail as well. In Indianapolis [as a reporter for the *Indianapolis Star*], I covered the cops for quite a while, which I actually loved, and often interviewed people in prison. So it wasn't necessarily writing *about* the prison, but I was in prison and jail both. Some people draw a distinction between the two.

CT: Police beat?

JH: That's it.

CT: Well, did you get—I don't suppose "comfortable" is the word—but did the environment seem normalized? Familiar? I guess I'm talking leading up to the kind of fieldwork that you did for *Going Up the River*. You didn't go into this cold. You did the police beat. It took you into scenes of incarceration, but at the same time, you were, I mean, a kind of immigrant in a new land.

JH: That's what journalism is. It's immigration into a new land. It's voyeurism. Call it what you will, but that's the fantastic thing. Where else can you get a chance to see this stuff? You don't. If you're a cop maybe, you get to do it. You get to go into other people's worlds, and ask questions, and people have to tell you answers. So, yeah—definitely an immigrant.

CT: Let's go to your beginnings as a writer. Did you read a lot as a boy?

JH: I started college in South Carolina where I grew up. And for the first part of my college career, I was an economics major and actually still love economics as a way to explain social phenomenon, not as the dry science everybody thinks it is, but as a way of explaining human behavior, which has always fascinated me. But it began to get a little too dry for me, and so I wanted to look for another way to do that, and writing was the way. I transferred to Boston University to study journalism.

CT: Were you encouraged by teachers early in your writing?

JH: In high school, I wrote a lot of short stories. In fact, I was very touched to learn through one of my sisters that after the [1991] Pulitzer had been announced, one of my English teachers back in high school had remembered a paper I had written and re-membered my name. And I had completely forgotten it—but that's another way of saying, yes, I had always written, even in high school.

CT: So you had an ability that you hadn't quite grasped.

JH: I guess not. My mother had always thought I would be a writer. She herself always admired writers, had books in the house. She had just a tremendous respect for the written word. And her fa-ther (my maternal grandfather, first-generation American) dropped out of school, but was a lifelong newspaper reader, *fer-vent* newspaper reader. I mean, read it front to back, obits., everything—very big believer in journalism, and I credit going into newspaper work partly to strong impressions of him read-ing the newspapers. So I guess it was latent, but always there.

CT: Were you a book reader too? On the phone you mentioned Dickens and Orwell.

JH: Somewhat in high school, but really in college. I was fortunate to have a couple of roommates who were big readers, probably a rarity among men. My roommates and one very good friend were good thinkers and good readers, and that was very important.

CT: So at B.U.—let me stop a little and ask you about the journal-ism program in the School of Public Communication. It's now the College of Communication.

JH: Early on I think it's very nuts and bolts, very by-the-books kind of stuff. They teach you the old inverted-pyramid way of writ-ing a news story, building your facts more broadly as you go down, the old five "w's": who, what, when, where, and why, very rudimentary kind of things . . . very vocational in a way. At the basic level, there's no real intellectual content. Only when you start to write and you take higher-level courses, then it's sort of like music, when the notes start to go together and you think, OK, this is beginning to sound like music and not just Chopsticks.

CT: Let me ask you then to reflect on what the trajectory was that got you from what you're just describing. You were certified by B.U.'s journalism program as a working newspaperman, but how did you get beyond the inverted pyramid to *Going Up the River*, which requires literary skills, creating character, adroit narrative handling? What's the trajectory?

JH: If you're half-way intelligent you wear out that inverted pyramid pretty fast. It's always a staple of what you do, but the challenge of repeating it wears off. All the things I read and admired that motivated me to think, "Gee, I'd like to be like that one day" or "I'd love to have a sentence like that one day," thinking of the E. B. Whites, the Joan Didions, the Tom Wolfes, the Dickenses, the Orwells—all of those people that I had read did nonfictional work. I just was looking for a way to take what I had learned and move it closer in their direction.

CT: What attracts you about nonfiction?

JH: It's true. I almost pause before I say that because it sounds so trite. But there is just something absolutely compelling, I think, about knowing, as it says on TV, "it's from a true story." I love fiction—don't get me wrong. But there is just something about knowing that this thing really happened, that it really, really did happen, that attracts me to this thing.

CT: While working for the *Indianapolis Star*, did you elbow out and do other kinds of writing? Was that on the side, off the books, or what?

JH: I always wrote on my own. I would take various writing classes, workshops, fiction, nonfiction. I have basically done this all my adult life.

CT: So you gave yourself a continuing ed. program.

JH: Absolutely. Did it in Indiana. Did it at the Nieman Fellows Program too. It's marvelously helpful, though hilarious after a while because you get to recognize certain types who always hang out in writers' groups. Not to go on about that, but I always took those courses on the side. And, in fact, I had been very fortunate to have a guy named Robert Vare teach an unofficial course to the Niemans on nonfiction writing. Literary nonfiction. He had been previously, I think, an editor at *Atlantic Monthly* and also at the *New York Times Magazine*. I haven't talked to him in a while but believe he's at the University of Chicago. Immensely talented guy. Very good. And we had long, long discussions about narrative.

The great thing that really differentiated me from most of the people in any of those [creative-writing] groups is that I was actually a real newspaper reporter. I got to see real life each day. I could come to a writers' meeting at night, and that day I had just seen dead bodies. I had been to crime scenes. I had actually seen real *lived* life that most people had to imagine. Which is fine if you're a fiction writer, but I was actually getting the raw material each day, which is marvelous. It's terrific training.

And so, even in Indianapolis, I could take some of that material. I could rearrange it in these writing groups, practice, basically, learn how to bend and shape and mold things and apply it to the newspaper. So they were very complementary efforts.

CT: Did you have any notion when you were working within writers' groups and taking creative-writing courses of some larger plan—I'm thinking, of course, of *Going Up the River*.

JH: I always knew that I wanted to write a book. I am fairly analytically oriented. I like to connect the dots, and that is what led to the malpractice series that I did with [*Indianapolis Star* colleague] Susan Headden. And that's what I really like to do, figure out problems that many people miss simply because they haven't started to connect the dots.

And you start amassing a lot of information, and trying to tell it in a compelling way that emphasizes people and their stories, and it gets back to that music I talked about before. You put it together, and pretty soon you start saying, "This thing moves. This has pace. It has narrative. It has oomph. It's got consequence. It's got drama. It's got all those things people like to read about, including me. And all right, this is good. This beats who, what, where, when, and why. This cooks." And that's when I really started to be able to put all those things together and start to write the kind of journalism that I like to do.

CT: When did the book moment come?

JH: I guess in [19]98. My agent called and said we had sold the book. Suddenly somebody hands you a check, and it's the real deal. So I guess if there's a book moment, that's it. Of course, I still had the work to do.

CT: Had you already done some substantial part of the fieldwork? This book takes us all over Texas, we're up in Elmira, New York, we're in Philadelphia, we're in Illinois, Washington state, California. Was Colorado in here? Did you plan a methodical series of trips or plan methodically?

JH: It would be nice to say "yes," but the truthful answer is "no"—at least until I was about halfway through. I wrote and rewrote and rewrote sample chapters while I was putting together the proposal. So, I had done some work, but that whole process helped crystallize the direction where I thought it needed to go.

CT: It seems to me that *Going Up the River* is about—well, about a quarter of the way through I thought, This book is about the *real* price—the human price—of a massive prison industry obsessed with costs. This is about the real human cost.

But to do it, because of this subject, because every page carries such human brutality to other human beings, you've got to handle your reader with some care. The reader, it struck me, begins as an outsider to the topic, and you bring the reader to insider status. And the critical, frank things that you can say at the end, straight out, you wouldn't dare say at the beginning because you might drive your reader away.

In our phone conversation before this interview, you said that you wanted to talk about some of the difficulty of telling this story, or call it the challenge, or call it tactics or necessary strategies. As a reader, I felt that at certain points I couldn't take any more, but just then you gave me another new aspect of the same issue. You took the foot off the gas, or you relieved the pressure a little bit, so the reader could get a little breathing room before we had to plunge into something so horrible that it was really unbearable.

JH: That's largely due to the two editors I had at Random House who were very good, Scott Moyers and Sunshine Lucas. They were very good about introducing those breathing spaces, if you will, but I struggled early on and Robert [Vare] was very helpful in those early stages of trying to put some architecture in this thing. That was the toughest part. I thought, The big picture: how do you tell a story that is not obviously a story?

I think narrative works very well and works best where you have what's clearly a story, a discrete event: a guy is killed. A murder is the classic. *In Cold Blood* would be classic. I don't want to say that was very easy to do, because that's an extremely hard book to do. But that situation is the type that lends itself to a narrative story. You can tell it chronologically.

CT: It's linear.

JH: Yeah. It's linear. It's very clear. A guy dies. There's the end. In a way, it sets itself, to do no disservice to *In Cold Blood* or others like it. It's much harder, I think (at least it was for me), to try a narrative on disparate stories, different parts of the country, different times. They're not obviously connected in any way, so you have to come up with a strategy for connecting those things and making them progress as if they were a part of a whole, and we settled on something like a travelogue, a narrative of moving around the country, all the while building some mass as the thing gets rolling.

Part of that, of course, is designed, as you mentioned, to pull the reader in. One of the things I struggled with very early on is the question of audience. You say, Who am I writing for? Who is going to buy it? If it's just a group of technical people or prison wardens or whatnot, you can write one way for specialized people, but if it's a general-interest book, you've got to write another way.

So I struggled with method and with the architecture. What form would attract a person who maybe has a passing interest in prisons but is a regular person, has a regular job, and just might pick this book up because "Mmm, it's kind of interesting?" And a travel narrative is one way to achieve that. My wife, who was an English major, spent many nights reading drafts. She had a lot of input in that as well, but I struggled tremendously, trying to figure out some form into which I could fit all of these stories and make it fairly, not seamless, but at least connected.

CT: Did you prep yourself by reading travel literature?

JH: Not consciously. For a while I did read certain works to try to get a sound and a rhythm and a feeling in my head.

CT: Any names that pop into mind?

JH: The usual suspects. George Orwell is a favorite of mine, and I read *Road to Wigan Pier*. I read and reread it. . . . *Elements of Style* because it's got an approach that I wanted to keep. So I would read . . . Dickens, actually, was quite wonderful. Dickens in his day used to love to go to criminal trials, for both professional and personal reasons. He loved them, thought they were great stages on which all of these human characters appeared. I love trials too. I love courts. I love prisons. I love the whole milieu. And so I read Dickens and a number of others. I'm a big fan of Joan Didion. And the early Tom Wolfe.

And then I think after a while I just stopped reading because I said, "None of these people are serving as an exact model I'm groping for." And if I tried to imitate them, that's probably failure at best and frustrating at least. So, I just finally set aside all the reading material and just tried to write.

CT: Of course, you have to be an historian of U.S. prisons and penology too.

JH: Which is fascinating, actually.

CT: And give readers several history lessons.

JH: Every so often I tried to set the IV back up and just drip a little in here and there.

CT: Let me ask this: in nonfiction investigative writing, you've got to present factual data, as well as keep the narrative going. Is that difficult?

JH: Yeah. In fact, I think they are mutually exclusive many times, if not most times, because the first thing you learn as any kind of reporter—a real reporter working at a newspaper or magazine— is how slippery facts are. There are always contradictory facts. I remember as a very young reporter going to see a police shooting and talking to people who claimed to be eyewitnesses but who provided me with diametrically opposite versions of the events. One person said the policeman (it was a policewoman, actually) was standing right over the victim with a foot on either side of his body and shot him directly in the back. I talked to somebody else, and he said, "No, the guy was running away, and she was about twenty feet away."

And so you learn very quickly as a reporter that some facts are not reconcilable. They are statements. I don't believe those witnesses were lying. They didn't have a motive to lie. But as a reporter, an investigative reporter, you learn early on that your facts are not always going to reconcile. You have to reach a question of fairness inside your own head about how you are going to present the material to a reader who wasn't there and is relying on you to vouchsafe what really happened.

CT: But even with facts that may not be in dispute, as when you say that to build a certain prison, the state of Virginia toppled six thousand trees—

JH: There's a fact nobody disputes.

CT: When it appears, it's a very powerful fact. The reader thinks, "Oh, my God!" Brutality toward the environment, and then a brutal institution to go up. But all the way through, I've marked passages where the narrative has to come to a halt so that you can offer documentation about construction costs, dates, numbers of inmates in or out, ratios of guards to inmates, this kind of thing. Is that change-off hard to handle? For one thing, you obviously can't give a reader a big block of such data.

JH: I had lots of talks with my editors about that. As a writer, you've got to balance it. But at some point in your narrative, you've got to offer proof of what you're saying. At some point, the reader says in his or her mind, "Show me. Put up or shut up." So you need the facts to do that, but you can't just drop them in with a big wrecking ball—brrrrrmmmm—because it just looks clumsy and breaks the narrative. So these two are always in tension.

The narrative is the good stuff, the dessert. Everybody loves it. It goes along, and there are characters and dialogue.

Then comes those nasty facts, which are the vegetables. You've got to give them the Brussels sprouts here, just a little bit, but they really need them. They're good for you, really they are. But you don't want to put too much on the plate because people will just stop eating, so you work those in as you can.

Facts are wonderful. Other nonfiction writers that I know are big fans of facts, because they realize that a certain fact, well presented, very concisely, very small—if you plop it down just right, it has tremendous power. Facts have power. They're like verbs in the sentence. They have a lot of *wham!* if you use them correctly. So you choose from a lot of the facts to find the one best: six thousand trees. And you say, OK, I'll use the tree fact, and I'll throw away the other facts. So they are always in contention, and you worry, on the one hand, if you use too many facts you'll slow down the narrative, but if you use too few people will say, "He really didn't prove his case."

CT: I want to ask how you present your own identity. You're the traveler, the "I" who gets into conversations. But at other times, you're conspicuously absent as a character in your own story. Is it difficult to decide when to come forward and be a part of the scene? And—a separate question really—is it also tough to create a persona that can gain your reader's confidence and not turn conviction into obsession?

JH: I've discussed these things with [Random House editor] Scott Moyers a lot. Scott always wanted me to put more of myself in the book. We had long discussions about that, and it's tough, because one of the things they teach you back in BU or any journalism program is, put yourself in the background. So when you come to write a book like this, after ten or fifteen years of that kind of training, it's extremely difficult. All your warning signs go off whenever you say "I" or "me."

And even when you overcome that, you do have to say, Well, what kind of companion am I going to be in this book, because people are going to read it as a travelogue? You're essentially a travel partner, and anybody who's been on a long road trip with someone knows that's a very touchy relationship. So I worked hard on that.

CT: I thought you did it superbly.

JH: Thanks.

CT: Let me ask you this: Did you ever find yourself cutting any literary language? Because one of the gifts that you give the reader along the way, to cite one brief example, and I quote, "The girders are covered with wire mesh giving the yard the feel of a human aviary." Now, you could have stopped with "girders covered with wire mesh." Period. Then here comes this nice metaphor, and it's just like a little present in the middle of the paragraph. Does that come naturally, that kind of thing, or do you find you have to rein in your tendencies to get literary?

JH: My old partner on the Pulitzer series (she's now an assistant managing editor, Investigative Projects, at *U.S. News and World Report*) used to joke with me about my writing. She'd take the phrase from *The New Yorker,* "block that metaphor," because I would always think in terms of metaphors, and she would get on me about that. It became a joke between us, but I always think of things like that and jot them down in my notebooks. My notebooks have all sorts of—a ton of literary references. Robert Vare scratched out whole pages of stuff that he thought just didn't move it forward. I would digress and go off on some beautiful little literary thing, but it just didn't move the story forward. So, yeah, there's a ton that got cut.

CT: You've referred several times to the help of editors along the way, so is this sort of a crucial partnership for any writer?

JH: I know reporters who would kill me for saying so. It would break the brotherly code, but surely in book writing as opposed to newspaper writing, that's the case. I leaned on these people greatly, and really, it's a very vulnerable relationship because you realize if you get the wrong kind of editor, if they're not your kind of person, it's like having the wrong kind of spouse. But actually they were marvelous with that.

CT: Tell me whether the book, as format, as venue—I'm kind of groping here, stumbling into a question of why *Going Up the River* has to be a book and could not possibly be a newspaper series. I also think everybody who reads newspapers is aware that we are really down to a handful of good papers. I'm shocked by the *Chicago Tribune,* the *Cleveland Plain Dealer*—I travel to these cities, I buy these papers, and it's just horrifying how thin the news content. I don't want to predetermine your response, but what's being said now is that TV and the Internet have it all, that books can't really have an impact. I'm thinking books *do* have an impact—or can. Who would have thought *The Feminine Mystique* or *Unsafe at Any Speed*—

JH: I love that book.

CT: —or *Silent Spring*—they seem to come out of nowhere and tap into something that people were broadly thinking. That kind of crystallizing moment belongs to the book.

JH: I know some of the books you cited are from ten, twenty, thirty years ago, and I love all of them. They are great books—and able to synthesize that information in a way that even the best newspapers still aren't quite able to because, among other reasons, I think all of those books you've just mentioned take a clear point of view and the author's voice is very important in them. Those two things, a clear point of view and author's voice, are almost always the two things deleted from any newspaper article—virtually always—so those two things can eviscerate the force even out of a lengthy series. So I think the book still has a tremendous impact. You can really affect, even in some small way, what people think about something. That's marvelous. It's a wonderful thing.

In this second Gilded Age, Hallinan reveals that newspaper reporting in the twenty-first century is as stimulating—and confining—as it was to journalist muckrakers of the last century. He seeks "intellectual content" beyond the regimented inverted pyramid, which is basic to news reporting. Yet he welcomes the reporter's firsthand experience—including a homicide scene—for the adrenaline and the credential. The satisfaction echoes Christopher Wilson's observation from early twentieth-century popular discourse on reporters: "The reporter became America's . . . high priest of 'experience,' the expert on 'real life' " (17).

Hallinan, however, is also heir to the era's rationalization of newspaper work and the standardization of reporting. The reporter's work, whether news gathering or writing, at that time became "routinized" or, in Lincoln Steffens's term, machinelike (C. Wilson 35; cf. 17–39). Recall the Chicago *Record* reporter Ray Stannard Baker's dismay, in 1894, at the inside-page burial of his daily assignments on the Pullman strike court proceedings. In frustration, Baker tried his experimental sketch of the Swedish striker's family at mealtime—and thereby exited boilerplate reporting.

Hallinan, too, says he first mastered the "nuts-and-bolts," "by-the-book" news-story format. Then he worked assiduously to gain the narrative skills of the journalists he had long admired, just as the first-generation muckrakers strove to expand their narrative abilities. *Going Up the River* measures its author's distance from journalism's rudiments. The narrative not only brings readers inside the razor wire, but wraps a brutal subject in overtly literary prose. Readers encounter such figurative language as this chilling description of a momentarily "lovely" western Virginia prison at sunset when "the peaks are limned with light . . . [and] the coils of razor wire gleam like gold" (218). Such figure is disciplined by the exegetical task at hand. Metaphors, similes, and symbols—figurative terms necessary to narrative must be integral to Hallinan's argument, bringing it forward, deepening it. The "gold" razor wire does not simply aestheticize the prison any more than does Ida Tarbell's image of excess oil production as a suicidal opening of nature's veins. Hallinan's image, like Tarbell's, is argumentive. Appearing at the close of this book on the waste of human and financial treasure on prisons, the "gold" razor wire signifies American society's rush to a collective fool's gold.

Going Up the River, like The Shame of the Cities and other muckraker texts, is a call to citizens' activism. "After spending years in America's correctional institutions," says Hallinan, "I had come to believe that they—and we—were capable of something more, that the limits of our ingenuity were not confined to building a $110,000 [per cell] human warehouse" (216). The critical key word, "warehouse," is the argument for new consideration of rehabilitation initiatives, treatment of nonviolent offenders, and judicial discretion in sentencing.

The public, however, must first be roused, and Hallinan's readers repeatedly encounter this bemused and bewildered statement on a somnolent American public in the new prison era: "no one seemed to mind" (176). Whether the subject is private prisons creating the unprecedented new homos economicus, "the prison millionaire," whether it is the imprisonment of seventy-five-year-old women for twenty-four years on drug distribution charges; or whether it is the linkage of religion with civics in a prison rodeo in which inmates on bulls and broncos are "slung to the dirt," "knocked out cold," and "trampled"— "nobody seems to care" (60, 113, 174, 200, 205 [emphasis added]). To care, to mind, is the narrative wake-up call, the nation's reveille, in Going Up the River: Travels in a Prison Nation. It was the summons of Hallinan's predecessors in the first muckraker era. It is the summons of his cohorts today.

Epilogue

Tipping Point, or the Long Goodbye?

Perhaps a pendulum is ready to swing. Perhaps, to use Malcolm Gladwell's title, things are approaching the shift that Gladwell defines as *The Tipping Point* (2000), the moment "when an idea, trend, or social behavior crosses a threshold, tips, and spreads like wildfire" (see introduction).

Social change may proceed slower than wildfire, but the actual conflagration, which was started by nineteen Middle Eastern jihadic terrorists, arguably launched the twenty-first century in the attacks of September 11, 2001. In the United States, the burning, collapsing World Trade Center twin towers became mental templates of ur-disaster. America's vulnerability was writ large in the tornadic dust boiling in the canyons of lower Manhattan and inscribed on the faces of firefighters and police, of residents and workers who got out—eyes blank because they saw too much.

Whether the towers were, or were not, *"Notre Dame de l'Argent,"* a cathedral to Our Lady of Money, as the French feminist theorist Julia Kristeva called them, the mood of post–9/11 Davos-in-New-York 2002 was unprecented in apprehensiveness. The exuberance of panel sessions of years past (for example, "Wiring the World") gave way in 2002 to a new theme, "Leadership in a Fragile World." This theme responded to the terrorist bombing of the symbols of global capitalist monetary power. Headquartered at the Waldorf-Astoria Hotel, Davos-in-New-York 2002 featured workshops and panels on such topics as "Who's Afraid of Globalization," "Understanding Global Anger," and "The Future of Terrorism: Understanding the Next Threats."

The more subdued tone also responded to the growing wage-equity and anti-globalization movement, which from 1999 marshaled tens of thousands of protesters in public streets during meetings of the World Trade Organization, the World Bank, and the G-7 meetings of the major industrial nations in Seattle, Quebec City, Genoa, and New York. Avoidance of organized protest now drove such political-financial

meetings into remote places inaccessible to protesters, who nonetheless staged street demonstrations and teach-ins in proximate cities.*

Indications were that news media, which for years had ignored or
ridiculed antiglobalist activists, might now approach the movement's
issues with new seriousness. The *New York Times*, the U.S. newspaper
of record, had been just one of many outlets to treat activists as mere
copycat residue of the 1960s counterculture. In May 2002, however,
the *Times* ran an editorial-page denunciation of "Sweatshops Under
the American Flag" (May 10, 2002: A34). It censored the system by
which "Made in America" labels for such brands as Gap and Limited
Brands masked the labor peonage in American territories overseas. In
August 2002, the *Times*'s Sunday magazine cover story analyzed the
failures of the globalization movement to improve the lives of the
world's poor (August 18, 2002, section 6: 28). Also in 2002, the Nobel
Prize–winning economist Joseph E. Stiglitz, former chief economist
for the World Bank, published a widely reviewed critique of global
economic policy, *Globalization and Its Discontents*.

Suddenly, Davos Man—even in Davos itself—seemed neither omniscient nor invincible. In May 2002, Bill Gates, on behalf of the Bill and
Melinda Gates Foundation, pledged $50 million for a global nutrition
program, declaring "market-based capitalism" to be insufficient to improve poor children's lives worldwide. By that fall, the foundation,
with Gates himself as its spokesman, would mount a $100-million anti-
AIDS project in India. In January 2003, at the World Economic Forum in Davos, the foundation announced a $200-million grant for
innovative approaches to solving leading critical health problems in
developing countries, including malaria, tuberculosis, and malnutrition. Bill Gates emphasized the need to shift priority to the four billion
people (two-thirds of the world's population) afflicted with diseases
largely ignored by Western medicine. "Market-based capitalism works
well in driving scientific research," said Gates, "but to accelerate research into diseases in the developing world, market forces alone
are often not enough." Philanthropy, he added, herein shows "its
ability to place a value on things that the market does not" (*Wall Street
Journal*, January 27, 2003: A16). Gates expressed the hope that such
initiatives as the foundation's might spur public investment in similar

* The June 2002 meeting site of the G-8—with Russia now the eighth nation—was
a western Canadian Rockies wilderness lodge accessible by one road only but nonetheless protected from protesters by 6,000 soldiers and 4,500 police, in addition to a 330-
mile-radius no-flight zone patrolled by fighter jets. The woodland trails had checkpoints,
but because the G-8 site is also the habitat of cougars, wolves, and grizzlies, wildlife
rangers were on duty, shown on TV network news explaining their expertise in bear
deterrence.

projects. His 2003 Davos panel was titled "Science for the Global Good."

Challenges to the hegemony of Davos Man were beginning to appear in such titles as David C. Korten's *When Corporations Rule the World* (2nd ed., 2001), in the business writer Marjorie Kelley's *The Divine Right of Capital: Dethroning the Corporate Aristocracy* (2001), and in the corporate law expert Lawrence Mitchell's *Corporate Irresponsibility: America's Newest Export* (2001).

The Enron scandals further discredited Davos Man, who was suddenly less the "ruthless competitor" than an outright crook. The collapse of the energy-trader Enron, the seventh-largest U.S. corporation, and its auditor Arthur Andersen, was the major news story of the winter of 2002. Congressional hearings were televised, and an *Economist* cover typified the saturation newsstand coverage; it pictured the company's tilted-E logo plunging like a meteorite.

How were citizens to know that Houston-based Enron was only the beginning? By the spring of 2002, a person could hardly keep up with the landslide of multinational corporate crimes, much less follow a money trail packed with staggering sums. A few trail markers caught the eye. Enron's top twenty-nine executives reportedly gained more than $1 billion for themselves as the corporation imploded. The company's employees, meanwhile, had been prohibited in the autumn of 2001 from selling the Enron stock in which their 401(k) pensions were invested. They watched, helpless, as their retirement stock sank into worthlessness and learned that their new company benefit would be the services of grief counselors. (Pensions financed with company stock in recent years had similarly collapsed at Global Crossing, Lucent Technologies, Waste Management, Family Golf, Nortel Networks, Carter Hawley Hale, and Color Tile.) It was reported that in four of the last five years of Enron's existence, the company had paid no taxes at all to the U.S. treasury.

That same spring, such companies as Dynergy, Global Crossing, WorldCom, and Xerox were shown to have misled the public about profits. In May 2002, the *New York Times* headlined a "Requiem" for the former celebrity stock analysts now under investigation for criminal behavior (May 5, 2002: section 3: 1). In the Internet start-up boom years, the analysts had urged investors—especially small investors lacking Wall Street insider savvy—to buy stocks that the analysts privately trashed. Corporate "outside" audits, moreover, were now shown to be corrupted by auditors acting in conflicting roles as consultants to their clients. A business writer called this "accounting legerdemain" in his postmortem of the 1990s entitled "The Long Boom's

Ugly Side." The *Wall Street Journal* headlined, "Main Street Loses Faith in Stocks," and reported that the financial-services industry worked to woo investors who were said to feel "shell shocked" (May 8, 2002: C1).

Corporate chiefs tumbled from their pedestals and became targets of investigation and suspicion. "The Imperial Chief Executive Is Suddenly in the Cross Hairs" headlined the *New York Times* in June 2002 (June 24, 2002: A1). On July 10, the *Wall Street Journal* announced "a swing of the pendulum away from a quarter-century of bipartisan deference to capitalists." By September 2002, the president of the Federal Reserve Bank of New York called the CEO pay scale of recent years "terribly bad social policy and perhaps even bad morals" (*Wall Street Journal*, September 12, 2002: A2).

All CEOs were tarred by the brush of cohorts disgraced in the wake of scandals, forced resignations, arrests, and indictments at Adelphia, Tyco, Rite Aid, ImClone, Qwest, Martha Stewart Living, Health-South, and other companies. The pharmaceutical titan Merck booked more than $12 billion in pharmacy co-payments as corporate income. WorldCom laid off a quarter of its eighty thousand employees upon disclosure that it had hid more than $9 billion in losses with accounting tricks (though its ex-CEO, Bernard Ebbers, who had headed the company during its crime time, left with a multimillion-dollar package). In May 2002, a *Wall Street Journal* columnist wrote, "Nothing disrobes an emperor like a crashing stock market," and the *New York Times* editorialized about "a crazed 'anything goes' mentality" fostering "outrageous executive compensation practices" at companies treated by CEOs and high-ranking executives as "private bank and casino" (*Wall Street Journal*, May 5, 2002: B1 and *New York Times*, May 19, 2002, section 4: 14). New business books appeared—*Why C.E.O.'s Fail*, by a Honeywell executive, and *Pigs at the Trough: How Corporate Greed and Political Corruption Are Undermining America*, by the political commentator Arianna Huffington. One *New York Times* business writer summed up the new reality: "Public trust in corporate America has been undeniably shattered" (June 2, 2002, section 3: 1).

Prophetic Internet CEO jokes began to circulate, one in which a roving band of CEOs, calling themselves the CEOnistas, were spotted near the Mexican border, leaving a trail of profit-inflation scams and yelling, "You'll never audit me alive!" CEO was said to be the abbreviation for "Chief Embezzlement Officer." In July and August 2002, executives of Adelphia and WorldCom, charged with conspiracy and fraud, were arrested, handcuffed, and led away by marshalls in the "perp walk" before TV cameras. Residents of Tennessee took special note of the arrests of Adelphia's John Rigas and his two sons, since the

14. *The Economist,* May 4–10, 2002. Courtesy *The Economist.*

corporation had spent millions to buy naming rights to Nashville's NFL stadium, home of the Titans. In early autumn 2002, with the telecommunications giant in bankruptcy, workers removed the huge red Adelphia "A" logo from the stadium. It had become a corporate scarlet letter.*

The public suddenly could see, crystal-clear, the sham "transparency" of the new U.S. capitalism and the failure of regulatory oversight by so-called watchdog agencies, the Securities and Exchange Commission and the Federal Energy Regulatory Commission. Citizen groups also protested corporate moves to save multimillions of U.S. federal tax dollars by registering company "shell" headquarters in such mail-drop tax havens as Bermuda and Barbados, a ploy that the *New York Times* called "the Tax Bermuda Triangle" (May 13, 2002: A16).

The business press, which had been so swept up in the 1990s bubble economy that its reporters were evangelists for the banks, financial-services industry, and "bad apple" corporations, now reflected and produced a *zeitgeist* shift. The *Wall Street Journal* now exposed corporate neologisms of Enron and faltering telecommunications companies as a lexical "dreamworld of corporate babble" in which "corporate chieftains and dot-commers . . . blathered in jargon" (May 15, 2002: B1). In June 2002, the *New York Times* swept aside a decade of pro-CEO business literature as "fawning" and "idolatrous" (June 24, 2002: A1). A business writer noted that the former "beloved technology entrepreneurs" now appeared, "not as heroes but as symbols of hubris" (*New York Times*, May 12, 2002: section 4: 1). "Three-card-monte" and "bubble" were the censorious phrases in the business press, and corporate mergers and acquisitions were suddenly termed "binges." The 2003 World Economic Forum in Davos, according to the *Times*, took place in a "darkened" mood because "corporate stars had fallen in disgrace" and economies had "slowed, stripping businesses of the self-confidence and supremacy they once enjoyed as champions of globalization" (January 23, 2003: A3).

The scandals touched the White House too, even though President George W. Bush traveled to the New York Stock Exchange on July 9, 2002, to call on Wall Street to "end the days of cooking the books, shading the truth, and breaking our laws." The market nonetheless sank even as Bush offered what, on the following day, the *New York Times*

---

* According to a Securities and Exchange Commission complaint filed on July 24, 2002, the *Wall Street Journal* reported, "After John J. Rigas racked up a personal debt of more than $66 million by early 2001, he was withdrawing so much money from [Adelphia] for personal use that his son Timothy had to limit him to $1 million a month—which he duly withdrew for 12 months, even as public filings listed his annual income at less than $1.9 million" (July 25, 2002: A3).

called "hard talk, softer plans" (and continued its decline on July 16 after Federal Reserve Chairman Alan Greenspan denounced business pathology of "infectious greed").

The infection threatened the White House, where reporters questioned President George W. Bush's own early 1990s business history at the Harken Energy Company and the Texas Rangers baseball team. The deals that made the president's fortune during the years of his own father's presidency suddenly seemed less exemplary of business acumen than of insider crony capitalism, proven by reports that Harvard University had rescued the failing Harken Energy with a multi-million-dollar cash infusion. Vice President Richard (Dick) Cheney's tenure as CEO of Halliburton, meanwhile, had come under investigation by the Securities and Exchange Commission and appeared to implicate Cheney in an accounting fraud by which the company falsely reported some $500 million in profits. The administration that had boasted of its corporate business origins and practices was now vulnerable to that very identity.

The historian Gary Cross in his *An All-Consuming Century* (2001) argues that Americans have forfeited the duties of citizenship for the pleasures of shopping. He makes the case that the U.S. middle class has asked only to be left alone to pursue consumer-based desires. He implies that Americans expect all authorities, whether in politics or business, mainly to preserve consumerism by bolting the lid on Pandora's box so that human ills cannot contaminate a consumerist world. Cross cautions, however, that this mentality may be unsustainable in the twenty-first century. Post–September 11, 2001, President George W. Bush, declaring the War on Terrorism, had urged that U.S. citizens show patriotic support by shopping. His advice prompted slack-jawed incredulity and the kinds of jokes that signal the psychological realization that Cross's caution may be well advised. In January 2003, international business leaders at the World Economic Forum (Davos encore) reported that they had lost confidence that "the American wallet can continue to save the day" because American consumers had ceased to be the " 'engine' of the global economy" (*Wall Street Journal*, January 27, 2003: A2). The previous June, Paul Krugman plaintively posed this question in his *New York Times* column: "Who will save that malfunctioning corporation called the U. S. A.?" (June 4, 2002: A19).

Perhaps the first muckraker era is instructive in this historical moment. In a long-admired book, *The Age of Reform* (1955), the historian Richard Hofstadter identified the elements necessary for successful progressive social change—for a successful tipping point. Widely read in American history classes in my own undergraduate days, *The Age of Reform* predates the Civil Rights and women's movements but remains useful in light of the parallels of the two Gilded Ages. At the close of *Exposés and Excess*, I have turned back to it.

Middle-class anxieties of the first Gilded Age, Hofstadter found, grew from a sense that personal character and hard work had become irrelevant: "When one observed the behavior of the plutocracy, it seemed to be inversely related to civic responsibility and personal restraint. The competitive process seemed to be drying up. All of society was felt to be threatened . . . by moral and social degeneration and the eclipse of democratic institutions. . . . The great corporation, the crass plutocrat, the calculating political boss" now served to thwart personal initiative and civic-minded effort (11).

Far from despairing, however, the c. 1900s reformers believed that "the nation could be redeemed if the citizens awoke to their responsibilities." In this great awakening, says Hofstadter, "the muckraker was a central figure." "Before there could be action," he goes on, "there must be information and exhortation. Grievances had to be given specific objects, and these the muckraker supplied. It was muckraking that brought the diffuse malaise of the public into focus" (11, 185).

Muckrakers, then, were architects. Their literature of exposure constituted a set of blueprints. The actual new societal construction, however, required the involvement of activist citizens from numerous walks of life—and assent on the part of those not directly driving social change. The motives of the many parties varied, as Hofstadter shows. These groups and individuals did not march in lockstep. Key to the change from the c.1900s Gilded Age to the Progressive era, however, was the complementary participation of administrators, lawmakers, judges (notably Justice Louis D. Brandeis), professionals (including those from the new social sciences), the clergy, academics, industrialists, workers, labor leaders and organizers, and even city machine bosses (134).

Artists and writers also contributed to the reformist public discourse. Contemporary to *The Age of Reform*, Robert H. Bremner's *From the Depths: The Discovery of Poverty in the United States* (1956) shows the extent to which the painters of the so-called Ashcan School, notably Robert Henri and John Sloan, educated the middle-class public in the cruel and destructive impact of vast wealth disparities and resulting poverty, as did the realist-naturalist writers, such as Jack London and O. Henry (see chs. 10 and 11). Says Bremner of the writers, "They were less given to pondering the mysterious workings of the universe than to attacking the inequities of a social system that imposed enormous disadvantages on the many while conferring extraordinary privileges on the few" (175).

Effective public communication was also crucial for social change, says Hofstadter: "The men who were in best rapport with public senti-ment were preaching to the whole nation the necessity of taking up, personally and individually, those civic burdens which the previous generation had forsaken" (205). Middle-class investors, for instance, were warned in 1914 by Louis Brandeis that their savings provided the wealth of the new plutocracy, which now disempowered them: "The fetters which bind the people are forged from the people's own gold" (qtd. in Hofstadter 219). In 1910, Woodrow Wilson similarly warned that ordinary stockholders were unknowingly "contributing money for the conduct of a business which other men run as they please." Wilson concluded that the decisions of the new corporations—the monopolistic trusts—were "autocratic" (qtd. in Hofstadter 220).

Though middle class in its values, the reform movement of the first Gilded Age also enlisted figures of wealth. "Progressive leaders in both major parties," Hofstadter shows, included "a large number of well-to-do men," among them the merchant E. A. Filene and the sugar magnate Rudolph Spreckels (143–44). Also included were wealthy "self-made men" like John P. Altgeld and Hazen Pingree, who became governor of Michigan. For all of them, "Progressive ideology distinguished be-tween 'responsible' and 'irresponsible' wealth" (145).

Hofstadter emphasizes that the agents of progressive change were a younger generation. He notes in his *Autobiography* that William Allen White recalled the "hundreds or thousands of young men in their twenties, thirties, and early forties" whose "quickening sense of the in-equities, injustices, and fundamental wrongs" of American society drove their efforts at reform (367). The election of Theodore Roo-sevelt, the youngest of the U.S. presidents, symbolized this new re-formist youthful vigor.

Reading *The Age of Reform* in these opening years of the twenty-first century, I immediately recognize Hofstadter's presumption of a cer-tain status quo in the United States It is crude to imply that *The Age of Reform* could be subtitled "The End of American History." But Hof-stadter's *given* was that the U.S. public, in its own self-interest, would support the attainment and continuation of civic social programs in the post-Progressive, post-New Deal era. He presumed public agree-ment that government was necessarily a major player in ensuring the common welfare, in regulating economic and social extremes of be-havior, and, through its revenues, in helping to provide the necessities of life—education, healthcare, and so on—for the citizenry.

Hofstadter wrote his book in the Eisenhower years, of course, when public funds were far more available for such programs. The historian did not foresee an economy in which 52 cents of every discretionary tax dollar was committed to the military. He did not foresee a late twentieth century of factory shutdowns and a starved U.S. treasury, with legislators in both parties gorged on special-interest campaign money and bevies of lawyers and lobbyists looking for legal loopholes to enable tax evasion, environmental pollution, the privatization of the airwaves, and so on. He did not anticipate the "extraordinary" upward redistribution of income in which, by 1998, "the top 1 percent garnered almost 15 per cent of the nation's income for itself, more income than was received by the more than 100 million people in the bottom 40 percent of the population taken together."* He did not foresee the spread of gated housing or the manufacture, announced in 2003, of production model Lincoln and Cadillac armored cars.

The Age of Reform is thus secure in its middle-class and positivist assumptions. Nowhere does it anticipate incipient ideological drives to dismantle the New Deal and return to social Darwinism and a new Gilded Age on the upramp to the twenty-first century. Written in what Henry Luce called "The American Century," *The Age of Reform* did not anticipate a *Pax Americana* of a global American empire, nor a perpetual War on Terror. Though *The Age of Reform* was written during the anti-communist hysteria of the McCarthy era, it did not anticipate an ongoing Orwellian "security" state of surveillance and curtailed civil liberties in the twenty-first century.

If the new muckraker narratives of c. 2000 are to be seen in Hofstadter's framework as a set of social guidelines, then their implementation remains an open question at this tipping point, even as the authors are praised, awarded prestigious prizes, and prominent on best-seller lists.

If the new muckrakers' narratives are blueprints, who might be the likely players driving new social movements? The young activists in the anti-sweatshop and wage-equity initiatives? The younger corporate careerists determined that ambition need not—must not—lead to handcuffs and a perp walk before TV-news cameras? Politically, could one of the aggressive young state attorneys general—perhaps a veteran of the tobacco settlement wars or the prosecution of Enron-era crimes—be planning even now to run for national office? At this writing, some men of wealth have come forward, as did those a century ago, to differentiate between "responsible" and "irresponsible" wealth. In 2001, a Boston-based group called Responsible Wealth enlisted a group of multimillionaires and billionaires to support estate taxation for the long-term good of the citizenry, among them George Soros,

---

* In the Eisenhower years, the top marginal tax of the wealthiest elites stood at 91 percent (versus 50 percent by the first Reagan administration). In the Eisenhower era, too, corporations paid an average 25 percent of the federal tax bill, in contrast to the 7 percent in 2001 (see Alperowitz, "Tax the Plutocrats!").

members of the Rockefeller family, and Paul Newman. Asked on TV by Bill Moyers whether he believes the United States has reverted to a second Gilded Age, William H. (Bill) Gates, Sr., replied, "I do" (*Now*, January 17, 2003). Gates and Chuck Collins have reprised Henry Demerest Lloyd's title in their plea to Congress to reinstate inheritance taxes. Their *Wealth and Our Commonwealth: Why America Should Tax Accumulated Fortunes* (2003) states that the United States "is now the most unequal society in the industrialized world" (14). Their book is a reasoned plea to redirect America away from plutocratic aristocracy.

As for public communication, the messages of the new muckraker narratives are distilled and circulated in sound bytes and op-eds, which reprise the themes of Ehrenreich, Schlosser, and the others. As the cabinet-level Department of Homeland Security was about to receive congressional approval and be signed into law in 2003, only one in eight Americans, according to a Gallup poll, believed they would be "a lot safer." One public figure who is, in Hofstadter's term, "in best rapport with public sentiment" suggests why. Vermont Senator James Jeffords's "Mandate for the Middle," a *New York Times* op-ed, defined U.S. homeland security in terms of higher-wage jobs, adequate childcare, environmental protection, healthcare, and education (November 30, 2002: A17). Failure to engage these issues, Jeffords warns, would be a "grave mistake." As the new muckrakers know, it would turn a tipping point into a long goodbye.

Bibliography

The First Muckrakers and Their Associates

Baker, Ray Stannard. *Following the Color Line: American Negro Citizenship in the Progressive Era*. 1908. New York: Harper, 1964.

Bellamy, Edward. *Looking Backward—2000–1887*. 1887. Ed. Cecelia Tichi. New York: Penguin, 1982.

Dreiser, Theodore. *Sister Carrie*. 1900. New York: Modern Library, 1999.

Lloyd, Henry Demarest. *Wealth Against Commonwealth*. New York: Harper and Brothers, 1899.

London, Jack. *The Human Drift*. New York: Macmillan, 1917.

———. *The Iron Heel*. New York: Macmillan, 1908.

———. *The People of the Abyss*. New York: Macmillan, 1903.

———. *Revolution and Other Essays*. New York: Macmillan, 1910.

———. *The War of the Classes*. New York: Macmillan, 1905.

Norris, Frank. *McTeague*. 1899. New York: NAL Signet, 1964.

———. *The Octopus: A Story of California*. New York: Grosset & Dunlap, 1901.

Phillips, David Graham. "The Treason of the Senate." *Cosmopolitan*. 1906. Reprinted in *The Muckrackers*. Ed. Arthur and Lila Weinberg 1961. Champaigne: University of Illinois Press, 2001.

Riis, Jacob. *How the Other Half Lives: Studies Among the Tenements of New York*. New York: Scribner, 1904, c.1890.

Sinclair, Upton. *The Brass Check: A Study of American Journalism*. 10th revised ed. Pasadena, Calif.: self-published, 1931.

———. *The Jungle*. 1906. New York: Penguin, 1996.

———. *Springtime and Harvest*. 1901. Republished as *King Midas*. New York, London: Funk & Wagnalls, 1901.

Steffens, Lincoln. *The Autobiography of Lincoln Steffens*. New York: Harcourt, Brace, 1931.

———. *The Shame of the Cities*. 1904. New York: Hill and Wang, 1957.

Tarbell, Ida M. *All in the Day's Work: An Autobiography*. New York: Macmillan, 1939.

———. *The History of the Standard Oil Company*. New York: McClure, Phillips, 1905. 2 vols.

The New Muckrakers and Their Antecedents

Bradsher, Keith. *High and Mighty: SUVs—The World's Most Dangerous Vehicle and How They Got That Way*. New York: Public Affairs, 2002.

Carson, Rachel. *Silent Spring*. Boston: Houghton Mifflin, 1962.

Cassidy, John. *Dot.con: The Greatest Story Ever Sold*. New York: HarperCollins, 2002.

Conover, Ted. *Newjack: Guarding Sing Sing*. New York: Random House, 2000.

Davis, Mike. *City of Quartz: Excavating the Future in Los Angeles*. London and New York: Verso, 1990.

Downie, Leonard, Jr., and Robert G. Kaiser. *The News About The News: American Journalism in Peril*. New York: Knopf, 2002.

Drew, Elizabeth. *The Corruption of American Politics: What Went Wrong and Why*. Woodstock, N.Y.: Overlook Press, 2000.

Ehrenreich, Barbara. *Fear of Falling: The Inner Life of the Middle Class*. New York: Pantheon, 1989.

———. *Nickel and Dimed: On (Not) Getting By in America*. New York: Holt Metropolitan, 2001.

Eisnitz, Gail. *Slaughterhouse: The Shocking Story of Greed, Neglect, and Inhumane Treatment Inside the U.S. Meat Industry*. Amherst, N.Y.: Prometheus Books, 1997.

Fallows, James M. *Breaking the News: How the Media Undermine American Democracy*. N.Y.: Pantheon Books, 1996.

Frank, Robert H., and Philip J. Cook. *The Winner-Take-All Society: How More and More Americans Compete for Ever Fewer and Bigger Prizes, Encouraging Economic Waste, Income Inequality, and an Impoverished Cultural Life*. New York: Free Press, 1995.

Frank, Thomas. *One Market Under God: Extreme Capitalism, Market Populism, and the End of Economic Democracy*. New York: Doubleday, 2000.

Fraser, Jill Andresky. *White-Collar Sweatshop: The Deterioration of Work and Its Rewards in Corporate America*. New York: W. W. Norton, 2001.

Friedan, Betty. *The Feminine Mystique*. New York: W. W. Norton, 1963.

Garrett, Laurie. *Betrayal of Trust: The Collapse of Global Public Health*. New York: Hyperion, 2000.

———. *The Coming Plague: Newly Emerging Diseases in a World out of Balance*. New York: Farrar, Straus and Giroux, 1994.

Hallinan, Joseph T. *Going Up the River: Travels in a Prison Nation*. New York: Random House, 2001.

Harrington, Michael. *The Other America: Poverty in the United States*. New York: Macmillan, 1962.

Hitchens, Christopher. *The Trial of Henry Kissinger*. London and New York: Verso, 2001.

Huffington, Arianna. *Pigs at the Trough: How Corporate Greed and Political Corruption Are Undermining America*. New York: Crown, 2003.

Kelley, Marjorie. *The Divine Right of Capital: Dethroning the Corporate Aristocracy*. San Francisco: Berrett-Koehler, 2001.

Klein, Naomi. *No Logo: Taking Aim at the Brand Bullies*. New York: Picador, 2000.

Johnson, Haynes. *Sleepwalking Through History: America in the Reagan Years*. New York: W. W. Norton, 1991.

Lapham, Lewis. "Notebook: *Res Publica*." *Harper's Magazine* 303. 1819 (December 2001): 8–11.

Levison, Iain. *A Working Stiff's Manifesto: A Memoir*. New York: Soho Press, 2002.

Lowenstein, Roger. *When Genius Failed: The Rise and Fall of Long-Term Capital Management*. New York: Random House, 2001.

Mitchell, Lawrence. *Corporate Irresponsibility: America's Newest Export*. New Haven, Conn.: Yale University Press, 2001.

Moody, Kim. *Workers in a Lean World: Unions in the International Economy*. London and New York: Verso, 1997.

Moore, Michael. *Downsize This!* New York: Crown Publishers, 1996.

Mosley, Walter. *Workin' on the Chain Gang: Shaking Off the Dead Hand of History*. New York: Ballantine, 2000.

Mueller, Rudolph. *As Sick as It Gets: The Shocking Reality of America's Health Care*. Dunkirk, N.Y.: Olin Frederick, 2001.

Nader, Ralph. *Unsafe at Any Speed: The Designed-In Dangers of the American Automobile*. New York: Grossman, 1965.

Orwell, George. *The Road to Wigan Pier*. 1937. New York: Berkeley, 1961.

Schlosser, Eric. *Fast Food Nation: The Dark Side of the All-American Meal*. Boston and New York: Houghton Mifflin, 2001.

Shilts, Randy. *And the Band Played On: Politics, People, and the AIDS Epidemic*. New York: St. Martin's Press, 1985.

Welsome, Eileen. *The Plutonium Files: America's Secret Medical Experiments in the Cold War*. New York: Dial Press, 1999.

Whitaker, Robert. *Mad in America: Bad Science, Bad Medicine, and the Enduring Mistreatment of the Mentally Ill*. Cambridge: Perseus, 2002.

Wilson, William Julius. *When Work Disappears: The World of the New Urban Poor*. New York: Knopf, 1996.

Wolfe, Tom. *The Bonfire of the Vanities*. New York: Farrar, Straus and Giroux, 1987.

———. *A Man in Full*. New York: Farrar, Straus and Giroux, 1998.

Woodward, Bob. *Maestro: Greenspan's Fed and the American Boom*. New York: Simon & Schuster, 2000.

Additional Works Cited

Adams, Henry. *The Education of Henry Adams*. 1907. Ed. Ira Nadel Oxford and New York: Oxford University Press, 1999.

Arnold, Matthew. *Culture and Anarchy: An Essay in Political and Social Criticism*. New York: Macmillan, 1920.

Baker, Ray Stannard. *American Chronicle: An Autobiography of Ray Stannard Baker*. New York: Scribner, 1945.

Belasco, David. *The Heart of Maryland and Other Plays*. Ed. Glenn Hughes and George Savage. Princeton, N.J.: Princeton University Press, 1941.

Blair, Walter, Theodore Hornberger, and Randall Stewart. *American Literature: A Brief History*. Revised ed. Chicago: Scott Foresman, 1964.

Blakely, Edward J., and Mary Gail Snyder. *Fortress America: Gated Communities in the United States*. Washington, D.C.: Brookings Institution Press; Cambridge, Mass.: Lincoln Institute of Land Policy, 1997.

Brady, Kathleen. *Ida Tarbell: Portrait of a Muckraker*. New York: Seaview/-Putnam, 1984.

Brands, H. W. *The Age of Gold: The California Gold Rush and the New American Dream*. New York: Doubleday, 2002.

Bremmer, Robert H. *From the Depths: The Discovery of Poverty in the United States*. New York: New York University Press, 1956.

Brooks, Peter. *The Melodramatic Imagination: Balzac, Henry James, Melodrama, and the Mode of Excess.* 1976. New Haven, Conn.: Yale University Press, 1995.

———. *Reading for the Plot: Design and Intention in Narrative.* New York: Knopf, 1984.

Brooks, Van Wyck. *The Confident Years: 1885–1915.* New York: Dutton, 1955.

Carlyle, Thomas. *Sartor Resartus.* Ed. Kerry McSweeney and Peter Sabor. and Oxford and New York: Oxford University Press, 1999.

Chernow, Ron. *Titan: The Life of John D. Rockefeller, Sr.* New York: Vintage, 1999.

Cleaver, Eldridge. *Soul on Ice.* New York: McGraw-Hill, 1967.

Cross, Gary S. *An All-Consuming Century: Why Commercialism Won in Modern America.* New York: Columbia University Press, 2000.

Crunden, Robert M. *Ministers of Reform: The Progressives' Achievement in American Civilization 1889–1920.* New York: Basic Books, 1982.

Darwin, Charles. *The Works of Charles Darwin.* Ed. Paul H. Barrett and R. B. Freeman. New York: New York University Press, 1987.

Davis, Rebecca Harding. *Bits of Gossip: Writing Cultural Autobiography.* Ed. Janice Milner Lasseter and Sharon M. Harris. Nashville, Tenn.: Vanderbilt University Press, 2001.

———. *Life in the Iron-Mills.* Ed. Cecelia Tichi. New York: Bedford, 1998.

Dickstein, Morris. *Double Agent: The Critic and Society.* Oxford and New York: Oxford University Press, 1992.

Didion, Joan. *Political Fictions.* New York: Knopf, 2001.

Dotlich, David L., and Peter C. Cairo. *Why CEOs Fail: The 11 Deadly Sins and How Not to Commit Them.* New York: Wiley, 2003.

Du Bois, W. E. B. *The Souls of Black Folk: Essays and Sketches.* Chicago: A. C. McClurg and Co., 1903.

Dumas, Alexander. *The Count of Monte Cristo.* 1845. Ed. David Coward. Oxford and New York: Oxford University Press, 1998.

Elliot, Emory, ed. *Columbia Literary History of the United States.* New York: Columbia University Press, 1988.

Empson, William. *Seven Types of Ambiguity.* 3rd ed. New York: New Directions Books, 1966.

Filler, Louis. *The Muckrakers.* 1939. University Park: Pennsylvania State University Press, 1976.

Fish, Stanley Eugene. *Is There a Text in This Class? The Authority of Interpretive Communities.* Cambridge, Mass.: Harvard University Press, 1980.

Fitch, Clyde. *Barbara Frietchie, the Frederick Girl: A Play in 4 Acts.* New York: Life Pub. Co., 1900.

Fitzgerald, F. Scott. *The Great Gatsby.* New York: Scribner, 1925.

Fussell, Paul. *Class: A Guide Through the American Status System.* New York: Simon & Schuster, 1983.

Garten, Jeffrey E. *The Mind of the CEO.* New York: Basic Books, 2001.

Gates, William H., Sr., and Chuck Collins. *Wealth and Our Commonwealth: Why America Should Tax Accumulated Fortunes.* Boston: Beacon Press, 2002.

Gilje, Paul. *Rioting in America.* Bloomington and Indianapolis: Indiana University Press, 1996.

Gladwell, Malcolm. *The Tipping Point: How Little Things Can Make a Big Difference.* New York: Back Bay Books, 2002.

Goldberg, Bernard. *Bias: A CBS Insider Exposes How the Media Distort the News.* Washington, D.C.: Regnery Publishing, 2002.

Goodwin, Jason. *Greenback: The Almighty Dollar and the Invention of America.* New York: Henry Holt, 2003.

Griffin, John Howard. *Black Like Me.* Boston: Houghton Mifflin, 1961.

Grimstead, David. *Melodrama Unveiled: American Theater and Culture, 1800–1850.* Chicago: University of Chicago Press, 1968.

Halberstam, David. *The Powers That Be.* New York: Knopf, 1979.

Harpham, Jeffrey Galt. "Ethics." *Critical Terms for Literary Study.* Ed. Frank Lentricchia and Thomas McLaughlin. 2nd ed. Chicago: University of Chicago Press, 1995. 387–405.

Hartsock, John C. *A History of American Literary Journalism.* Amherst: University of Massachusetts Press, 2000.

Hofstadter, Richard. *The Age of Reform: From Bryan to F.D.R.* 1955. New York: Knopf, 1969.

Howells, William Dean. *The Rise of Silas Lapham.* Centenary ed. Boston: Houghton Mifflin, 1937.

Hubbell, Jay. *Who Are the Major American Writers?* Durham, N.C.: Duke University Press, 1972.

James, C. L. R. *Mariners, Renegades, and Castaways: The Story of Herman Melville and the World We Live In.* 1952. London and New York: Alison and Busby, 1985.

James, Henry. *The American Scene.* New York: Harper and Brothers, 1907.

Jones, Laurie Beth. *Jesus CEO: Using Ancient Wisdom for Visionary Leadership.* New York: Hyperion, 1996.

Josephson, Matthew. *The Robber Barons: The Great American Capitalists, 1861–1901.* New York: Harcourt, Brace, 1934.

Kammen, Michael G. *Mystic Chords of Memory: The Transformation of Tradition in American Culture.* New York: Knopf, 1991.

Kaplan, Justin. *Lincoln Steffens: A Biography.* New York: Simon & Schuster, 1974.

Kazin, Alfred. *On Native Grounds: An Interpretation of Modern American Prose Literature.* New York: Harcourt, Brace and World, 1942.

Khurana, Rakesh. *Searching for a Corporate Savior: The Irrational Quest for Charismatic CEOs.* Princeton, N.J.: Princeton University Press, 2002.

Korten, David C. *When Corporations Rule the World.* 2nd ed. West Hartford, Conn.: Kumarian Press, 2001.

Kouwenhoven, John. *Made in America: The Arts in Modern Civilization.* Garden City, N. Y.: Doubleday, 1948.

Lansburgh, Richard H., ed. *Industrial Safety.* Philadelphia: American Academy of Political and Social Science, 1926.

Lichtenstein, Nelson, Susan Strasser, Roy Rosenzweig, Stephen Brier, and Joshua Brown, eds. *Who Built America: Working People & the Nation's Economy, Politics, Culture & Society.* Vol. 2. New York: Pantheon, 1992.

Liss, David. *A Conspiracy of Paper: A Novel.* New York: Random House, 2000.

Maass, Donald. *Writing the Breakout Novel.* Cincinnati, Oh.: Writer's Digest Books, 2002.

Mailer, Norman. "Birds and Lions: Writing from the Inside Out." *The New Yorker*, December 23 and 30, 2002.

Marchand, Roland. *Creating the Corporate Soul: The Rise of Public Relations and Corporate Imagery in American Big Business.* Berkeley and Los Angeles: University of California Press, 1998.

Martin, Jay. *Harvests of Change: American Literature 1865–1914.* Englewood Cliffs, N.J.: Prentice-Hall, 1967.

McLean, George N. *The Rise and Fall of Anarchy in America*. Chicago and Philadelphia: R.G. Badoux, 1888.

Mason, Jeffrey D. *Melodrama and the Myth of America*. Bloomington: Indiana University Press, 1993.

McChesney, Robert W. *Rich Media, Poor Democracy: Communication Politics in Dubious Times*. Urbana: University of Illinois Press, 1999.

McDonald, John D. *Condominium: A Novel*. Philadelphia: Lippincott, 1977.

McLean, George N. *The Rise and Fall of Anarchy in America*. Chicago and Philadelphia: R. G. Badoux, 1888.

McLoughlin, Emma, and Nicola Kraus. *The Nanny Diaries*. New York: St. Martin's Press, 2002.

Melville, Herman. *Moby-Dick*. 1851. New York: Penguin, 1986.

Miller, J. Hillis. "Narrative." *Critical Terms for Literary Study*. Ed. Frank Lentricchia and Thomas McLaughlin. 2nd ed. Chicago: University of Chicago Press, 1995.

Miraldi, Robert, ed. *The Muckrakers: Evangelical Crusaders*. Westport, Conn.: Praeger, 2000.

Morrison, Toni. *Beloved*. New York: Knopf, 1987.

———. *Jazz*. New York: Knopf, 1992.

———. *Paradise*. New York: Knopf, 1998.

———. *Song of Solomon*. New York: Knopf, 1977.

Mott, Frank Luther. *A History of American Magazines*. Cambridge, Mass.: Harvard University Press, 1938.

Nash, Christopher, ed. *Narrative in Culture: The Uses of Storytelling in the Sciences, Philosophy, and Literature*. London and New York: Routledge, 1990.

New York Times, *The Downsizing of America*. New York: Times Books, 1996.

Nye, Russell. *The Unembarrassed Muse: The Popular Arts in America*. New York: Dial Press, 1970.

Orman, Suze. *The Courage to Be Rich: Creating a Life of Material and Spiritual Abundance*. New York: Penguin Putnam, 2001.

———. *The 9 Steps to Financial Freedom: Practical and Spiritual Steps So You Can Stop Worrying*. New York: Three Rivers Press, 2000.

———. *The Road to Wealth: A Comprehensive Guide to Your Money—Everything You Need to Know in Good and Bad Times*. New York: Riverhead Books, 2001.

Pattee, Fred Lewis. *The New American Literature, 1890–1930*. New York and London: Century, 1930.

Phelan, James. *Narrative as Rhetoric: Technique, Audiences, Ethics, Ideology*. Columbus: Ohio State University Press, 1996.

Philips, Kevin. *Wealth and Democracy: A Political History of the American Rich*. New York: Broadway Books, 2002.

Pratt, Mary Louise. "Travel Narrative and Imperialist Vision." *Understanding Narrative*. Ed. James Phelan and Peter J. Rabinowitz. Columbus: Ohio State University Press, 1994.

Price, Kenneth M., and Susan Belasco Smith. *Periodical Literature in Nineteenth-Century America*. Charlottesville: University Press of Virginia, 1995.

Putnam, Robert D. *Bowling Alone: The Collapse and Revival of American Community*. New York: Simon & Schuster, 2000.

Rand, Ayn. *The Fountainhead*. 1943. New York: Scribner Classics, 2000.

Regier, C. C. *The Era of the Muckrakers*. 1932. Gloucester, Mass.: Peter Smith, 1957.

Salinger, J. D. *The Catcher in the Rye*. Boston: Little, Brown, 1951.

Schulman, Bruce J. *The Seventies: The Great Shift in American Culture, Society, and Politics*. New York: Free Press, 2001.

Sennett, Richard. *Corrosion of Character: The Personal Consequences of Work in the New Capitalism*. New York: W. W. Norton, 1998.

Serrin, Judith, and William Serrin, eds. *Muckraking! The Journalism That Changed America*. New York: New Press, 2002.

Smiley, Jane. *Horse Heaven*. New York: Knopf, 2000.

———. *Moo*. New York: Knopf, 1995.

Sommers, Christina Hoff. *The War Against Boys: How Misguided Feminism is Harming Our Young Men*. New York: Simon & Schuster, 2000.

Spiller, Richard. *Literary History of the United States*. 1946. New York: Macmillan, 1953.

Steinbeck, John. *The Grapes of Wrath*. 1939. New York: Viking, 1986.

Stiglitz, Joseph E. *Globalization and Its Discontents*. New York: W. W. Norton, 2002.

Stowe, Harriet Beecher. *Uncle Tom's Cabin*. Boston: Houghton Mifflin, 1899.

Stowe, Harriet Beecher, and Catherine Beecher. *An American Woman's Home*. Ed. Nicole Tonkovich. New Brunswick, N.J.: Rutgers University Press, 2002.

Sullivan, Mark. *Our Times: The United States, 1900–1925*. New York and London: n.p., 1927.

Thoreau, Henry David. *Walden*. Ed. Stephen Allen Fender. New York and London: Oxford University Press, 1997.

Tindell, George Brown, and David Shi. *America: A Narrative*. 3rd ed. New York: W. W. Norton, 1984.

Twain, Mark and Charles Dudley Warner. *The Gilded Age*. 1873. Oxford and New York: Oxford University Press, 1996.

Vidal, Gore. *1876*. New York: Random House, 1976.

———. *Empire*. New York: Random House, 1987.

Weinberg, Arthur, and Lila Weinberg. ed. *The Muckrakers*. 1961. Champaign: University of Illinois Press, 2001.

Weinstein, Cindy. "How Many Others Are There in the Other Half? Jacob Riis and the Tenement Population." *Nineteenth Century Contexts* 24.2 (2002): 195–216.

Wharton, Edith. *The House of Mirth*. New York: Scribner, 1905.

White, Hayden. *The Content of the Form: Narrative Discourse and Historical Representation*. 1987. Baltimore: Johns Hopkins University Press, 1997.

White, William Allen. *The Autobiography of William Allen White*. New York: Macmillan, 1946.

Whitman, Walt. *Leaves of Grass*. Ed. Sculley Bradley and Harold W. Blodgett. New York: W. W. Norton, 1973.

Wilson, Bruce. *The Prayer of Jabez: Breaking Through to the Blessed Life*. Sisters, Ore.: Multnomah Publishers, 2000.

Wilson, Christopher. *The Labor of Words: Literary Professionalism in the Progressive Era*. Athens: University of Georgia Press, 1985.

Wilson, Harold S. *McClure's Magazine and the Muckrakers*. Princeton, N.J.: Princeton University Press, 1970.

Index

Acknowledgments

Expressions of appreciation often begin with thanks to friends, colleagues, and family, while institutions round out the tribute, like ballast. This time, I reverse the order to thank, first, Vanderbilt University—named, of course, for its founder, Cornelius Vanderbilt—which gave me academic leave and travel funds for the interviews included in *Exposés and Excess*. Lifelong, ironic as it may be, given the nature of my project, I have been a beneficiary of the largesse of philanthropic fortunes, beginning with the Carnegie Library, where I borrowed books in Pittsburgh as a child. More recently, I have been the grateful recipient of a William R. Kenan, Jr., professorship in English, funded by the William R. Kenan, Jr. Charitable Trust. And I have enjoyed a residency at the Rockefeller Foundation study and conference center at Bellagio, Italy. This book on a literature of exposé—of muckraking—is indebted to the benefaction of several of America's great fortunes.

My ability to write this book, in addition, is a tribute to U.S. public education in Pittsburgh, in Florida, and in West Virginia. It is a tribute to two public universities where I studied as an undergraduate and graduate student, Pennsylvania State University and the University of California at Davis. It is, moreover, a tribute to a U.S. government education initiative from the 1950s and 1960s. Graduate students of my generation were eligible for a fellowship program financed under the National Defense Education Act. This was legislation enacted mainly to catapult the United States ahead of the Soviet Union in science and technology, but it provided graduate fellowships in all disciplines, including the humanities. So my Ph.D. at the University of California at Davis, 1965–68, was sponsored by a government welfare program. Specific to *Exposés and Excess*, I give thanks first to Jerome Singerman, Humanities Editor at the University of Pennsylvania Press, who understood and welcomed this book and guided it with great deftness. Richard McCarty, Dean of the College of Arts and Science, and Dennis Hall, Associate Provost for Research, Vanderbilt University, have generously supported this work. I am thankful also to

Daniel Horowitz for his excellent suggestions and to Miles Orvell. Carolyn Levinson of the Vanderbilt University Department of English proved her patience, her keen ear, and her skills at superb transcription of the interview tapes. Claire Tichi helped substantially and with good grace as research assistant in the summer of 2002. Friends and colleagues were supportive, too, and I thank Teresa Goddu, Carol Burke, Thadious Davis, Wendy Martin, Amy Lang, and Julia Abraham, and Meg Stroup. As always, Bill Tichi buoyed my efforts on the homefront.